LIFE OF MUḤAMMAD[sa]

BY

ḤAḌRAT MIRZĀ BASHĪRUDDĪN MAḤMŪD AḤMAD

ISLAM INTERNATIONAL PUBLICATIONS LIMITED

Life of Muḥammad[sa]

BY: ḤAḌRAT MIRZĀ BASHĪRUDDĪN MAḤMŪD AḤMAD
KHALĪFATUL-MASĪḤ II

First published in UK in 1990
Second edition published in UK in 2005
Third edition published in UK in 2009
Fourth edition published in UK in October 2012
Fifth edition published in UK in new format in November 2012
Sixth edition published in UK in March 2013
Re-printed in UK in January 2014

PUBLISHED BY:
Additional Wakālat-e-Taṣnīf (United Kingdom)
Islamabad
Sheephatch Lane,
Tilford, Surrey, GU10 2AQ, UK

Printed and bound in Great Britain by Polestar Wheatons (UK) Ltd

British Library Cataloguing in Publication Data
Aḥmad, Mirzā Bashīruddīn Maḥmūd 1889–1965
The Life of Muḥammad
1. Islam Muḥammad (Prophet[sa])
I. Title
297.63

ISBN (hardback): 1- 85372- 045- 3
ISBN (paperback): 978-1-84880-081-6

Contacts for Further Information:
International: www.alislam.org
UK: www.ukmuslimsforpeace.com
USA: www.muslimsforpeace.org

About the Author

The Promised Son[ra] of the Promised Messiah and Mahdi[as]; the manifest Sign of Allah, the Almighty; the Word of God whose advent was prophesied by the Holy Prophet Muhammad[sa] and the Promised Messiah[as] as well as the past Prophets; a Star in the spiritual firmament for the like of which the world has to wait for hundreds of years to appear; the man of God, crowned with a spiritual halo from which radiated such scintillating rays of light as would instil spiritual life into his followers and captivate and enthral those who were not fortunate to follow him; an orator of such phenomenal quality that his speeches would make his audience stay put for hours on end, come rain or shine, deep into the late hours of the evenings while words flowed from his tongue like honey dripping into their ears to reach the depths of their soul to fill them with knowledge and invigorate their faith; the ocean of Divine and secular knowledge; the Voice Articulate of the age; without doubt the greatest genius of the 20th century; a man of phenomenal intelligence and memory; an epitome of the qualities of leadership; the one whose versatility cannot be comprehended—Ḥaḍrat Mirzā Bashīruddīn Maḥmūd Aḥmad[ra] (1889-1965), *Muṣliḥ Mau'ūd* (the Promised Reformer) was the eldest son and the second successor (Khalifah) of the Promised Messiah[as]. He took charge of the *Aḥmadiyya Jamā'at* at the young age of 24 when the *Jamā'at* was still in its infancy and nourished it to its maturity for more than 50 years with his spiritual guidance, prayers, tears, toil and blood. Not only did he fortify the foundations of the community laid down by the Promised Messiah[as], but expanded the structure of the *Jamā'at* by initiating various schemes, organizations, and programs taking his inspiration from the Promised Messiah[as] and under the Divine guidance. His foremost concern, to which he devoted all his life, was to accomplish the mission of the Promised Messiah—the daunting task of spreading the message of true Islam in its pristine purity to the ends of the world. To achieve this, he initiated *Taḥrīk-e-Jadīd* through which spread, and continues to spread, the missionary work all over the globe. His acute intelligence, keen intellect, deep and extensive scholarship and above all his God-given knowledge enabled him to produce a vast corpus of writings, speeches etc. His oeuvre is so vast that it will take many years to see the light of publication.

When the promised Messiah[as] fervently prayed to God to grant him a Sign in support of Islam, Allah gave him the good tiding about this son of his and said:

> **"...He will be extremely intelligent...and will be filled with secular and spiritual knowledge...Son, delight of the heart, high ranking, noble. A manifestation of the First and the Last, a manifestation of the True and the High; as if Allah has descended from heaven...Behold a light comes...We shall pour Our Spirit into him"** [Revelation of 20th February 1886]*

* Translation from Urdu by Sir Muḥammad Ẓafrullāh Khān in his English translation of *Tadhkirah*—the book containing dreams, visions and verbal revelations vouchsafed to the Promised Messiah[as]. (Revised edition, 2009.) [Publisher]

CONTENTS

Foreword

Life of Muḥammad[sa] is part of *Introduction to the study of the Holy Qur'an* by Haḍrat Mirzā Bashīrduddīn Maḥmūd Aḥmad[ra]. The Introduction was translated into English by Qāḍī Muḥammad Aslam and was first published in 1949 from London. Since then it has appeared in several editions. *Life of Muḥammad*[sa] has also appeared in several editions and is out of stock now. We are publishing it again with an index which the original English edition did not have. We have also reset it to make it more attractive. Needless to say that it is much in demand and we very much hope that the present edition will meet this demand. Some minor corrections have also been made.

The name of Muḥammad[sa], the Holy Prophet of Islam, has been followed by the symbol [sa], which is an abbreviation for the salutation 'may peace and blessings of Allah be upon him.' The names of other prophets and messengers are followed by the symbol [as], an abbreviation for 'on whom be peace.' The actual salutations have not generally been set out in full, but they should nevertheless, be understood as being repeated in full in each case. The symbol [ra] is used with the name of the Disciples of the Holy Prophet[sa] and those of the Promised Messiah[as]. It stands for *Raḍī Allāhu 'anhu/'anhā/'anhum* (May Allah be pleased with him/with her/with them).

In transliterating Arabic words we have followed the following system adopted by the Royal Asiatic Society.

ا at the beginning of a word, pronounced as *a*, *i*, *u* preceded by a very slight aspiration, like *h* in the English word 'honour'.
ث *th*, pronounced like th in the English word 'thing'.
ح *ḥ*, a guttural aspirate, stronger than h.
خ *kh*, pronounced like the Scotch ch in 'loch'.
ذ *dh*, pronounced like the English th in 'that'.
ص *ṣ*, strongly articulated s.

ض *ḍ*, similar to the English th in 'this'.
ط *ṭ*, strongly articulated palatal t.
ظ *ẓ*, strongly articulated z.
ع ', a strong guttural, the pronunciation of which must be learnt by the ear.
غ *gh*, a sound approached very nearly in the r '*grasseye*' in French, and in the German r. It requires the muscles of the throat to be in the 'gargling' position whilst pronouncing it.
ق *q*, a deep guttural k sound.
ء ', a sort of catch in the voice.

Short vowels are represented by:

a for ——َ—— (like *u* in 'bud');
i for ——ِ—— (like *i* in 'bid');
u for ——ُ—— (like *oo* in 'wood');

Long vowels by:

ā for ——ا—— or آ (like *a* in 'father');
ī for ى ——ِ—— or ——ٖ—— (like *ee* in 'deep');
ū for و ——ُ—— (like *oo* in 'root');

Other:

ai for ى ——َ—— (like *i* in 'site')♦;
au for و ——َ—— (resembling *ou* in 'sound').

The consonants not included in the above list have the same phonetic value as in the principal languages of Europe.

We have not transliterated Arabic, Persian and Urdu words which have become part of English language, e.g., Islam, Mahdi, Qur'an, Hijra, Ramadan, Rahman, Hadith, Zakat, ulema, umma, sunna, kafir etc.

For quotes straight commas (straight quotes) are used to differentiate them from the curved commas used in the system of transliteration, ' for ع, ' for ء. Commas as punctuation marks are used according to the normal usage.

The Publishers

♦ In Arabic words like شيخ (Shaikh) there is an element of diphthong which is missing when the word is pronounced in Urdu.

بسم الله الرحمن الرحيم

Life of Muḥammad[sa]

ARABIA AT THE TIME OF THE PROPHET'S[sa] BIRTH

The Prophet[sa] was born in Mecca in August 570 A.D. He was given the name Muḥammad[sa] which means, the Praised One. To understand his life and character we must have some idea of the conditions which obtained in Arabia at the time of his birth.

When he was born almost the whole of Arabia believed in a polytheistic form of religion. The Arabs traced their descent to Abraham[as]. They knew that Abraham[as] was a monotheistic Teacher. In spite of this, they entertained polytheistic beliefs and were given to polytheistic practices. In defence, they said that some human beings are outstanding in their contact with God. Their intercession on behalf of others is accepted by God. To reach Him is difficult for ordinary human beings. They must have others to intercede for them in order to obtain God's pleasure and help. Thus they were able to combine their reverence for Abraham[as] with their own polytheistic beliefs. Abraham[as], they said, was a holy man. He was able to reach God without intercession, whilst ordinary Meccans could not do so. The people of Mecca, therefore, had made idols of holy and righteous persons, and these they worshipped and to these they made offerings in order to please God through them. This attitude was primitive, illogical and full of defects. But the Meccans were not worried by these. They had not had a monotheistic Teacher for a long time, and polytheism, once it takes root, spreads and knows no bounds. The number of gods begins to increase. At the time of the Prophet's[sa] birth, it is said that in the Ka'ba alone, the Sacred Mosque of all Islam and the house of worship built by Abraham[as] and his son Ishmael, there were 360 idols. It seems that for every day of the lunar year the Meccans had an idol. In other big centres there were other idols, so that we can say that every part of Arabia was steeped in polytheistic belief. The Arabs were devoted to the culture of speech. They were much interested in their spoken language and were very keen on its advance. Their intellectual ambitions, however, were scant. Of History, Geography, Mathematics, etc., they knew nothing. But as they were a desert people and had to find their way about in the desert without the assistance of landmarks, they had developed a keen interest in Astronomy. There was in the whole of Arabia not a single school. It is said that in Mecca only a few individuals could read and write.

From the moral point of view the Arabs were a contradictory people. They suffered from some extreme moral defects but at the same time they possessed some admirable qualities. They were given to excessive drinking. To become drunk and to run wild under the effect of drink was for them a virtue, not a vice. Their conception of a gentleman was one who should entertain his friends and neighbours to drinking bouts. Every rich man would hold a drinking party at least five times a day. Gambling was their national sport. But they had made of it a fine art. They did not gamble in order to become rich. Winners were expected to entertain their friends. In times of war, funds were collected through gambling. Even today we have the institution of prize-bonds to raise money for war. The institution has been resuscitated in our time by the people of Europe and America. But they should remember that in this they only imitate the Arabs. When war came, Arabian tribes would hold a gambling party. Whoever won had to bear the greater part of the expenses of the war.

Of the amenities of civilized life, the Arabs knew nothing. Their chief occupation was trade, and to this end they sent their caravans to far-off places, such as

Abyssinia, Syria, Palestine and even India. The rich among them were great admirers of Indian swords. Their clothing needs were supplied largely by Yemen and Syria. The trading centres were the towns. The rest of Arabia, excepting Yemen and some northern parts, was Bedouin. There were no permanent settlements, or places of habitation. The tribes had divided the country between them so that members of a tribe wandered about freely in their part of the country. When the water supply in any place was exhausted, they would move on to some other place and settle down. Their capital consisted of sheep, goats and camels. From the wool they made cloth, and from the skins they made tents. What was left over they sold in the market. Gold and silver were not unknown, but they were certainly very rare possessions. The poor and the common folks made ornaments of cowries and sweet-smelling substances. Seeds of melons were cleaned, dried and strung together to make necklaces. Crime and immoralities of various kinds were rampant. Theft was rare but dacoity was common. To attack and to dispossess one another was regarded a birthright. But, at the same time, they honoured their word more than any other people. Should an individual go to a powerful leader or tribe and ask for protection, that leader or tribe was honour-bound to protect that individual. If this was not done, the tribe lost caste throughout Arabia. Poets commanded great prestige. They were honoured as national leaders. Leaders were expected to possess great powers of speech and even to be able to compose verse. Hospitality had developed into a national virtue. A forlorn traveller on arrival at the headquarters of a tribe would be treated as an honoured guest. The best animals would be slaughtered for him and the utmost consideration shown. They did not care who the visitor was. It was enough that a visitor had arrived. The visit meant an increase of status and prestige for the tribe. It became the tribe's duty, therefore, to honour the visitor. By honouring him it honoured itself. Woman in this

Arab society had no status and no rights. Among them it was thought honourable to put baby girls to death. It is a mistake, however, to think that infanticide was practised on a country-wide scale. Such a dangerous institution could not flourish throughout a country. That would have meant the extinction of the race. The truth is that in Arabia—or for that matter in India or any other country where infanticide has ever existed, it has been confined only to certain families. The Arab families who practised it either had an exaggerated notion of their social status or they were constrained in other ways. Possibly they were unable to find suitable young men for their daughters to marry; knowing this, they put to death their baby girls. The evil of this institution lies in its savageness and its cruelty, not in the results which it has in terms of a nation's population. Different methods were used for killing baby girls, among them burying alive and strangulation.

Only the real mother was regarded as a mother in Arab society. Step-mothers were not regarded as mothers and there was no ban on a son's marrying his step-mother on the death of his father. Polygamous marriages were very common, and there was no limit to the number of wives a man could take. More than one sister could also be taken to wife by the same person at one and the same time.

The worst treatment was meted out by combatant sides to one another in war. Where hatred was strong, they did not hesitate to split the bodies of the wounded, take out parts and eat them in cannibal fashion. They did not hesitate to mutilate the bodies of their enemies. Cutting off the nose or ears, or plucking out an eye was a common form of cruelty practised by them. Slavery was widespread. Weak tribes were made slaves. The slave had no accepted status. Every master did as he liked with his slaves. No action could be taken against a master who maltreated his slave. A master could murder his slave without having to answer for it. If one master murdered another's slave, even then the penalty was not death. All that was required of him was to compensate the aggrieved master suitably. Women-slaves were used to satisfy sexual desires. The children born of such unions were also treated as slaves. Women-slaves who became mothers remained slaves. In terms of civilization and social advance the Arabs were a very backward people. Kindness and consideration to one another were unknown. Woman had the worst status possible. Still the Arabs possessed some virtues. Individual bravery, for instance, sometimes reached a very high level.

It was among such people that the Holy Prophet[sa] of Islam was born. His father 'Abdullāh had died before his birth. Accordingly, he and his mother Āmina had to be looked after by the grandfather, 'Abdul Muṭṭalib. The child Muḥammad[sa] was suckled by a countrywoman who lived in a place near Ṭā'if. It was a custom in Arabia in those days to hand over children to women in the country, whose duty was to bring up the children, to train their speech and to give them a good start in bodily health. When the Prophet[sa] was in his first year*, his mother died while travelling from Medina to Mecca and had to be buried *en route*. The child was brought to Mecca by a woman-servant and handed over to the grandfather. When he was in his eighth year, his grandfather also died, after which Abū Ṭālib, his uncle, became his guardian, this being the wish expressed in a will by the grandfather. The Prophet[sa] had two or three opportunities to travel out of Arabia. One of these occurred when at the age of twelve he went in the company of Abū Ṭālib to Syria. It seems that this journey took him only to the south-eastern towns of

---

* A: In *Biḥārul-Anwār* Imām Bāqir narrates on the authority of Wāqidī that Āminah, the mother of the Holy Prophet[sa], died when he was four months old, thus, he was an orphan when he was only four months old. (*Biḥārul-Anwāril-Jāmi'ati li-Durari Akhbāril-A'immatil-Aṭhār, Bābu Manshā'ihī wa Raḍā'ihī wa mā ẓahara min I'jāzihī 'inda dhālika ilā Nubuwwatihī* by Sheikh Muḥammad Bāqir Majlisī, vol.15, p.194; published by Al-Amīrah Beirut, First edition 2008.)

B: However, according to Ibni Hishām, Ḥaḍrat Āminah, the mother of the Holy Prophet[sa], died when he was six years old. (*Sīratun-Nabawiyyah* by Ibni Hishām, *Bābu Wafāti Āminata wa Ḥāli Rasūlillāhi ma'a Jaddihī 'Abdil Muṭṭalib ba'dahā*, p.134, published by Dārul-Kutubil-'Ilmiyyah Beirut, Lebanon, First edition 2001.)

Syria, for in historical references to this journey there is no mention of places like Jerusalem. From now onwards until he grew up to young manhood he remained in Mecca. From very childhood he was given to reflection and meditation. In the quarrels and rivalries of others he took no part, except with a view to putting an end to them. It is said that the tribes living in Mecca and the territories around, tired of unending blood-feuds, resolved to found an association the purpose of which was to help victims of aggressive and unjust treatment. When the Holy Prophet[sa] heard of this, he gladly joined. Members of this association gave an undertaking in the following terms:

> **They will help those who were oppressed and will restore them their rights, as long as the last drop of water remained in the sea. And if they do not do so, they will compensate the victims out of their own belongings (*Sīrat Ibni Hishām by Imām Suhailī*).**

It seems that no other member of this association was ever called upon to discharge the undertaking solemnly entered into by members of this association. But opportunity came to the Holy Prophet[sa] when he had announced his Mission. His worst enemy was Abū Jahl, a chief of Mecca. He preached social boycott and public humiliation of the Prophet[sa]. About that time a person from outside came to Mecca. Money was due to him from Abū Jahl, but Abū Jahl refused to pay. He mentioned this to people in Mecca. Some young men, out of sheer mischief, suggested that he should approach the Prophet[sa]. They thought that the Prophet[sa] would refuse to do anything for fear of the general opposition to him and particularly for fear of the opposition of Abū Jahl. If he refused to help this man, he would be said to have broken his pledge to the association. If, on the other hand, he did not refuse and chose to approach Abū Jahl for the restitution of this loan, Abū Jahl was certain to turn him away with contempt. This man went to the Prophet[sa] and complained to him about Abū Jahl. The Prophet[sa], hesitating not a minute, stood up, went with the man and knocked at Abū Jahl's door. Abū Jahl came out and saw that his creditor was standing with the Prophet[sa]. The Prophet[sa] mentioned the loan and suggested its payment. Abū Jahl was taken aback and, making no excuses, paid at once. When the other chiefs of Mecca heard of this they reproved Abū Jahl, telling him how weak and self-contradictory he had proved. He preached the social boycott of the Prophet[sa], yet he himself accepted direction from the Prophet[sa] and paid a loan on his suggestion. In self-defence, Abū Jahl pleaded that any other person would have done the same. He told them that as he saw the Prophet[sa] standing at his door, he also saw two wild camels standing one on each side, ready to attack. We cannot say what this experience was. Was it a miraculous appearance designed to upset Abū Jahl or was it the awe-inspiring presence of the Prophet[sa] which produced this hallucination? A man hated and oppressed by a whole town had taken the courage to go alone to the leader of that town and demand the restitution of a loan. Maybe this very unexpected sight frightened Abū Jahl and for a moment made him forget what he had sworn to do against the Prophet[sa], and forced him to do as the Prophet[sa] suggested (*Hishām*).

HOLY PROPHET'S[sa] MARRIAGE WITH KHADĪJA[ra]

When the Prophet[sa] was about twenty-five years old, his reputation for integrity and fellow-feeling had spread over the whole of the town. People would point admiring fingers at him and say, here was a man who could be trusted. This reputation reached the ears of a rich widow who approached the Prophet's[sa] uncle, Abū Ṭālib, to let his nephew lead a trading caravan of hers to Syria. Abū Ṭālib mentioned this to the Prophet[sa] and the Prophet[sa] agreed. The expedition met with great success and brought unexpected profits. The rich widow, Khadīja[ra], was convinced that the success of the caravan was due not only to the conditions of the market in

Syria, but also to the integrity and efficiency of its leader. She interrogated her slave, Maisara, on this subject, and Maisara supported her view and told her that the honesty and sympathy with which this young leader of the caravan had managed her affairs would not be shown by many persons. Khadīja[ra] was much impressed by this account. She was forty years of age and had already been widowed twice. She sent a woman friend of hers to the Prophet[sa] to find out whether he would be persuaded to marry her. This woman went to the Prophet[sa] and asked why he had not married. The Prophet[sa] replied he was not rich enough to do so. The visitor suggested whether he would agree, if a rich and respectable woman were found whom he could marry. The Prophet[sa] asked who this woman could be, and the visitor said she was Khadīja[ra]. The Prophet[sa] apologized, saying that Khadīja[ra] was too highly placed for him. The visitor undertook to deal with all difficulties. In that case, said the Prophet[sa], there was nothing for him to say but to agree. Khadīja[ra] then sent a message to the Prophet's[sa] uncle. Marriage between the Prophet[sa] and Khadīja[ra] was settled and solemnized. A poor man orphaned in, childhood had his first peep into prosperity. He became rich. But the use he made of his riches is an object-lesson to all mankind. After the marriage Khadīja[ra] felt that she was rich and he was poor and that this inequality between them would not make for happiness. So she proposed to make over her property and her slaves to the Prophet[sa]. The Prophet[sa], making sure that Khadīja[ra] was in earnest, declared that as soon as he had any of Khadīja's[ra] slaves, he would set them free. And he did so. Moreover, the greater part of the property which he received from Khadīja[ra] he distributed among the poor. Among the slaves whom he thus set free was one Zaid[ra]. He appeared to be more intelligent and more alert than others. He belonged to a respectable family, had been kidnapped as a child and sold from place to place until he reached Mecca.

Young Zaid[ra], newly freed, saw at once that it was better to sacrifice freedom for the sake of slavery to the Prophet[sa]. When the Prophet[sa] set the slaves free, Zaid[ra] refused to be freed and asked leave to continue to live with the Prophet[sa]. He did so, and as time went on his attachment to the Prophet[sa] grew. But in the meantime Zaid's[ra] father and his uncle were on his track and they ultimately heard that he was in Mecca. In Mecca they traced him in the house of the Prophet[sa]. Coming to the Prophet[sa], they asked for the liberty of Zaid[ra] and offered to pay as much ransom as the Prophet[sa] should demand. The Prophet[sa] said that Zaid[ra] was free and could go with them as he liked. He sent for Zaid[ra] and showed him his father and uncle. After the parties had met and dried their tears, Zaid's[ra] father told him that he had been freed by his kind Master and, as his mother was much afflicted by the separation, he had better return home. Zaid[ra] replied, "Father! who does not love his parents? My heart is full of love for you and mother. But I love this man Muḥammad[sa] so much that I cannot think of living elsewhere than with him. I have met you and I am glad. But separation from Muḥammad[sa] I cannot endure." Zaid's[ra] father and his uncle did their utmost to persuade Zaid[ra] to return home with them but Zaid[ra] did not agree. Upon this the Holy Prophet[sa] said, "Zaid[ra] was a freedman already, but from today he will be my son." Seeing this affection between Zaid[ra] and the Prophet[sa], Zaid's[ra] father and uncle went back and Zaid[ra] remained with the Prophet[sa] (*Hishām*).

THE PROPHET[sa] RECEIVES HIS FIRST REVELATION

When the Prophet[sa] was over thirty years of age, love of God and love of His worship began to possess him more and more. Revolting against the mischiefs, misdeeds and the many vices of the people of Mecca, he chose a spot two or three miles away for his meditations. This was on top of a hill, a sort of cave shaped out of stone. His wife Khadīja[ra] would prepare food enough for several days, and with this he would repair to the cave Ḥirā. In the cave he would worship God day and night. When he was forty years of age, he saw a vision. It was in this very cave. He saw some one commanding him to recite.

The Prophet[sa] said in reply he did not know what or how to recite. The figure insisted and at last made the Prophet[sa] recite the following verses:

> **Recite thou in the name of thy Lord Who created, created man from a clot of blood. Recite! And thy Lord is the Most Beneficent, Who taught man by the pen, taught man what he knew not (96:2-6).**

These verses, the first ever revealed to the Prophet[sa], became part of the Qur'an as did other verses which were revealed later. They have tremendous meaning. They command the Prophet[sa] to stand up and be ready to proclaim the name of the One God, the One Creator—of the Prophet[sa] and of all others—Who has made man and sowed the seed of His own love and that of fellow-men in his nature. The Prophet[sa] was commanded to proclaim the Message of this God, and was promised help, and protection by Him in the proclamation of this Message. The verses foretold a time when the world would be taught all manner of knowledge through the instrumentality of the pen, and would be taught things never heard of before. The verses constitute an epitome of the Qur'an. Whatever the Prophet[sa] was to be taught in later revelations is contained in embryo in these verses. The foundation was laid in them of a great and heretofore unknown advance in the spiritual progress of man. The meaning and explanation of these verses will be found in their place in this Commentary. We refer to them here because their revelation constitutes a great occasion in the life of the Prophet[sa]. When the Prophet[sa] received this revelation, he was full of fear of the responsibility which God had decided to place on his shoulders. Any other person in his place would have been filled with pride—he would have felt that he had become great. The Prophet[sa] was different. He could achieve great things but could take no pride in his achievement. After this great experience he reached home greatly agitated, his face drawn. On Khadīja's[ra] enquiry, he narrated the whole experience to her and summed up his fears, saying, "Weak man that I am, how can I carry the responsibility which God proposes to put on my shoulders." Khadīja[ra] replied at once:

> **God is witness, He has not sent you this Word that you should fail and prove unworthy, that He should then give you up. How can God do such a thing, while you are kind and considerate to your relations, help the poor and the forlorn and bear their burdens? You are restoring the virtues which had disappeared from our country. You treat guests with honour and help those who are in distress. Can you be subjected by God to any trial? (*Bukhārī*).**

Having said this, Khadīja[ra] took the Prophet[sa] to her cousin, Waraqa bin Naufal, a Christian. When he heard the account Waraqa said:

> **"The angel who descended on Moses[as], I am sure, has descended on you" (*Bukhārī*).**

FIRST CONVERTS

Waraqa evidently referred to the prophecy in Deuteronomy 18:18. When the news reached Zaid[ra], the Prophet's[sa] freed slave, now about thirty years of age, and his cousin 'Alī[ra], about eleven, they both declared their faith in him. Abū Bakr[ra], friend of his childhood, was out of town. As he returned he began to hear of this new experience which the Prophet[sa] had had. He was told that his friend had gone mad and had begun to say that angels brought him messages from God. Abū Bakr[ra] trusted the Prophet[sa] completely. He did not doubt for a minute that the Prophet[sa] must be right—he had known him to be both sane and sincere. He knocked at the Prophet's[sa] door and on admission into his company asked him what had happened. The Prophet[sa], fearing lest Abū Bakr[ra] should misunderstand, began a long explanation. Abū Bakr[ra] stopped the Prophet[sa] from doing so, and insisted that all he wanted to know was whether an angel had really descended upon him from God and had given him a Message. The Prophet[sa] wanted to explain again, but Abū Bakr[ra] said he wanted to hear no explanation. He wanted only an answer to the question whether he had had a Message from God. The Prophet[sa] said, "Yes" and Abū Bakr[ra] at once declared his faith. Having declared his faith, he said, argument would have detracted from the value of his faith. He had known the Prophet[sa] long and intimately. He could not doubt him, and he wanted no argument to be convinced of his truth. This small group of the Faithful then were the first believers of Islam: a woman full of years, an eleven-year-old boy, a freed slave living among strangers, a young friend and the Prophet[sa] himself. This was the party which made the silent resolve to spread the light of God all over the world. When the people and their leaders heard of this, they laughed and declared that these men had gone mad. There was nothing to fear and nothing to worry about. But as time went on, the truth began to dawn and as the Prophet Isaiah[as] (28:13) said long ago, precept upon precept, precept upon precept; line upon line, line upon line; here a little, and there a little; began to descend upon the Prophet[sa].

THE FAITHFUL PERSECUTED

God began to talk to Muḥammad[sa] in "another tongue". The youth of the country began to wonder. Those in search of truth became excited. Out of scorn and derision began to grow approval and admiration. Slaves, young men, and hapless women began to collect around the Prophet[sa]. In his Message and in his teaching there was hope for the degraded, the depressed and the young. Women thought the time for the restoration of their rights was near. Slaves thought the day of their liberation had come and young men thought the avenues of progress were going to be thrown open to them. When derision began to change into approval and indifference into attachment, the chiefs of Mecca and the officials began to take fright. They assembled and took counsel. They decided that derision was no method to deal with this menace. A more serious remedy had to be applied. The new influence had to be put down by force. It was decided that persecution and some form of boycott must be instituted. Practical steps were soon taken, and Mecca was pitched against Islam in a serious conflict. The Prophet[sa] and his small following were no longer considered mad, but a growing influence which, if allowed to grow unimpeded, would prove a danger to the faith, prestige, customs and traditions of Mecca. Islam threatened to pull down and rebuild the old structure of Meccan society, to create a new heaven and a new earth, the coming of which must mean the disappearance of the old heaven of Arabia and its old heart. Meccans could no longer laugh at Islam. It was a question now of life and death for them. Islam was a challenge and Mecca accepted the challenge, as enemies of Prophets had always accepted the challenge of their Prophets. They decided not to meet argument by argument but to draw the sword and put down the dangerous teaching by force; not to match the good example of the Prophet[sa] and his followers by their own, nor to reply to kind words in kind, but to maltreat the innocent and to abuse those who spoke kindly. Once again in the world a conflict started between belief and disbelief; the forces of Satan declared war on the angels. The Faithful, still a handful, had no power to resist the onslaughts and violence of the disbelievers. A most cruel campaign began. Women were butchered shamelessly. Men were slaughtered. The slaves who had declared their faith in the Prophet[sa] were dragged over burning sands and stones. Their skins became hardened like those of animals. A long time after, when Islam had become established far and near, one of these early converts named Khabbāb bin Al-Arat[ra] had his body exposed. His friends saw his skin hardened like an animal's and asked him why it was so. Khabbāb[ra] laughed and said it was nothing; only a memory of those early days when slaves converted to Islam were dragged through the streets of Mecca over hard and hot sands and stones (*Musnad*, Vol. 5, p. 110).

The slaves who believed came from all communities. Bilāl[ra] was a negro, Ṣuhaib[ra] a Greek. They belonged to different faiths. Jabr[ra] and Ṣuhaib[ra] were Christians, Bilāl[ra] and 'Ammar[ra], idol-worshippers. Bilāl[ra] was made to lie on hot sand, loaded with stones, and boys were made to dance on his chest, and his master, Umayya bin Khalf, tortured him thus and then asked him to renounce Allah and the Prophet[sa] and sing the praises of the Meccan gods, Lāt and 'Uzzā. Bilāl[ra] only said, *Aḥad, Aḥad* ... (God is One).

Exasperated, Umayya handed Bilāl[ra] over to street boys, asking them to put a cord round his neck and drag him through the town over sharp stones. Bilāl's[ra] body bled, but he went on muttering, *Aḥad, Aḥad*... Later, when Muslims settled in Medina and were able to live and worship in comparative peace, the Holy Prophet[sa] appointed Bilāl[ra] a Mu'adhdhin, the official who calls the worshippers to prayers. Being an African, Bilāl[ra] missed the (h), in the Arabic *Ashhadu* (I bear witness). Medinite believers laughed at his defective pronunciation, but the Prophet[sa] rebuked them and told them how dear Bilāl[ra] was to God for the stout faith he showed under Meccan tortures. Abū Bakr[ra] paid ransom for Bilāl[ra] and many other slaves and secured their release. Among them was Ṣuhaib[ra], a prosperous merchant, whom the Quraish continued to belabour even after his release. When the Holy Prophet[sa] left Mecca to settle down in Medina, Ṣuhaib[ra] wanted to go with him. But the Meccans stopped him. He could not take away from Mecca, they said, the wealth he had earned in Mecca. Ṣuhaib[ra] offered to surrender all his property and earnings and asked whether they would then let him go. The Meccans accepted the arrangement. Ṣuhaib[ra] reached Medina empty-handed and saw the Prophet[sa], who heard him and congratulated him, saying, "This was the best bargain of your life."

Most of these slave-converts remained steadfast in outer as well as inner professions of faith. But some were weak. Once the Holy Prophet[sa] found ‘Ammār[ra] groaning with pain and drying his tears. Approached by the Prophet[sa], ‘Ammār[ra] said he had been beaten and compelled to recant. The Prophet[sa] asked him, "But did you believe at heart?" ‘Ammār[ra] declared that he did, and the Prophet[sa] said that God would forgive his weakness.

‘Ammār's[ra] father, Yāsir[ra], and his mother, Samiyya[ra], also were tormented by disbelievers. On one such occasion the Prophet[sa] happened to pass by. Filled with emotion, he said, "Family of Yāsir[ra], bear up patiently, for God has prepared for you a Paradise." The prophetic words were soon fulfilled. Yāsir[ra] succumbed to the tortures, and a little later Abū Jahl murdered his aged wife, Samiyya[ra], with a spear.

Zinbīra[ra], a woman slave, lost her eyes under the cruel treatment of disbelievers.

Abū Fukaih[ra], Ṣafwān bin Umayya's slave, was laid on hot sand while over his chest were placed heavy and hot stones, under pain of which his tongue dropped out.

Other slaves were mishandled in similar ways.

These cruelties were beyond endurance. But early believers bore them because their hearts were made stout by assurances received daily from God. The Qur'an descended on the Prophet[sa], but the reassuring voice of God descended on all believers. Were not this so, the Faithful could not have withstood the cruelties to which they were subjected. Abandoned by fellow-men, friends and relations, they had none but God with them, and they cared not whether they had anyone else. Because of Him, the cruelties seemed nothing, abuse sounded like prayers and stones seemed like velvet.

The free citizens who believed were not less cruelly treated. Their elders and chiefs tormented them in different ways. ‘Uthmān[ra] was a man of forty, and prosperous. Yet when the Quraish resolved upon general persecution of Muslims, his uncle, Ḥakam, tied him up and beat him. Zubair bin al-'Awwām[ra], a brave young lad who later became a great Muslim general, was wrapped up in a mat by his uncle, smoked from underneath and tortured by suffocation. But he would not recant. He had found Truth and would not give it up.

Abū Dharr[ra], of the tribe of Ghaffār, heard of the Prophet[sa] and went to Mecca to investigate. The Meccans dissuaded him, saying that they knew Muḥammad[sa] well and that his Movement was only a selfish design. Abū Dharr[ra] was not impressed; so he went to the Prophet[sa], heard the Message of Islam straight from him and was converted. Abū Dharr[ra] asked if he could keep his faith secret from his tribe. The Prophet[sa] said he could do so for a few days. But as he passed through the streets of Mecca he heard a party of Meccan chiefs abuse the Holy Prophet[sa] and make vile attacks. No longer could he keep his faith secret, and he declared at once: "I bear witness that there is no God but Allah, and that there is no one like Allah; and Muḥammad[sa] is His Servant and Prophet[sa]." This cry raised in an assembly of disbelievers seemed to them an effrontery. They rose in wrath and belaboured him until he fell down senseless. The Prophet's[sa] uncle 'Abbās[ra], not a convert yet, passed by and began to remonstrate on behalf of the victim. "Your food caravans pass through Abū Dharr's[ra] tribe," he said, "and angered at your treatment, his people can starve you to death." The following day Abū Dharr[ra] stayed at home. But the day after he went again to the same assembly and found them abusing the Holy Prophet[sa] as before. He went to the Ka'ba and found people doing the same. He could not restrain himself, stood up and made a loud declaration of his faith. Again he was severely handled. The same thing happened a third time, and Abū Dharr[ra] went back to his tribe.

The Holy Prophet[sa] himself was no exception to the cruel treatment meted out to the Faithful. On one occasion he was in prayer. A party of disbelievers put a mantle round his neck and dragged him; his eyes seemed protruded. Abū Bakr[ra] happened to come and rescued him, saying, "You seek to kill him, because he says, God is his Master?" On another occasion he lay prostrate in prayer and they laid the entrails of a camel on his back. He could not rise until the weight was removed. On yet another occasion he was passing through a street and a group of street boys followed him. They went on slapping his neck and telling the people that he called himself a Prophet[sa]. Such was the hatred and enmity against him, and such was his helplessness.

The Prophet's[sa] house was stoned from surrounding houses. Garbage and the remains of slaughtered animals were thrown into his kitchen. On many occasions dust was thrown on him while he was praying so that he had to retire to a safe spot for his public prayers.

These cruelties, perpetrated against a weak and innocent group and their honest, well-meaning but helpless Leader[sa], were not wasted, however. Decent men saw all this and became drawn to Islam. The Prophet[sa] was once resting on Ṣafā, a hill near the Ka'ba. The Meccan chief Abū Jahl, the Prophet's[sa] arch-enemy, passed by and began to pour vile abuse on him. The Prophet[sa] said nothing and went home. A woman-slave of his household was a witness to this distressing scene. Ḥamza[ra], the Prophet's[sa] uncle, a brave man feared by all his townsmen, returned home from a hunt in the jungle and entered the house proudly, his bow hung on his shoulder. The woman-slave had not forgotten the morning scene. She was disgusted to see Ḥamza[ra] walk home thus. She taunted him, saying that he thought himself brave and went about armed but knew not what Abū Jahl had done to his innocent nephew in the morning. Ḥamza[ra] heard an account of the morning incident. Though not a believer, he possessed nobility of character. He may have been impressed by the Prophet's[sa] Message, but not to the extent of joining openly. When he heard of this wanton attack by Abū Jahl, he could not hold back. His hesitancy about the new Message was gone. He began to feel that so far he had been too casual about it. He made straight for the Ka'ba, where the chiefs of Mecca were wont to meet and confer. He took his bow and struck Abū Jahl hard. "Count me from today a follower of Muḥammad[sa]," he said. "You abused him this morning because he would say nothing. If you are brave, come out and fight me." Abū Jahl was dumbfounded. His friends rose to help but, afraid of Ḥamza[ra] and his tribe, Abū Jahl stopped them, thinking an open fight would cost too dearly. He was really to blame, he said, about the morning incident (*Hishām* and *Ṭabarī*).

THE MESSAGE OF ISLAM

Opposition continued to mount. At the same time the Prophet[sa] and his followers were doing all they could to make plain to the Meccans the Message of Islam. It was a many-sided Message and of great ultimate significance, not only for Arabs but for the whole world. It was a Message from God. It said:

The Creator of the world is One. None else is worthy of worship. The Prophets have ever believed Him to be One, and taught their followers so. Meccans should give up all images and idols. Did they not see that the idols could not even remove the flies which dropped on the offerings laid at their feet? If they were attacked they could not repel. If they had a question put to them, they could not answer. If they were asked for help, they could do nothing. But the One God helped those who asked for His help, answered those who addressed Him in prayer, subjugated His enemies, and raised those who abased themselves before Him. When light came from Him, it illumined His devotees. Why then did the Meccans neglect Him and turn to lifeless images and idols and waste their lives? Did they not see that their want of faith in the One True God had made them utterly superstitious and incompetent? They had no idea of what was clean and what was unclean, of right and wrong. They did not honour their mothers. They treated savagely their sisters and daughters, and denied them their due. They did not treat their wives well. They tormented widows, exploited orphans, the poor and the weak, and sought to build their prosperity on the ruins of others. Of lying and cheating they were not ashamed, nor of burgling and loot. Gambling and drinking were their delight. For culture and national advance they did not care. How long were they going to ignore the One True God, and continue to lose and lose, and suffer and suffer? Had they not better reform? Had they not better give up all forms of exploitation of one another, restore rights to whom they were due, spend their wealth on national needs and on improving the lot of the poor and the weak, treat orphans as a trust and regard their protection as a duty, support widows and establish and encourage good works in the whole community, cultivate not merely justice and equity, but compassion and grace? Life in this world should be productive of good. "Leave good works behind", the Message further said, "that they may grow and bear fruit after you are gone. There is virtue in giving to others, not in receiving from them. Learn to surrender that you may be nearer to your God. Practise self-denial for the sake of your fellow-men, that you may multiply your credit with God. True, the Muslims are weak, but do not go after their weakness, Truth will triumph. This is the decree of Heaven. Through the Prophet[sa] a new measure and a new criterion of good and evil, of right and wrong, will be set up in the world. Justice and mercy will reign. No constraint will be allowed in the matter of religion, and no interference. The cruelties to which women and slaves have been subjected will be obliterated. The Kingdom of God will be instituted in place of the kingdom of Satan."

When this Message was preached to the people of Mecca and the well-meaning and reflective among them began to be impressed by it. The elders of Mecca took a serious view of what was happening. They went in a deputation to the Prophet's[sa] uncle, Abū Ṭālib, and addressed him thus:

You are one of our chiefs and for your sake we have so far spared your nephew, Muḥammad[sa]. The time has come, however, when we should put an end to this national crisis, this conflict, in our midst. We ask and demand that he should desist from saying anything against our idols. Let him proclaim that God is One, but let him not say anything against our idols. If he agrees to this, our conflict and controversy with him will be over. We urge you to persuade him. But if you are unable to do so, then one of two things must happen. Either you will have to give up your nephew, or we, your people, will give you up *(Hishām)*.

Abū Ṭālib was confronted with a hard choice. To give up his nephew was hard. Equally hard was it to be disowned by his people. Arabs had little in the way of money. Their prestige lay in their leadership. They lived for their people, and their people for them. Abū Ṭālib was much upset. He sent for the Prophet[sa] and explained to him the demand made by the elders of Mecca. "If you do not agree," he said with tears in his eyes, "then either I have to give you up or my people will give me up." The Prophet[sa] was in evident sympathy with his uncle. Tears came to his eyes and he said:

I ask you not to give up your people. I ask you not to stand by me. Instead, you may give me up and stand by your people. But the One and Only God is my witness when I say that even if they were to place the sun on my right and the moon on my left, I would not desist from preaching the truth of the One God. I must go on doing so until I die. You can choose your own pleasure (*Hishām* and *Zurqānī*).

This reply, firm, straight and sincere, opened the eyes of Abū Ṭālib. He sank deep in thought. Though he did not have the courage to believe, he thought he was lucky to have lived to see this grand demonstration of belief and regard for duty. Turning to the Prophet[sa], he said:

> **"My nephew, go your way. Do your duty. Let my people give me up. I am with you" (*Hishām*).**

EMIGRATION TO ABYSSINIA

When tyranny reached its extreme limit the Prophet[sa] assembled his followers, and pointing to the west told them of a land across the sea where men were not murdered because of a change of faith, where they could worship God unmolested, and where there was a just king. Let them go there; maybe the change would bring them relief. A party of Muslim men, women and children, acting on this suggestion, went to Abyssinia. The migration was on a small scale and very pathetic. The Arabs regarded themselves as keepers of the Ka'ba, and so they were. To leave Mecca was for them a great wrench, and no Arab could think of doing so unless living in Mecca had become absolutely impossible. Nor were the Meccans prepared to tolerate such a movement. They would not let their victims escape and have the least chance to live elsewhere. The party, therefore, had to keep its preparations for the journey a close secret and to depart without even saying good-bye to their friends and relations. Their departure, however, became known to some and did not fail to impress them. 'Umar[ra], subsequently the Second Khalifah of Islam, was still a disbeliever, a bitter enemy and persecutor of Muslims. By sheer chance, he met some members of this party. One of these was a woman, Ummi 'Abdullah[ra]. When 'Umar[ra] saw household effects packed up and loaded on animals, he understood at once that it was a party leaving Mecca to take refuge elsewhere. "Are you going?" he asked. "Yes, God is our witness," replied Ummi 'Abdullah[ra]. "We go to another land, because you treat us most cruelly here. We will not return now until Allah pleases to make it easy for us." 'Umar[ra] was impressed and said, "God be with you." There was emotion in his voice. This silent scene had upset him. When the Meccans got to know of it, they sent a party in chase. This party went as far as the sea but found that the Muslims had already embarked. Not being able to overtake them, they decided to send a delegation to Abyssinia to excite the king against the refugees and to persuade him to hand them over again to Meccans. One of the delegates was 'Amr bin al-'Āṣ[ra], who later joined Islam and conquered Egypt. The delegation went to Abyssinia, met the king and intrigued with his court. But the king proved very firm and, in spite of the pressure which the Meccan delegation and his own courtiers were able to put upon him, he refused to hand over the Muslim refugees to their persecutors. The delegation returned disappointed, but in Mecca they soon thought of another plan to force the return of Muslims from Abyssinia. Among the caravans going to Abyssinia they set afloat the rumour that all Mecca had accepted Islam. When the rumour reached Abyssinia, many Muslim refugees joyfully returned to Mecca but found on arrival that the rumour which had reached them was a fabrication. Some Muslims went back again to Abyssinia but some decided to stay. Among the latter was 'Uthmān bin Maz'ūn[ra], son of a leading Meccan chief. 'Uthmān[ra] received protection from a friend of his father, Walīd bin Mughīra, and began to live in peace. But he saw that other Muslims continued to suffer brutal persecution. It made him very unhappy. He went to Walīd and renounced his protection. He felt he should not have such protection while other Muslims continued to suffer. Walīd announced this to the Meccans.

One day, Labīd, poet-laureate of Arabia, sat among the chiefs of Mecca, reciting his verse. He read a line which meant that all graces must ultimately come to an end. 'Uthmān[ra] boldly contradicted him and said, "The graces of Paradise will be everlasting." Labīd, not used to such contradictions, lost his temper and said, "Quraish, your guests were not insulted like this before. Whence has this fashion begun?" To appease Labīd, a man from among the audience rose and said, "Go on and take no notice of this fool". 'Uthmān[ra] XE "Persecution to the Muslims:'Uthmān bin Maz'ūn[ra] insisted that he had said nothing foolish. This exasperated the Quraishite, who sprang upon 'Uthmān[ra] and gave him a sharp blow, knocking out an eye. Walīd was present at the scene. He was a close friend of 'Uthmān's[ra] father. He could not endure such treatment of his deceased friend's son. But 'Uthmān[ra] was no longer under his formal protection and Arab custom now forbade him to take sides. So he could do nothing. Half in anger, half in anguish he turned to 'Uthmān[ra], and said, "Son of my friend, you would have saved your eye, had you not renounced my protection. You have to thank yourself for it."

'Uthmān[ra] replied,

> **"I have longed for this. I lament not over the loss of one eye, because the other waits for the same fate. Remember, while the Prophet[sa] suffers, we want no peace" (*Ḥalbiyya*, Vol. 1, P. 348).**

'UMAR[ra] ACCEPTS ISLAM

About this time, another very important event took place. 'Umar[ra], who later became the Second Khalifah of Islam, was still one of the fiercest and the most feared enemies of Islam. He felt that no effective step had yet been taken against the new Movement and decided to put an end to the Prophet's[sa] life. He took his sword and set out. A friend was puzzled to see him going and asked where he was going and with what intent. "To kill Muḥammad[sa]," said 'Umar[ra].

"But would you be safe from his tribe after this? And do you really know how things are going? Do you know that your sister and her husband have joined Islam?"

It came like a bolt from the blue and greatly upset 'Umar[ra]. He decided to go and have done with his sister and her husband first. As he reached their house he heard a recitation going on inside. The voice was that of Khabbab[ra] who was teaching them the Holy Book. 'Umar[ra] entered the house swiftly. Khabbab[ra], alarmed by the hurried steps, had already hid himself. 'Umar's[ra] sister, Fāṭima[ra], put away the leaves of the Qur'an. Confronting her and her husband, 'Umar[ra] said, "I hear you have renounced your own faith," and, saying this, he raised his hand to strike her husband, who was incidentally his own cousin. Fāṭima[ra] threw herself between 'Umar[ra] and her husband; so 'Umar's[ra] hand fell on Fāṭima's[ra] face and struck her on the nose, from which blood flowed freely. The blow made Fāṭima[ra] all the braver. She said, "Yes, we are Muslims now and shall remain so; do what you may." 'Umar[ra] was a brave man, though rough. His sister's face, dyed red by his own hand, filled him with remorse. Soon he was a changed man. He asked to be shown those leaves of the Qur'an they were reading from. Fāṭima[ra] refused lest he should tear them up and throw them away. 'Umar[ra] promised not to do so. But, said Fāṭima[ra], he was not clean. 'Umar[ra] offered to have a bath. Clean and cooled, he took the leaves of the Qur'an in his hand. They contained a portion of the Chapter Ṭā Hā. And he came upon the verses:

"Verily I am Allah; there is no God beside Me. So serve Me, and observe prayer for My remembrance. Surely the Hour is coming, and I am going to manifest it, that every soul may be recompensed for its endeavour" (20:15, 16).

The firm assertion of God's existence, the clear promise that Islam would soon establish genuine worship in place of the customary one current in Mecca—these and a host of other associated ideas must have moved 'Umar[ra]. He could contain himself no longer. Faith welled up in his heart and he said, "How wonderful, how inspiring!" Khabbāb[ra] came out of his hiding, and said, "God is my witness, only yesterday I heard the Prophet[sa] pray for the conversion of 'Umar[ra] or 'Amr ibn Hishām. Your change is the result of that prayer." 'Umar'sra mind was made up. He asked where the Prophetsa was and made straight for him at Dari Arqam, his bare sword still in his hand. As he knocked at the door, the Prophet'ssa Companions could see 'Umarra through the crevices. They feared lest he should have some evil design. But the Prophetsa said, "Let him come in." 'Umarra entered, sword in hand. "What brings you?" inquired the Prophetsa. "Prophetsa of God," said 'Umarra, "I am here to become a Muslim." *Allāhu Akbar*, cried the Prophetsa. *Allāhu Akbar*, cried the Companions. The hills around Mecca echoed the cries. News of the conversion spread like wild fire and henceforward 'Umarra, the much-feared persecutor of Islam, himself began to be persecuted along with other Muslims. But 'Umarra had changed. He delighted now in suffering as he had delighted before in inflicting suffering. He went about Mecca, a much harassed person.

PERSECUTION INTENSIFIES

Persecution became more and more serious and more unbearable. Many Muslims had already left Mecca. Those who stayed behind had to suffer more than ever before. But Muslims swerved not a bit from the path they had chosen. Their hearts were as stout as ever, their faith as steadfast. Their devotion to the One God was on the increase and so was their hatred for the national idols of Mecca. The conflict had become more serious than ever. The Meccans convened another big meeting. At this they resolved on an all-out boycott of the Muslims: The Meccans were to have no normal dealings with Muslims. They were neither to buy from them, nor to sell them anything. The Prophetsa, his family and a number of relations who, though not Muslims, still stood by him, were compelled to take shelter in a lonely place, a possession of Abū Ṭālib. Without money, without means and without reserves, the Prophet'ssa family and relations suffered untold hardships under this blockade. For three years there was no slackening of it. Then at last, five decent members of the enemy revolted against these conditions. They went to the blockaded family, offered to annul the boycott, and asked the family to come out. Abū Ṭālib came out and reproved his people. The revolt of the five became known all over Mecca, but good feeling asserted itself again, and Meccans decided they must cancel the savage boycott. The boycott was over, but not its consequences. In a few days the Prophet's[sa] faithful wife, Khadīja[ra], met her death, and a month later his uncle, Abū Ṭālib.

The Holy Prophet[sa] had now lost the companionship and support of Khadīja[ra], and he and the Muslims had lost the good offices of Abū Ṭālib. Their passing away naturally also resulted in the loss of some general sympathy. Abū Lahab, another uncle of the Prophet[sa], seemed ready at first to side with the Prophet[sa]. The shock of his brother's death and regard for his dying wish were still fresh in his mind. But the Meccans soon succeeded in antagonizing him. They made use of the usual appeals. The Prophet[sa] taught that disbelief in the Oneness of God was an offence, punishable in the Hereafter; his teaching contradicted everything they had learnt from their forefathers, and so on. Abū Lahab decided to oppose the Prophet[sa] more than ever. Relations between Muslims and Meccans had become strained. A three-year boycott and blockade had enlarged the gulf between them. Meeting and preaching seemed impossible. The Prophet[sa] did not mind the ill-treatment and the persecution; these were nothing so long as he had the chance to meet and address people. But now it seemed that he had no such chance in Mecca. General antagonism apart, the Prophet[sa] now found it impossible to appear in any street or public place. If he did, they threw dust at him and sent him back to his house. Once he returned home, his head covered with dust. A daughter wept as she removed the dust. The Prophet[sa] told her not to weep for God was with him. Ill-treatment did not upset the Prophet[sa]. He even welcomed it as evidence of interest in his Message. One day, for instance, the Meccans by a general intrigue said nothing to him nor did they ill-treat him in any way. The Prophet[sa] retired home disappointed, until the reassuring voice of God made him go to his people again.

THE PROPHET[sa] GOES TO ṬĀ'IF

It seemed that in Mecca now nobody would listen to him and this made him sad. He felt he was stagnating. So he decided to turn elsewhere for the preaching of his Message, and he chose Ṭā'if, a small town about sixty miles to the south-east of Mecca and famed for its fruit and its agriculture. The Prophet's[sa] decision was in keeping with the traditions of all Prophets[as]. Moses[as] turned now to the Pharaoh, now to Israel, and now to Midian. Jesus[as], similarly, turned now to Galilee, now to places across the Jordan, and now to Jerusalem. So the Holy Prophet[sa] of Islam, finding that Meccans would ill-treat but not listen, turned to Ṭā'if. In polytheistic beliefs and practices Ṭā'if was not behind Mecca. The idols to be found in the Ka'ba were not the only, nor the only important, idols in Arabia. One important idol, al-Lāt, was to be found in Ṭā'if; because of it Ṭā'if also was a centre of pilgrimage. The inhabitants of Ṭā'if were connected with those of Mecca by ties of blood; and many green spots between Ṭā'if and Mecca were owned by Meccans. On arrival at Ṭā'if, the Prophet[sa] had visits from its chiefs but none seemed willing to accept the Message. The rank and file obeyed their leaders and dismissed the teaching with contempt. This was not unusual. People immersed in worldly affairs always regard such a Message as something of an interference and even an offence. Because the Message is without visible support—such as numbers or arms—they also feel they can dismiss it with contempt. The Prophet[sa] was no exception. Reports of him had already reached Ṭā'if, and here he now was, without arms or following, a lone individual with only one companion, Zaid[ra]. The towns folk thought him a nuisance which should be ended, if only to please their chiefs. They set vagabonds of the town and street boys at him who pelted him with stones and drove him out of the town. Zaid[ra] was wounded and the Prophet[sa] began to bleed profusely. But the pursuit continued until this defenceless party of two was several miles out of Ṭā'if. The Prophet[sa] was sorely grieved and dejected when an angel descended upon him and asked if he would like his persecutors to be destroyed. "No," said the Prophet[sa]. "I hope that of these very tormentors would be born those who would worship the One True God." (*Bukhārī, Kitāb Bad'ul-Khalq.*)

Exhausted and dejected, he stopped at a vineyard owned by two Meccans who happened to be present. They were among his persecutors at Mecca, but on this occasion they became sympathetic. Was it because a Meccan had been ill-treated by the people of Ṭā'if, or was it because a spark of human kindness suddenly glowed in their hearts? They sent to the Prophet[sa] a tray full of grapes with a Christian slave, 'Addas[ra] by name and belonging to Nineveh. 'Addas[ra] presented the tray to the Prophet[sa] and his companion. While he looked wistfully at them, he became more curious than ever when he heard the Prophet[sa] say, "In the name of Allah, the Gracious, the Merciful." His Christian background was enlivened and he felt he was in the presence of a Hebrew Prophet[as]. The Prophet[sa] asked him where he belonged and 'Addas[ra] said Nineveh, upon which the Prophet[sa] said, "Jonah[as], son of Amittai, who belonged to Nineveh, was a holy man, a Prophet like me." The Prophet[sa] also told 'Addās[ra] of his own Message. 'Addās[ra] felt charmed and believed at once. He embraced the Prophet[sa] with tears in his eyes and started kissing his head, hands and feet. The meeting over, the Prophet[sa] turned again to Allah and said:

Allah, I submit my plaint to Thee. I am weak, and without means. My people look down upon me. Thou art Lord of the weak and the poor and Thou art my Lord. To whom wilt Thou abandon me—to strangers who push me about or to the enemy who oppresses me in my own town? If Thou art not angered at me, I care not for my enemy. Thy mercy be with me. I seek refuge in the light of Thy face. It is Thou Who canst drive away darkness from the world and give peace to all, here and hereafter. Let not Thy anger and Thy wrath descend on me. Thou art never angry except when Thou art pleased soon after. And there is no power and no refuge except with Thee (*Hishām* and *Ṭabarī*).

Having said this prayer, he set back for Mecca. He stopped en route at Nakhla for a few days and set out again. According to Meccan tradition he was no longer a citizen of Mecca. He had left it because he thought it hostile and could not return to it except with the permission of the Meccans. Accordingly, he sent word to Muṭ'im bin 'Adī—a Meccan chief, to ask if Meccans would permit him to come back. Muṭ'im, though as bitter an enemy as any other, possessed nobility of heart. He collected his sons and relatives. Arming themselves, they went to the Ka'ba. Standing in the courtyard he announced he was permitting the Prophet[sa] to return. The Prophet[sa] then returned, and made a circuit of the Ka'ba. Muṭ'im, his sons and relatives, with swords unsheathed, then escorted the Prophet[sa] to his house. It was not protection in the customary Arabian sense which had been extended to the Prophet[sa]. The Prophet[sa] continued to suffer and Muṭ'im did not shield him. Muṭ'im's act amounted to a declaration of formal permission for the Prophet[sa] to return.

The Prophet's[sa] journey to Tā'if has extorted praise even from the enemies of Islam. Sir William Muir, in his biography of the Prophet[sa], writes (speaking of the journey to Ṭā'if):

> **There is something lofty and heroic in this journey of Muḥammad[sa] to Aṭ-Ṭā'if; a solitary man, despised and rejected by his own people, going boldly forth in the name of God, like Jonah to Nineveh, and summoning an idolatrous city to repent and support his mission. It sheds a strong light on the intensity of his belief in the divine origin of his calling (*Life of Muḥammad[sa]* by Sir W. Muir, 1923 edition, pp. 112-113).**

Mecca returned to its old hostility. The Prophet's[sa] home town again became hell for him. But he continued to tell people of his Message. The formula, "God is One", began to be heard here and there. With love and regard, and with a sense of fellow-feeling, the Prophet[sa] persisted in the exposition of his Message. People turned away but he addressed them again and again. He made his proclamation, whether the people cared or not, and persistence seemed to pay. The handful of Muslims who had returned from Abyssinia and had decided to stay, preached secretly to their friends, neighbours and relations. Some of these were persuaded to declare themselves openly and to share the sufferings of other Muslims. But many, though persuaded at heart, did not have the courage to confess openly; they waited for the kingdom of God to come to the earth.

In the meantime revelations received by the Prophet[sa] began to hint at the near possibility of migration from Mecca. Some idea of the place they were to migrate to was also given to him. It was a town of wells and date-groves. He thought of Yamāma. But soon the thought was dismissed. He then waited in the assurance that whatever place they were destined to go to would certainly become the cradle of Islam.

ISLAM SPREADS TO MEDINA

The annual Hajj drew near, and from all parts of Arabia pilgrims began to arrive in Mecca. The Prophet[sa] went wherever he found a group of people, expounded to them the idea of One God and told them to give up excesses of all kinds and prepare for the Kingdom of God. Some listened and became interested. Some wished to listen but were sent away by the Meccans. Some who had already made up their minds, stopped to ridicule. The Prophetsa was in the valley of Minā when he saw a group of six or seven people. He found that they belonged to the Khazraj tribe, one in alliance with the Jews. He asked them if they would listen to what he had to say. They had heard of him and were interested; so they agreed. The Prophetsa spent some time telling them that the Kingdom of God was at hand, that idols were going to disappear, that the idea of One God was due to triumph, and piety and purity were once again going to rule. Would they not, in Medina, welcome the Message? The group became much impressed. They accepted the Message and promised, on their return to Medina, to confer with others and report next year whether Medina would be willing to receive Muslim refugees from Mecca. They returned and conferred with their friends and relations. There were, at the time, two Arab and three Jewish tribes at Medina. The Arab tribes were the Aus and the Khazraj and the Jewish tribes the Banū Quraiẓa, the Banū Naḍīr, and the Banū Qainuqā'. The Aus and the Khazraj were at war. The Quraiẓa and the Naḍīr were in alliance with the Aus and the Qainuqā' with the Khazraj. Tired of unending warfare, they were inclined to peace. At last they agreed to acknowledge the Khazraj Chief, 'Abdullāh bin Ubayy bin Salūl, as King of Medina. From the Jews, the Aus and the Khazraj had heard of prophecies in the Bible. They had heard Jewish tales of the lost glory of Israel and of the advent of a Prophetsa "like unto Mosesas." This advent was near at hand, the Jews used to say. It was to mark the return to power of Israel and the destruction of their enemies. When the people of Medina heard of the Prophetsa, they became impressed and began to ask if this Meccan Prophetsa was not the Prophetsa they had heard of from the Jews. Many young men readily believed. At the next

Hajj twelve men from Medina came to Mecca to join the Prophet[sa]. Ten of these belonged to the Khazraj and two to the Aus tribe. They met the Prophet[sa] in the valley of Minā and, holding the Prophet's[sa] hand, solemnly declared their belief in the Oneness of God and their resolve to abstain from all common evils, from infanticide, and from making false accusations against one another. They also resolved to obey the Prophet[sa] in all good things. When they returned to Medina, they started telling others of their New Faith. Zeal increased. Idols were taken out of their niches and thrown on the streets. Those who used to bow before images began to hold their heads high. They resolved to bow to none except the One God. The Jews wondered. Centuries of friendship, exposition and debate had failed to produce the change which this Meccan Teacher had produced in a few days. The people of Medina would go to the few Muslims in their midst and make inquiries about Islam. But the few Muslims could not cope with the large numbers of inquiries, nor did they know enough. They decided, therefore, to address a request to the Prophet[sa] to send them some one to teach Islam. The Prophet[sa] agreed to send Muṣ'ab[ra], one of the Muslims who had been in Abyssinia. Muṣ'ab[ra] was the first missionary of Islam to go out of Mecca. At about this time, the Prophet[sa] had a grand promise from God. He had a vision in which he saw that he was in Jerusalem and Prophets had joined behind him in congregational worship. Jerusalem only meant Medina, which was going to become the centre of the worship of the One God. Other Prophets congregating behind the Prophet[sa] of Islam meant that men following different Prophets would join Islam, and Islam would thus become a universal religion.

Conditions in Mecca had now become most critical. Persecution had assumed the worst possible form. Meccans laughed at this vision and described it as wishful thinking. They did not know that the foundations of the New Jerusalem had been laid.

Nations of the East and the West were agog. They wanted to hear the Last Great Message of God. In those very days the Kaiser and the Chosroes of Iran went to war with each other. Chosroes was victorious. Syria and Palestine were overrun by Iranian armies. Jerusalem was destroyed. Egypt and Asia Minor were mastered. At the mouth of the Bosphorus, only ten miles from Constantinople, Iranian Generals were able to pitch their tents. Meccans rejoiced over Iranian victories and said the judgement of God had been delivered—the idol-worshippers of Iran had defeated a People of the Book. At that time, the Holy Prophet[sa] received the following revelation:

> **The Romans have been defeated in the land nearby, and they, after their defeat, will be victorious in a few years—Allah's is the command before and after that—and on that day will the believers rejoice with the help of Allah. He helps whom He pleases; and He is the Mighty, the Merciful. Allah has made this promise. Allah breaks not His promise, but most men know not (30: 3-7).**

The prophecy was fulfilled in a few years. The Romans defeated the Iranians and recovered the territories they had lost to them. The part of the prophecy which said, "On that day the believers shall rejoice with the help of God", was also fulfilled. Islam began to advance. The Meccans believed they had put an end to it by persuading people not to listen to Muslims but to show active hostility instead. Right at this time the Prophet[sa] received in his revelations news of victories for Muslims, and destruction for Meccans. The Prophet[sa] announced the following verses:

> **And they say, "Why does he not bring us a Sign from his Lord?" Has there not come to them the clear evidence in what is contained in the former books? And if We had destroyed them with a punishment before it, they would have surely said, "Our Lord, wherefore didst Thou not send to us a Messenger that we might have followed Thy commandments before we were humbled and disgraced?"**

Say, "Each one is waiting; wait ye, therefore, and you will know who are the people of the right path and who follow true guidance" (20: 134-136).

The Meccans complained of lack of Signs. They were told that the prophecies about Islam and the Prophet[sa] recorded in earlier books should be enough. Had Meccans been destroyed before the Message of Islam could be explained to them, they would have complained of lack of chance to consider the Signs. The Meccans must, therefore, wait.

Revelations promising victory for believers and defeat for disbelievers were being received every day. When the Meccans looked at their own power and prosperity and at the powerlessness and poverty of Muslims, and then heard of the promises of divine help and of Muslim victories in the Prophet's[sa] daily revelations, they wondered and wondered. Were they mad or was the Prophet[sa] mad? They were hoping that persecution would compel the Muslims to give up their faith and return to the Meccans, that the Prophet[sa] himself and his closest followers would begin to have doubts about his claims. But instead of this they had to listen to confident affirmations like the following:

Nay, I swear by all that you see, and by all that you see not that it is surely the message brought by an honoured Messenger[sa]. And it is not the word of a poet; little is it that you believe; nor is it the utterance of a soothsayer; little is it that you heed. It is a revelation from the Lord of the worlds. And if he had forged any sayings in Our name, We would surely have seized him by the right hand, and then surely would We have severed his life-artery, and not one of you could have held Us off from him. And surely it is an admonition for the God-fearing. And, surely, We know that some of you reject Our Signs. And, surely, it is a source of anguish for the disbelievers. And, surely, it is the true certainty. So glorify the name of thy Lord, the Great (Qur'an 69:39-53).

Meccans were warned that all their fond hopes would be smashed. The Prophet[sa] was neither a poet, nor a soothsayer nor a pretender. The Qur'an was a reading for the pious. True, it had its deniers. But it also had its secret admirers, those who were jealous of its teaching and its truths. The promises and prophecies contained in it would all be fulfilled. The Prophet[sa] was asked to ignore all opposition and go on celebrating his Mighty God.

The third Hajj arrived. Among the pilgrims from Medina was a large party of Muslims. Owing to Meccan opposition these Muslims from Medina wished to see the Prophet[sa] in private. The Prophet's[sa] own thoughts were turning more and more to Medina, as a likely place for migration. He mentioned this to his closest relations but they tried to dissuade him from all thoughts of this kind. They pleaded that though Mecca was full of opposition, it offered the support of several influential relations. The prospects at Medina were all uncertain and, should Medina prove as hostile as Mecca, would the Prophet's[sa] Meccan relations be able to help? The Prophet[sa], however, was convinced that migration to Medina had been decreed. So he rejected the advice of his relations and decided to migrate to Medina.

FIRST PLEDGE OF 'AQABA

After midnight, the Prophet[sa] again met the Muslims from Medina in the valley of 'Aqaba. His uncle 'Abbās[ra] was with him. The Muslims from Medina numbered seventy-three, out of whom sixty-two belonged to the Khazraj tribe and eleven to the Aus. The party included two women, one being Ummi 'Ammāra[ra], of the Banū Najjār. They had been taught Islam by Muṣ'ab[ra], and were full of faith and determination. They all proved to be pillars of Islam. Ummi 'Ammāra[ra] is an example. She instilled in her children undying loyalty to Islam. One of her sons, Ḥabīb[ra], was taken prisoner by Musailima, the

Pretender, in an encounter after the Prophet's[sa] death. Musailima tried to unsettle Ḥabīb's[ra] faith. "Do you believe Muḥammad[sa] to be a Messenger of God?" he asked. "Yes," was the reply. "Do you believe me to be a Messenger of God?" asked Musailima. "No," replied Ḥabīb[ra]. Upon this Musailima ordered one of his limbs to be cut off. This done, he asked Ḥabīb[ra] again, "Do you believe Muḥammad[sa] to be a Messenger of God?" "Yes," replied Ḥabīb[ra]. "Do you believe me to be a Messenger of God?" "No." Musailima ordered another limb to be cut off Ḥabīb's[ra] body. Limb after limb was cut off in this way and Ḥabīb's[ra] body was reduced to many pieces. He died a cruel death, but left behind an unforgettable example of personal heroism and sacrifice for the sake of religious conviction (*Ḥalbiyya*, Vol. 2, p. 17).

Ummi 'Ammāra[ra] accompanied the Prophet[sa] in several wars.

This party of Medina Muslims, in short, attained to great distinction for their loyalty and faith. They came to Mecca not for wealth, but for faith; and they had it in abundance.

Moved by family ties and feeling legitimately responsible for the safety of the Prophet[sa], 'Abbās[ra] thus addressed the party:

> **O Khazraj, this my relation is respected here by his people. They are not all Muslims, yet they protect him. But he has chosen now to leave us and go to you. O Khazraj, do you know what will happen? All Arabia will be against you. If you realize the risks entailed by your invitation, then take him away; if you do not, then give up your intention and let him stay here.**

The leader of this party Al-Barā'[ra] replied assuredly:

> **We have heard you. Our resolution is firm. Our lives are at the disposal of the Prophet[sa] of God. We are decided, and only await his decision (*Ḥalbiyya*, Vol. 2, p. 18).**

The Prophet[sa] gave a further exposition of Islam and its teaching. Explaining this, he told the party that he would go to Medina if they would hold Islam as dear as they held their wives and children. He had not quite finished when this party of seventy-three devotees cried, 'Yes,' 'Yes,' in one voice. In their zeal they forgot that they could be overheard. 'Abbās[ra] cautioned them to speak low. But the party was full of faith. Death now was nothing in their eyes. When 'Abbas[ra] cautioned the party, one of them said aloud, "We are not afraid, O Prophet of God[sa]. Permit us, and we can deal with the Meccans right now and avenge the wrongs they have done you." But the Prophet[sa] said he had not yet been commanded to fight.

The party then took the oath of fealty and the meeting dispersed.

The Meccans did get to know of this meeting. They went to the Medina encampment to complain against these visitors to their chiefs. 'Abdullāh bin Ubbayy bin Salūl—Chief of chiefs—knew nothing of what had happened. He assured the Meccans that it must be some false rumour which they had heard. The people of Medina had accepted him as their leader and could not do anything without his knowledge and permission. He did not know that the people of Medina had cast off the rule of Satan and accepted the rule of God instead.

THE HIJRA

The party returned to Medina and the Prophet[sa] and his followers started preparations for migration. Family after family began to disappear. Muslims, certain that the Kingdom of God was near, were full of courage. Sometimes a whole lane would be emptied in the course of a night. In the morning Meccans would see the doors locked and realize that the residents had migrated to Medina. The growing influence of Islam amazed them.

At last not a single Muslim remained in Mecca save a few slave converts, the Prophet[sa] himself, Abū Bakr[ra] and 'Alī[ra]. The Meccans realized that their prey was about to escape. The chiefs assembled again and decided they should now kill the Prophet[sa]. By a special divine design, it seems, the date they appointed for killing the Prophet[sa] was appointed for his escape. When the Meccan party was collecting in front of the Prophet's[sa] house with intent to kill, the Prophet[sa] was moving out in the secrecy of the night. The Meccans must have feared anticipation of their foul design by the Prophet[sa]. They proceeded cautiously and when the Prophet[sa] himself passed by, they took him for someone else, and withdrew to avoid being noticed. The Prophet's[sa] closest friend Abū Bakr[ra] had been informed of the Prophet's[sa] plan the day before. He duly joined and then both left Mecca, and took shelter in a cave called Thaur, about three or four miles from Mecca over a hill. When the Meccans learnt of the Prophet's[sa] escape, they collected and sent a force in pursuit. Led by a tracker, they reached Thaur. Standing at the mouth of the cave in which the Prophet[sa] and Abū Bakr[ra] sat hiding, the tracker said that Muḥammad[sa] was either in the cave or had ascended to heaven. Abū Bakr[ra] heard this and his heart sank. "The enemy has nearly got us," he whispered. "Fear not, God is with us," replied the Prophet[sa]. "I fear not for myself," went on Abū Bakr[ra], "but for you. For, if I die, I am but an ordinary mortal; but if you die, it will mean death to faith and spirit" (*Zurqānī*). "Even so, fear not," assured the Prophet[sa], "We are not two in this cave. There is a third—God" (*Bukhārī*).

Meccan tyranny was destined to end. Islam was to have the chance to grow. The pursuers were deceived. They ridiculed the tracker's judgement. It was too open a cave, they said, for anybody to take shelter in, for with snakes and vipers it was none too safe. If they had but bent a little, they could have sighted the two. But they did not, and dismissing the tracker, they returned to Mecca.

For two days the Prophet[sa] and Abū Bakr[ra] waited in the cave. On the third night, according to the plan, two fleet camels were brought to the cave, one for the

Prophet[sa] and the guide; the other for Abū Bakr[ra] and his servant, 'Āmir bin Fuhaira[ra].

SURAQA[ra] PURSUES THE PROPHET

Before setting out, the Prophet[sa] looked back at Mecca. Emotions welled up in his heart. Mecca was his birthplace. He had lived there as child and man and had received there the Divine Call. It was the place where his forefathers had lived and flourished since the time of Ishmael. With these thoughts, he had a last long look at it and then said, "Mecca, thou art dearer to me than any other place in the world, but thy people would not let me live here." Upon this Abū Bakr[ra] said, "The place hath turned out its Prophet[sa]. It only awaiteth its destruction." The Meccans, after the failure of their pursuit, put a prize on the heads of the two fugitives. Whoever captured and restored to the Meccans the Prophet[sa] or Abū Bakr[ra] dead or alive was to have a reward of a hundred camels. The announcement was made among the tribes around Mecca. Tempted by the reward, Surāqa bin Mālik[ra], a Bedouin chief, started in pursuit of the party and ultimately sighted them on the road to Medina. He saw two mounted camels and, feeling sure they were bearing the Prophet[sa] and Abū Bakr[ra], spurred on his horse. The horse reared and fell before it had gone very far and Surāqa[ra] fell with it. Surāqa's[ra] own account of what happened is interesting. He says:

> **After I fell from the horse, I consulted my luck in the superstitious fashion common with Arabs by a throw of the arrows. The arrows boded ill-luck. But the temptation of the reward was great. I mounted again and resumed my pursuit and nearly overtook the party. The Prophet[sa] rode with dignity, and did not look back. Abū Bakr[ra], however, looked back again and again (evidently, out of fear for the safety of the Prophet[sa]). As I neared them, my horse reared again, and I fell off. I consulted the arrows again; and**

again they boded ill-luck. My horse's hoofs sank deep into the sand. Mounting again and resuming the pursuit seemed difficult. I then understood that the party was under divine protection. I called out to them and entreated them to stop. When near enough I told them of my evil intention and of my change of heart. I told them I was giving up the pursuit and returning. The Prophet[sa] **let me go, but made me promise not to reveal their whereabouts to anybody. I became convinced that the Prophet**[sa] **was a true one, destined to succeed. I requested the Prophet**[sa] **to write me a guarantee of peace to serve me when he became supreme. The Prophet**[sa] **asked 'Āmir bin Fuhaira**[ra] **to write me a guarantee, and he did. As I got ready to return with it, the Prophet**[sa] **received a revelation about the future and said, "Surāqa**[ra]**, how wilt thou feel with the gold bangles of the Chosroes on thy wrists?" Amazed at the prophecy I asked, "Which Chosroes? Chosroes bin Hormizd, the Emperor of Iran?" The Prophet**[sa] **said, "Yes" (*Usud al-Ghāba*).**

Sixteen or seventeen years later the prophecy was literally fulfilled. Surāqa[ra] accepted Islam and went to Medina. The Prophet[sa] died, and after him, first Abū Bakr[ra], and then 'Umar[ra] became the Khalifahs of Islam. The growing influence of Islam made the Iranians jealous and led them to attack the Muslims but, instead of subjugating the Muslims, they were themselves subjugated by them. The capital of Iran fell to the Muslims who captured its treasures, including the gold bangles which the Chosroes wore at State functions. After his conversion, Surāqa[ra] used to describe his pursuit of the Prophet[sa] and his party and to tell of what passed between him and the Prophet[sa]. When the spoils of the war with Iran were placed before 'Umar[ra], he saw the gold bangles and remembered what the Prophet[sa] had told Surāqa[ra]. It was a grand prophecy made at a time of utter helplessness. 'Umar[ra] decided to stage a visible fulfilment of the prophecy. He, therefore, sent for Surāqa[ra] and ordered him to put on the gold bangles. Surāqa[ra] protested that the wearing of gold by men had been forbidden by Islam. 'Umar[ra] said that this was true, but that the occasion was an exception. The Prophet[sa] had foreseen Chosroes' gold bangles on his wrists; therefore he had to wear them now, even on pain of punishment. Surāqa[ra] was objecting out of deference to the Prophet's[sa] teaching; otherwise he was as eager as anyone else to provide visible proof of the fulfilment of the great prophecy. He put on the bangles and Muslims saw the prophecy fulfilled (*Usud al-Ghāba*). The fugitive Prophet[sa] had become a king. He himself was no longer in this world. But those who succeeded him could witness the fulfilment of his words and visions.

THE PROPHET[sa] ARRIVES AT MEDINA

To return to our narrative of the Hijra. After the Prophet[sa] had dismissed Surāqa[ra] he continued his journey to Medina unmolested. When he reached Medina, the Prophet[sa] found the people waiting impatiently. A more auspicious day could not have dawned for them. For, the sun which had risen for Mecca had come instead to shine on Medina.

News that the Prophet[sa] had left Mecca had reached them, so they were expecting his arrival. Parties of them went miles out of Medina to look for him. They went in the morning and returned disappointed in the evening. When at last the Prophet[sa] did reach Medina, he decided to stop for a while in Qubā, a nearby village. A Jew had seen the two camels and had decided that they were carrying the Prophet[sa] and his Companions. He climbed an eminence and shouted, "Sons of Qaila, he for whom you waited has come." Everyone in Medina who heard this cry rushed to Qubā, while the people of Qubā, overjoyed at the arrival of the Prophet[sa] in their midst sang songs in his honour.

The utter simplicity of the Prophet[sa] is illustrated by an incident which took place at this time at Qubā. Most people in Medina had not seen the Prophet[sa] before.

When they saw his party sitting under a tree, many of them took Abū Bakr[ra] for the Prophet[sa]. Abū Bakr[ra], though younger, had a greyer beard and was better dressed than the Prophet[sa]. So they turned to him and sat in front of him, after showing him the obeisance due to the Prophet[sa]. When Abū Bakr[ra] saw that he was being mistaken for the Prophet[sa], he rose, took his mantle and hung it against the sun and said, "Prophet[sa] of God, you are in the sun. I make this shade for you" (*Bukhārī*). With tact and courtesy he made plain to visitors from Medina their error. The Prophet[sa] stopped at Quba for ten days, after which the people of Medina took him to their city. When he entered the town, he found that all the people, men, women and children, had turned out to receive him. Among the songs they sang was:

> **Moon of the fourteenth night has risen on us from behind al-Widā'. So long as we have in our midst one who calls us to God, it is incumbent upon us to tender our thanks to God. To you who have been sent to us by God we present our perfect obedience (*Ḥalbiyya*).**

The Prophet[sa] did not enter Medina from the eastern side. When the people of Medina described him as a "moon of the fourteenth night", they meant that they were living in the dark before the Prophet[sa] came to shed his light upon them. It was a Monday when the Prophet[sa] entered Medina. It was a Monday when he left the cave Thaur and, strange as it may seem, it was a Monday on which he took Mecca about ten years later.

ABŪ AYYŪB ANṢĀRĪ[ra] AS PROPHET'S[sa] HOST

While the Prophet[sa] was in Medina, everybody longed to have the honour of being his host. As his camel passed through a lane, families would line up to receive him. With one voice they would say, "Here we are with our homes, our property and our lives to receive you and to offer our protection to you. Come and live with us."

Many would show greater zeal, go forward and held the reins of the camel and insist on the Prophet's[sa] dismounting in front of their doors and entering their houses. Politely the Prophet[sa] would refuse saying, "Leave my camel alone. She is under the command of God; she will stop where God wants her to stop." Ultimately it stopped on a site which belonged to orphans of the Banū Najjār tribe. The Prophet[sa] dismounted and said, "It seems that this is where God wants us to stop." He made enquiries. A trustee of the orphans came forward and offered the site for the use of the Prophet[sa]. The Prophet[sa] replied that he would not accept the offer unless he were allowed to pay. A price was settled and the Prophet[sa] decided to build a mosque and some houses on it. This settled, the Prophet[sa] asked who lived nearest to the site. Abū Ayyūb Anṣārī[ra] came forward and said that his house was the nearest and that his services were at the Prophet's[sa] disposal. The Prophet[sa] asked him to prepare a room in his house for him. Abū Ayyūb's[ra] house was double-storeyed. He offered to let the Prophet[sa] have the upper storey. But the Prophet[sa] preferred to have the lower storey for the convenience of his visitors.

The devotion which the people of Medina had for the Prophet[sa] showed itself again. Abū Ayyūb[ra] agreed to let the Prophet[sa] have the lower storey, but refused to go to sleep on a floor under which lived the Prophet[sa]. He and his wife thought it discourteous to do so. A pitcher of water was accidentally broken and water flowed on the floor. Abū Ayyūb[ra], fearing lest some water should drip through to the room occupied by the Prophet[sa], took his quilt and with it dried up the water before any could drip through. In the morning he called on the Prophet[sa] and narrated the events of the night before, upon hearing which the Prophet[sa] agreed to occupy the upper storey. Abū Ayyūb[ra] prepared meals and sent them up. The Prophet[sa] ate whatever he wanted and Abū Ayyūb[ra] whatever remained. After a few days, others demanded a share in entertaining the Prophet[sa]. Until the Prophet[sa] settled in his own house and made his own arrangements he was entertained by the people of Medina in turn. A widow had an only son named Anas[ra], aged about eight or nine. She brought the boy to the Prophet[sa] and offered him for the Prophet's[sa] personal service. This Anas[ra] became immortalized in the annals of Islam. He became a very learned man, and also rich. He attained to over one hundred years of age and in the days of the Khalifahs was held in great esteem by everybody. Anas[ra] is reported to have said that although he went into the service of the Prophet[sa] as a boy and remained with him until the Prophet[sa] died, never did the Prophet[sa] speak unkindly to him, nor did he ever admonish him, nor did he ever set him a duty harder than he could perform. During his stay in Medina, the Prophet[sa] had only Anas[ra] with him. The testimony of Anas[ra], therefore, reveals the Prophet's[sa] character as it developed in the days of his growing power and prosperity at Medina.

Later, the Prophet[sa] sent his freedman Zaid[ra] to Mecca to fetch his family and relations. The Meccans had been stupefied by the sudden and well-planned departure of the Prophet[sa] and his followers. For some time, therefore, they did nothing to vex him. When the Prophet's[sa] family and the family of Abū Bakr[ra] left Mecca they raised no difficulty. The two families reached Medina unmolested. In the meantime the Prophet[sa] laid the foundations of a mosque on the site he had bought for the purpose. After this, he built houses for himself and for his Companions. About seven months were spent on their completion.

LIFE UNSAFE AT MEDINA

Within a few days of the Prophet's[sa] arrival in Medina, the pagan tribes there became interested in Islam and a majority of them joined. Many, not persuaded at heart, also joined. In this way a party joined the fold of Islam who were not Muslims at heart. Its members played a very sinister part in subsequent history. Some of them became sincere Muslims. Others remained insincere and kept intriguing against Islam and Muslims. Some refused to join at all. But they could not stand the growing influence of the New Faith, so they migrated from Medina to Mecca. Medina became a Muslim town. In it was established the worship of the One God. There was not a second town in the world then which could make this claim. It was no small joy to the Prophet[sa] and his friends that within a few days of their migration a whole town had agreed to give up the worship of idols and to establish instead the worship of the One Invisible God. But there was no peace yet for Muslims. In Medina itself a party of Arabs had only outwardly joined Islam. Inwardly, they were the sworn enemies of the Prophet[sa]. Then there were the Jews, who continuously intrigued against him. The Prophet[sa] was aware of these dangers. He remained alert and urged his friends and followers to be on their guard. He often remained awake the whole night (*Bārī*, Vol. 6, p. 60). Tired by night-long vigilance he once expressed a desire for help. Soon he heard the sound of armour. "What is this?" he asked. "It is Sa'd bin Waqqāṣ[ra], O Prophet[sa], who has come to do sentinel duty for you" (*Bukhārī* and *Muslim*). The people of Medina were alive to their great responsibility. They had invited the Prophet[sa] to come and live in their midst and it was now their duty to protect him. The tribes took counsel and decided to guard the Prophet's[sa] house in turn.

In the unsafety of his person and in the absence of peace for his followers, there was no difference between the Prophet's[sa] life at Mecca and his life at Medina. The only difference was that at Medina Muslims were able to worship in public in the mosque which they had built in the name of God. They were able to assemble for this purpose five times in the day without let or hindrance.

Two or three months passed. The people of Mecca recovered from their bewilderment and started making plans for the vexation of Muslims. They soon found that it did not fulfil their purpose merely to trouble Muslims in and around Mecca. It was necessary to attack the Prophet[sa] and his followers at Medina and turn them out of their new refuge. Accordingly they addressed a letter to 'Abdullāh bin Ubayy ibn Salūl, a leader of Medina, who, before the Prophet's[sa] arrival, had been accepted as king of Medina by all parties. They said in this letter that they had been shocked at the Prophet's[sa] arrival at Medina and that it was wrong on the part of the people of Medina to afford refuge to him. In the end they said:

> **Now that you have admitted our enemy in your home, we swear by God and declare that we, the people of Mecca, will join in an attack on Medina unless you, the people of Medina, agree to turn him out of Medina or give him a joint fight. When we attack Medina, we will put to the sword all able-bodied men and enslave all women (*Abū Dawūd, Kitāb al-Kharāj*).**

'Abdullāh bin Ubayy ibn Salūl thought this letter a God-send. He consulted other hypocrites in Medina and persuaded them that if they allowed the Prophet[sa] to live in peace among them they would invite the hostility of Mecca. It behoved them, therefore, to make war upon the Prophet[sa], if only in order to appease the Meccans. The Prophet[sa] got to know of this. He went to 'Abdullāh bin Ubayy ibn Salūl and tried to convince him that such a step would prove suicidal. Many people in Medina had become Muslims and were prepared to lay down their lives for Islam. If 'Abdullāh declared war upon Muslims, the majority of the people of Medina would fight on the side of Muslims. Such a war would, therefore, cost him dear and spell his own destruction. 'Abdullāh, impressed by this advice, was dissuaded from his plans.

At this time, the Prophet[sa] took another important step. He collected the Muslims and suggested that every two Muslims should become linked together as two brothers. The idea was well received. Medinite took Meccan as his brother. Under this new brotherhood, the

Muslims of Medina offered to share their property and their belongings with the Muslims of Mecca. One Medinite Muslim offered to divorce one of his two wives and to have her married to his Meccan brother. The Meccan Muslims declined to accept the offers of the Muslims of Medina out of regard for the needs of the latter. But the Muslims of Medina remained insistent, and the point had to be referred to the Prophet[sa]. The Muslims of Medina urged that the Meccan Muslims were their brothers; so, they had to share their property with them. The Meccan Muslims did not know how to manage land. But they could share the produce of the land if not the land itself. The Meccan Muslims declined with thanks this incredibly generous offer, and preferred to stick to their own vocation of trade. Many Meccan Muslims became rich again. But Muslims of Medina always remembered their offer to share their property with Meccan Muslims. Many a time when a Medinite Muslim died, his sons divided the inheritance with their Meccan brothers. For many years, the practice continued, until the Qur'an abolished it by its teaching about the division of inheritance (*Bukhārī* and *Muslim*).

PACT BETWEEN VARIOUS TRIBES OF MEDINA

Besides uniting Meccan and Medinite Muslims in a brotherhood, the Holy Prophet[sa] instituted a covenant between all the inhabitants of Medina. By this covenant, Arabs and the Jews were united into a common citizenship with Muslims. The Prophet[sa] explained to both Arabs and Jews that before the Muslims emerged as a group in Medina, there were only two groups in their town, but with Muslims now, there were three groups. It was but proper that they should enter into an agreement which should be binding upon them all, and which should assure to all of them a measure of peace. Eventually an agreement was arrived at. The agreement said:

Between the Prophet[sa] of God and the Faithful on the one hand, and all those on the other, who voluntarily agree to enter. If any of the Meccan Muslims is killed, the Meccan Muslims will themselves be responsible. The responsibility for securing the release of their prisoners will also be theirs. The Muslim tribes of Medina similarly will be responsible for their own lives and their prisoners. Whoever rebels or promotes enmity and disorder will be considered a common enemy. It will be the duty of all the others to fight against him, even though he happens to be a son or a close relation. If a disbeliever is killed in battle by a believer, his Muslim relations will seek no revenge. Nor will they assist disbelievers against believers. The Jews who join this covenant will be helped by Muslims. The Jews will not be put to any hardship. Their enemies will not be helped against them. No disbeliever will give quarter to anybody from Mecca. He will not act as a trustee for any Meccan property. In a war between Muslims and disbelievers he will take no part. If a believer is maltreated without cause, Muslims will have the right to fight against those who maltreat. If a common enemy attack Medina, the Jews will side with the Muslims and share the expenses of the battle. The Jewish tribes in covenant with the other tribes of Medina will have rights similar to those of Muslims. The Jews will keep to their own faith, and Muslims to their own. The rights enjoyed by the Jews will also be enjoyed by their followers. The citizens of Medina will not have the right to declare war without the sanction of the Prophet[sa]. But this will not prejudice the right of any individual to avenge an individual wrong. The Jews will bear the expenses of their own organization, and Muslims their own. But in case of war, they will act with unity. The city of Medina will be regarded as sacred and inviolate by those who sign the covenant. Strangers who come under the protection of its citizens will be treated as citizens. But the people of Medina will not be allowed to admit a woman to its citizenship without the permission of her relations. All disputes will be referred for decision to God and the

Prophet[sa]. Parties to this covenant will not have the right to enter into any agreement with the Meccans or their allies. This, because parties to this covenant agree in resisting their common enemies. The parties will remain united in peace as in war. No party will enter into a separate peace. But no party will be obliged to take part in war. A party, however, which commits any excess will be liable to a penalty. Certainly God is the protector of the righteous and the Faithful and Muḥammad[sa] is His Prophet[sa] (*Hishām*).

This is the covenant in brief. It has been prepared from scraps to be found in historical records. It emphasizes beyond any doubt that in settling disputes and disagreements between the parties at Medina, the guiding principles were to be honesty, truth and justice. Those committing excesses were to be held responsible for those excesses. The covenant makes it clear that the Prophet[sa] of Islam was determined to treat with civility and kindness the other citizens of Medina, and to regard them and deal with them as brethren. If disputes and conflicts arose later, the responsibility rested with the Jews.

As we have already said, two or three months passed away before Meccans could renew their planned hostility against Islam. An occasion was provided by Sa'd bin Mu'ādh[ra], chief of the Aus tribe of Medina, who arrived at Mecca for the circuit of the Ka'ba. Abū Jahl saw him do this and said, "After giving protection to this apostate Muḥammad[sa], do you expect you can come to Mecca and circuit the Ka'ba in peace? Do you think you can protect and save him? I swear by God, that had it not been for Abū Sufyān[ra], you could not have returned safe to your family."

Sa'd bin Mu'ādh[ra] replied, "Take it from me, if you Meccans stop us from visiting and circuiting the Ka'ba, you will have no peace on your road to Syria." At about that time Walīd bin Mughīra, a Meccan chief, became seriously ill. He apprehended that his end had come. The other chiefs of Mecca were sitting around. Walīd could not control himself and began to cry. The Meccan chiefs wondered at this and asked him why he was crying. "Do you think I am afraid of death? No, it is not death I fear. What I fear is lest the Faith of Muḥammad[sa] should spread and even Mecca go under him." Abū Sufyān[ra] assured Walīd that as long as they lived they would resist with their lives the spread of this Faith (*Khamīs*, Vol. I).

MECCANS PREPARING TO ATTACK MEDINA

From this narration of events it is quite clear that the lull in Meccan hostility was only temporary. The leaders of Mecca were preparing for a renewed attack on Islam. Dying chiefs bound their survivors to oaths of hostility against the Prophet[sa], and roused them to war against him and his followers. The people of Medina were invited to take up arms against the Muslims and were warned that, if they refused to do so, the Meccans and their allied tribes would attack Medina, kill their men and enslave their women. If the Prophet[sa] had stood aside and done nothing for the defence of Medina, he would have incurred a terrible responsibility. The Prophet[sa], therefore, instituted a system of reconnaissance. He sent parties of men to places round about Mecca to report on signs of preparations for war. Now and then, there were incidents—scuffles and fights—between these parties and Meccans. European writers say these incidents were initiated by the Prophet[sa] and that, therefore, in the wars which ensued, he was the aggressor. But we have before us the thirteen years of Meccan tyranny, their intrigues for antagonizing the people of Medina against the Muslims, and the threatened attack upon Medina itself. Nobody who remembers all this can charge the Prophet[sa] with the responsibility for initiating these incidents. If he sent out parties of Muslims for purpose of reconnaissance, it was in self-defence. Thirteen years of tyranny were justification enough for the preparations of Muslims for self-defence. If wars ensued between them and their Meccan enemy, the responsibility did not lie with Muslims. The slender grounds on which Christian nations today declare war against one another are well known. If half of what the Meccans did to Muslims is done today to a European people, they would feel justified in going to war. When the people of one country organize on a large scale the killing of another, when one people compels another to leave their homes, does it not give the victims the right to make war? After Muslims had migrated to Medina, no further ground was needed for them to declare war on the Meccans. But the Prophet[sa] declared no war. He showed tolerance and confined his defensive activities to reconnaissance. The Meccans, however, continued to irritate and harass the Muslims. They excited the people of Medina against them and interfered with their right of pilgrimage. They changed their normal caravan routes and started going through tribal areas around Medina, to rouse the tribes against the Muslims. The peace of Medina was threatened; so it was the obvious duty of Muslims to accept the challenge of war which the Meccans had been throwing down for fourteen years. Nobody under the circumstances could question the right of Muslims to accept this challenge.

While the Prophet[sa] was busy reconnoitring, he was not neglecting the normal and spiritual needs of his following in Medina. A great majority of the people of Medina had become Muslims, by outward profession as well as by inward faith. Some had joined by outward profession only. The Prophet[sa], therefore, started instituting the Islamic form of government in his small following. In earlier days, Arabs had settled their disputes by the sword and by individual violence. The Prophet[sa] introduced juridical procedures. Judges were appointed to settle claims which individuals or parties brought against one another. Unless a judge declared a claim to be just and true, it was not admitted. In the old days intellectual pursuits had been looked upon with contempt. The Prophet[sa] took steps to promote literacy and love of learning. Those who could read and write were asked to teach others the same arts. Injustice and cruelty were ended. The rights of women were established. The rich were to pay for the needs of the poor and for improving the social amenities of Medina. Labourers were protected from exploitation. For weak and incompetent heirs, arrangements were made for the appointment of trustees. Loan transactions began to be committed to writing. The importance of fulfilling all undertakings began to be impressed. The excesses committed against slaves were abolished. Hygiene and public sanitation began to receive attention. A census of the population was undertaken. Lanes and highways were ordered to be widened, and steps were taken to keep them clean. In short, laws were instituted for the promotion of an ideal family and social life. The savage Arabs for the first time in their history were introduced to the rules of politeness and civilized existence.

BATTLE OF BADR

While the Prophet[sa] planned for the practical institution of laws which were to serve not only his own generation of Arabs but all mankind for all time to come, the people of Mecca made their plans for war. The Prophet[sa] planned for a law which was to bring to his own people and all the others peace, honour and progress; his Meccan enemy planned for the destruction of that law. The Meccan plans eventually resulted in the Battle of Badr. It was the eighteenth month after the Hijra. A commercial caravan led by Abū Sufyān[ra] was returning from Syria. Under pretence of protecting this caravan, the Meccans raised a large army and decided to take it to Medina. The Holy Prophet[sa] came to know of these preparations. He also had revelations from God which said that the time to pay back the enemy in his own coin had come. He went out of Medina with a number of followers. Nobody at the time knew whether this party of Muslims would have to confront the caravan which was coming from Syria or the army which was coming from Mecca. The party numbered about three hundred. A commercial caravan in those days did not consist only of camels loaded with merchandise. It also included armed men who guarded the caravan and escorted it through its journey. Since tension had arisen between Meccans and the Muslims of Medina, the Meccan chiefs had begun to take special care about arming the escort. History records the fact of two other caravans which passed by this route a short while before. In one of these, two hundred armed men were provided as guard and escort, and in the other three hundred. It is wrong to suggest, as Christian writers do, that the Prophet[sa] took three hundred followers and set out to attack an undefended commercial caravan. The suggestion is mischievous and unfounded. The caravan which was now coming from Syria was a large one and, considering its size and the armed escort provided for other caravans, it seems reasonable to think that about four to five hundred armed guards must have been provided to serve as its escort. To say that the Muslim party of three hundred poorly-armed men were led by the Prophet[sa] to attack such a well-armed caravan in the hope of looting it is unjust in the extreme. Only rank prejudice and determined ill-will against Islam can prompt such a thought. If the Muslim party was out to confront only this caravan, their adventure could have been described as an adventure of war, although war in self-defence, for the Muslim party from Medina was small and ill-armed and the Meccan caravan was large and well-armed, and for a long time they had been carrying on a campaign of hostility against the Muslims of Medina.

In point of fact the conditions under which this small party of Muslims set out of Medina were far more grave. As we have said, they did not know whether it was the caravan from Syria or the army from Mecca which they would have to confront. The uncertainty under which the Muslims laboured is hinted at in the Qur'an. But the Muslims were prepared for both. The uncertainty under which the Muslims left Medina redounds to the credit of their faith and their tremendous sincerity. It was after they had gone some distance from Medina that the Prophet[sa] made it known to them that they would have to confront the large Meccan army rather than the small Syrian caravan.

Speculations had reached Muslims about the size of the Meccan army. The most moderate of these speculations placed the number at one thousand, all of them seasoned soldiers skilled in the art of war. The number accompanying the Prophet[sa] was only three hundred and thirteen, and of these many were unskilled and inexperienced, and most were ill-armed. A great majority of them went on foot, or mounted on camels. There were only two horses in the whole party. This party, which was as poorly equipped with the weapons of war as it was raw in experience, had to confront a force three times its number, consisting mostly of experienced fighters. It was quite obviously the most dangerous thing ever undertaken in history. The Holy Prophet[sa] was wise enough to ensure that nobody took part in it without due knowledge and without his will and heart in it. He told his party clearly that it was no longer the caravan they had to confront but the army from Mecca. He asked the party for their counsel. One after another, his Meccan followers stood up and assured the Prophet[sa] of their loyalty and zeal, and of their determination to fight the Meccan enemy who had come to attack the Muslims of Medina in their homes. Every time the Prophet[sa] heard a Meccan Muslim, he asked for more counsel and more advice. The Muslims of Medina had been silent. The aggressors were from Mecca, with blood relations to many of those Muslims who had migrated with the Prophet[sa] to Medina and who were now in this small party. The Muslims of Medina were afraid lest their zeal to fight the Meccan enemy should injure the feelings of their Meccan brethren. But when the Prophet[sa] insisted on more and more counsel, one of the Medinite Muslims stood up and said, "Prophet[sa] of God, you are having all the counsel you want, but you continue to ask for more. Perhaps you refer to us, the Muslims of Medina. Is that true?"

"Yes," said the Prophet[sa].

"You ask for our counsel," he said, "because you think that when you came to us, we agreed to fight on your side only in case you and your fellow emigrants from Mecca were attacked in Medina. But now we seem to have come out of Medina, and you feel that our agreement does not cover the conditions under which we find ourselves today. But O Prophet[sa] of God, when we entered into that agreement we did not know you as well as we do now. We know now what high spiritual station you hold. We care not for what we agreed to. We now stand by you, whatever you ask us to do. We will not behave like the followers of Moses[as] who said, 'Go you and your God and fight the enemy, we remain here behind.' If we must fight, we will and we will fight to the right of you, to the left of you, in front of you and behind you. True, the enemy wants to get at you. But we assure you that he will not do so, without stepping over our dead bodies. Prophet[sa] of God, you invite us to fight. We are prepared to do more. Not far from here is the sea. If you command us to jump into it, we will hesitate not." (*Bukhārī, Kitāb al-Maghāzī,* and *Hishām*).

This was the spirit of devotion and sacrifice which early Muslims displayed, and the like of which is not to be found in the history of the world. The example of the followers of Moses[as] has been cited above. As for the disciples of Jesus, we know they abandoned Jesus at a critical time. One of them gave him away for a paltry sum. Another cursed him, and the remaining ten ran away. The Muslims who joined the Prophet[sa] from Medina had been in his companionship only for a year and a half. But they had attained to such strength of faith that, had the Prophet[sa] but ordered, they would have plunged themselves heedlessly into the sea. The Prophet[sa] took counsel. But he had no doubt at all as to the devotion of his following. He took counsel in order to sift the weaklings and send them away. But he found that the Meccan and the Medinite Muslims vied with one another in the expression of their devotion. Both were determined that they would not turn their backs to the enemy, even though the enemy was three times their number and far better equipped, armed and experienced. They would rather put their faith in the promises of God, show their regard for Islam, and lay down their lives in its defence.

Assured of this devotion by both Meccan and Medinite Muslims, the Prophet[sa] advanced. When he reached a place called Badr, he accepted the suggestion of one of his followers and ordered his men to settle near the brook of Badr. The Muslims took possession of this source of water, but the land on which they took up their positions was all sand, and therefore unsuitable for the manoeuvres of fighting men. The followers of the Prophet[sa] showed natural anxiety over this disadvantage. The Prophet[sa] himself shared the anxiety of his followers and spent the whole night praying. Again and again he said:

> **My God, over the entire face of the earth just now, there are only these three hundred men who are devoted to Thee and determined to establish Thy worship. My God, if these three hundred men die today at the hands of their enemy in this battle, who will be left behind to glorify Thy name? (*Ṭabarī*).**

God heard the supplication of His Prophet[sa]. Rain came over-night. The sandy part of the field which the Muslims occupied became wet and solid. The dry part of the field occupied by the enemy became muddy and slippery. Maybe the Meccan enemy chose this part of the field and left the other for the Muslims because their experienced eye preferred dry ground to facilitate the movements of their soldiers and cavalry. But the tables were turned upon them by a timely act of God. The rain which came overnight made the sandy part of the field which was in the possession of the Muslims hard and the hard field where the Meccans had encamped slippery. During the night the Prophet[sa] had a clear intimation from God that important members of the enemy would meet with their death. He even had individual names revealed to him. The spots at which they were to drop dead were also revealed. They died as they were named and dropped where it had been foretold.

In the battle itself this little party of Muslims displayed wonderful daring and devotion. One incident proves this. One of the few Generals which the Muslim force included was 'Abdur Raḥmān bin 'Auf[ra], one of the chiefs of Mecca and an experienced soldier in his own way. When the battle began, he looked to his right and to his left to see what kind of support he had. He found to his amazement, that he had only two lads from Medina on his flanks. His heart sank and he said to himself, "Every General needs support on his sides. More so I on this day. But I only have two raw boys. What can I do with them?" 'Abdur Raḥmān bin 'Auf[ra] says he had hardly finished saying this to himself when one of the boys touched his side with his elbow. As he bent over to hear the boy, the latter said, "Uncle, we have heard of one Abū Jahl, who used to harass and torment the Prophet[sa]. Uncle, I want to fight him; tell me where he is." 'Abdur Raḥmān bin 'Auf[ra] had not yet replied to this youthful inquiry, when his attention was similarly drawn by the boy on the other side, who asked him the same question. 'Abdur Raḥmān[ra] was not a little amazed at the courage and determination of these two boys. A seasoned soldier, he did not think that even he would select the commander of the enemy for an individual encounter. 'Abdur Raḥmān[ra] raised his finger to point at Abū Jahl—armed to the teeth and standing behind the lines protected by two senior Generals, with drawn swords. 'Abdur Raḥmān[ra] had not dropped his finger, when the two boys dashed into the enemy ranks with the speed of an eagle, making straight for their chosen target. The attack was sudden. The soldiers and guards were stupefied. They attacked the boys. One of the boys lost an arm. But they remained unnerved and unbeaten. They attacked Abū Jahl, with such violence that the great commander fell to the ground, mortally wounded. From the spirited determination of these two boys, one can judge how deeply the followers of the Prophet[sa], both old and young, had been stirred by the cruel persecution to which they and the Prophet[sa] had been subjected. We only read about them in history, but yet are deeply stirred. The people of Medina heard of these cruelties from eye-witnesses. The feelings they must have had, can well be imagined. They heard of Meccan cruelties on the one hand and of the forbearance of the Prophet[sa] on the other. No wonder their determination mounted high to avenge the wrongs done to the Prophet[sa] and to the Muslims of Mecca. They looked only for an opportunity to tell the Meccan tormentors that if the Muslims did not retaliate, it was not because they were powerless; it was because they had not been permitted by God to do so. How determined this small Muslim force was to die fighting can be gauged from another incident. Battle had not yet been joined when Abū Jahl sent a Bedouin chief to the Muslim side to report on their numbers. This chief returned and reported that the Muslims were three hundred or more. Abū Jahl and his followers were glad. They thought the Muslims easy prey. "But," said the Bedouin chief, "my advice to you is—Don't fight these men, because every one of them seems determined to die! I have seen not men but death mounted on camels" (*Ṭabarī* and *Hishām*). The Bedouin chief was right—those who are prepared to die do not easily die.

A GREAT PROPHECY FULFILLED

The time of the battle drew near. The Prophet[sa] came out of the little hut in which he had been praying, and announced:

"The hosts will certainly be routed and will show their backs."

These were the words revealed to the Prophet[sa] some time before in Mecca. Evidently they related to this battle. When Meccan cruelty had reached its extreme limit, and Muslims were migrating to places where they could have peace, the Prophet[sa] had the following verses revealed to him by God:

> **And surely to the people of Pharaoh also came Warners. They rejected all Our Signs. So We seized them as the seizing of One Who is Mighty and Omnipotent. Are your disbelievers better than those? Or have you an exemption in the Scriptures? The hosts will certainly be routed and will show their backs. Nay, the Hour is their appointed time; and the Hour will be most calamitous and most bitter. Surely the offenders will be in bewilderment and flaming fire. On the day when they will be dragged into the Fire on their faces and it will be said to them, "Taste ye the touch of burning" (54:42-49).**

These verses are part of Sūrah Al-Qamar and this Sūrah, according to all reports, was revealed in Mecca. Muslim authorities place the date of its revelation somewhere between the fifth and tenth year of the Prophet's[sa] Call, that is, at least three years before the Hijra (i.e. the year of the Prophet's[sa] migration from Mecca to Medina). More likely, it was revealed eight years before. European authorities have the same view. According to Noldeke, the whole of this Chapter was revealed after the fifth year of the Prophet's[sa] Call. Wherry thinks this date a little too early. According to him, the Chapter belongs to the sixth or seventh year before the Hijra, or after the Prophet's[sa] Call. In short, both Muslim and non-Muslim authorities agree that this Chapter was revealed years before the Prophet[sa] and his followers migrated from Mecca to Medina. The prophetic value of the Meccan verses is beyond dispute. There is in these verses a clear hint of what was in store for the Meccans in the battlefield of Badr. The fate they were going to meet is clearly foretold. When the Prophet[sa] came out of his hut, he reiterated the prophetic description contained in the Meccan Chapter. He must have been put in mind of the Meccan verses, during his prayers in the hut. By reciting one of the verses he reminded his followers that the Hour promised in the Meccan revelation had come.

And the Hour had really come. The Prophet Isaiah[as] (21:13-17) had foretold this very hour. The battle began, even though Muslims were not ready for it and non-Muslims had been advised against taking part in it. Three hundred and thirteen Muslims, most of them inexperienced and unused to warfare, and nearly all of them unequipped, stood before a number three times as large, and all of them seasoned soldiers. In a few hours, many noted chiefs of Mecca met their end. Just as the Prophet Isaiah[as] had foretold, the glory of Kedar faded away. The Meccan army fled in miserable haste, leaving behind their dead as well as some prisoners. Among the prisoners was the Prophet's[sa] uncle, 'Abbās[ra], who generally stood by the Prophet[sa] during the days at Mecca. 'Abbas[ra] had been compelled to join the Meccans and to fight the Prophet[sa]. Another prisoner was Abu'l 'Āṣ[ra], a son-in-law of the Prophet[sa]. Among the dead was Abū Jahl, Commander-in-chief of the Meccan army and, according to all accounts, arch-enemy of Islam.

Victory came, but it brought mixed feelings to the Prophet[sa]. He rejoiced over the fulfilment of divine promises, repeated during the fourteen years which had gone by, promises which had also been recorded in some of the earliest religious writings. But at the same time he grieved over the plight of the Meccans. What a pitiable end had they met! If this victory had come to another in his place, he would have jumped with joy. But the sight of the prisoners before him, bound and handcuffed, brought tears to the eyes of the Prophet[sa] and his faithful friend Abū Bakr[ra]. ‘Umar[ra], who succeeded Abū Bakr[ra] as the Second Khalifah of Islam, saw this but could not understand. Why should the Prophet[sa] and Abū Bakr[ra] weep over a victory? ‘Umar[ra] was bewildered. So he made bold to ask the Prophet[sa], "Prophet[sa] of God, tell me why you weep when God has given you such a grand victory. If we must weep, I will weep with you, or put on a weeping face at least." The Prophet[sa] pointed to the miserable plight of the Meccan prisoners. This was what disobedience of God led to.

The Prophet Isaiah[as] spoke again and again of the justice of this Prophet[sa], who had emerged victorious from a deadly battle. Of this there was a grand demonstration on this occasion. Returning to Medina the Prophet[sa] rested for the night on the way. The devoted followers who watched him could see that he turned from side to side and could not sleep. They soon guessed that it was because he heard the groans of his uncle, ‘Abbās[ra], who lay nearby, bound tight as a prisoner of war. They loosened the cord on ‘Abbās[ra].‘Abbās[ra] stopped groaning. The Prophet[sa], no longer disturbed by his groans, went to sleep. A little later he woke up and wondered why he no longer heard ‘Abbās[ra] groan. He half thought ‘Abbās[ra] had gone into a swoon. But the Companions guarding ‘Abbās[ra] told him they had loosened the cord on ‘Abbās[ra] to let him (the Prophet[sa]) sleep undisturbed. "No, no," said the Prophet[sa], "there must be no injustice. If ‘Abbās[ra] is related to me, other prisoners are related to others. Loosen the cords on all of them or tie the cord tight on ‘Abbās[ra] also." The Companions heard this admonition and decided to loosen the cords on all the prisoners, and themselves bear the responsibility for their safe custody. Of the prisoners, those who were literate were promised freedom if they each undertook to make ten Meccan boys literate—this being their ransom for liberty. Those who had nobody to pay ransom for them, obtained their liberty for the asking. Those who could afford to pay ransom, were set free after they had paid it. By setting the prisoners free in this way, the Prophet[sa] put an end to the cruel practice of converting prisoners of war into slaves.

BATTLE OF UḤUD

When the Meccan army fled from Badr they announced that they would attack Medina again and avenge upon the Muslims for what the Meccans had suffered in the battle; and only a year later they did attack Medina again in full force. They felt so humiliated and disgraced at their defeat that the Meccan chiefs forbade surviving relations to weep over those who had died in the battle. They also laid down that profits from commercial caravans would be constituted into a war fund. With full preparations, therefore, an army of three thousand under the command of Abū Sufyān[ra] attacked Medina. The Prophet[sa] held a council and asked his followers whether they would meet the enemy in Medina or outside. He himself favoured the former alternative. He preferred to let the Muslims stay in Medina and let the enemy come and attack them in their homes. This, he thought, would place the responsibility for aggression and attack on the enemy. But at the council were many Muslims who had not had the chance to take part in the Battle of Badr, and who now longed to fight for God. They insisted on having a straight and open fight and on having the chance to die fighting. The Prophet[sa] accepted the general advice (*Ṭabaqāt*).

While this was being debated, the Prophet[sa] related a vision of his. He said, "I had a vision. I saw a cow, and I also saw my sword with its point broken. I saw the cow being butchered, and that I had put my hand inside a coat of armour. I also saw myself riding a ram." The Companions asked the Prophet[sa] how he interpreted the vision.

"The butchering of the cow" said the Prophet[sa], "indicates that some of my Companions will be killed in battle. The broken point of my sword indicates that some important one among my relations will meet his death, or maybe, I myself will suffer pain or injury of some kind. Putting my hand in a coat of armour seems to mean that if we stay in Medina it is better for us. The fact that I have seen myself riding a ram means that we will overpower the commander of the disbelievers, and that he will die at our hands" (*Bukhārī, Hishām* and *Ṭabaqāt*).

It was made clear by this vision and its interpretation that it was better for Muslims to stay in Medina. The Prophet[sa], however, did not insist upon this, because the interpretation of the vision was his own, not a part of revealed knowledge. He accepted the advice of the majority and decided to go out of Medina to meet the enemy. As he set out, the more zealous section of His following realizing their mistake, approached the Prophet[sa] and said, "Prophet[sa] of God, the way you advised seems better. We ought to stay in Medina and meet the enemy in our streets."

"Not now," said the Prophet[sa]. "Now the Prophet[sa] of God has put on his armour. Come what may, now we shall go forward. If you prove steadfast and persevering, God will help you" (*Bukhārī* and *Ṭabaqāt*). So saying, he went forward with a force of a thousand. At a small distance from Medina they camped for the night. It was the Prophet's[sa] custom to let his fighting force rest a while before they met the enemy. At the time of the morning prayers, he made a round. He found that some Jews also had joined the Muslims. They pretended they had treaties of alliance with the Medina tribes. As the Prophet[sa] had had knowledge of Jewish intrigues, he sent off the Jews. As soon as he did so, 'Abdullāh bin Ubayy ibn Salūl, chief of the hypocrites, withdrew with his three hundred followers. He said the Muslim army was now no match for the enemy. To take part in the battle was now certain death. The Prophet[sa] had made a mistake in sending off his own allies. The result of this eleventh-hour desertion was that only seven hundred Muslims were left under the Prophet's[sa] command. The seven hundred stood against an army more than four times their number, and many more times better in equipment. In the Meccan army were seven hundred fighters in armour; in the Muslim army only one hundred. The Meccans had a mounted force of two hundred horses, Muslims had only two horses. The Prophet[sa] reached Uḥud. Over a narrow hilly pass there, he posted a guard of fifty, charged with the duty of repelling any attack on it by the enemy or any attempt to possess it. The Prophet[sa] told them clearly their duty. It was to stand where they had been posted, and not to move from the spot until they were commanded to do so, no matter what happened to the Muslims. With the remaining six hundred and fifty men, the Prophet[sa] went to do battle with an army about five times as large. But, with the help of God, in a short time the six hundred and fifty Muslims drove away three thousand skilled Meccan soldiers. The Muslims ran in pursuit. The hilly pass on which fifty Muslims had been posted was in the rear. The guard said to the commander, "The enemy is beaten. It is time we took some part in the battle and won our laurels in the next world." The commander stopped them, reminding them of the clear orders of the Prophet[sa]. But the men explained that the Prophet's[sa] order was to be taken in the spirit and not in the letter. There was no meaning in continuing to guard the pass while the enemy was running for life.

VICTORY CONVERTED INTO DEFEAT

Arguing thus they left the pass and plunged into the battle. The fleeing Meccan army included Khālid bin Walīd[ra], who later became a great Muslim general. His keen eye fell on the unguarded pass. There were only a few men guarding it now. Khālid[ra] shouted for another

Meccan general 'Amr bin al-'Āṣ[ra], and asked him to have a look at the pass behind. 'Amr[ra] did so, and thought it the chance of his life. Both generals stopped their men and climbed on to the hill. They killed the few Muslims who were still guarding the pass and from the eminence started an attack upon the Muslims. Hearing their war cries, the routed Meccan army collected itself again, and returned to the field. The attack on the Muslims was sudden. In their pursuit of the Meccan army they had dispersed over the whole of the field. Muslim resistance to this new attack could not be assembled. Only individual Muslim soldiers were seen engaging the enemy. Many of these fell fighting. Others fell back. A few made a ring round the Prophet[sa]. They could not have been more than twenty in all. The Meccan army attacked this ring fiercely. One by one, the Muslims in the ring fell under the blows of Meccan swordsmen. From the hill, the archers sent volleys of arrows. At that time, Ṭalḥa[ra], one of the Quraish and the Muhājirīn (Meccan Muslims who had taken refuge in Medina), saw that the enemy arrows were all directed to the face of the Prophet[sa]. He stretched out his hand and held it up against the Prophet's[sa] face. Arrow after arrow struck Talha's[ra] hand, yet it did not drop, although with each shot it was pierced through. Ultimately it was completely mutilated. Ṭalḥa[ra] lost his hand and for the rest of life went about with a stump. In the time of the Fourth Khalifah of Islam when internal dissensions had raised their head, Ṭalḥa[ra] was tauntingly described by an enemy as the handless Ṭalḥa[ra]. A friend of Ṭalḥa[ra] replied, "Handless, yea, but do you know where he lost his hand? At the Battle of Uḥud, in which he raised his hand to shield the Prophet's[sa] face from the enemy's arrows."

Long after the Battle of Uḥud friends of Ṭalḥa[ra] asked him, "Did not your hand smart under the arrow shots and the pain make you cry?" Ṭalḥa[ra] replied, "It made me smart, and it almost made me cry, but I resisted both because I knew that if my hand shook but slightly, it would expose the Prophet's[sa] face to the volley of enemy arrows." The few men who were left with the Prophet[sa] could not have stood the army which they faced. A party of the enemy advanced forward and pushed them off. The Prophet[sa] then stood alone like a wall, and soon a stone struck his forehead and made a deep gash in it. Another blow drove the rings of his helmet into his cheeks. When the arrows were falling thick and fast and the Prophet[sa] was wounded he prayed, "My God, forgive my people for they know not what they are doing" (*Muslim*). The Prophet[sa] fell on the dead, the dead who had lost their lives in his defence. Other Muslims came forward to defend the Prophet[sa] from more attacks. They also fell dead. The Prophet[sa] lay unconscious among these dead bodies. When the enemy saw this, they took him for dead. They withdrew in the certainty of victory, and proceeded to line up again. Among the Muslims who had been defending the Prophet[sa] and who had been pushed by the avalanche of enemy forces, was 'Umar[ra]. The battlefield had now cleared. 'Umar[ra] who saw this, became certain that the Prophet[sa] was dead. 'Umar[ra] was a brave man. He proved it again and again; best of all, in fighting simultaneously the great Empires of Rome and Iran. He was never known to blench under difficulties. This 'Umar[ra] sat on a stone with drooping spirits, crying like a child. In the meantime another Muslim, Anas bin Naḍr[ra] by name, came wandering along in the belief that the Muslims had won. He had seen them overpower the enemy but, having had nothing to eat since the night before, had withdrawn from the battlefield, with some dates in his hand. As soon as he saw 'Umar[ra] crying, he stood amazed and asked, "'Umar[ra], what is the matter with you that instead of rejoicing over a magnificent victory won by the Muslims, you are crying?"

'Umar[ra] replied, "Anas[ra], you do not know what has happened. You only saw the first part of the battle. You do not know that the enemy captured the strategic point on the hill and attacked us fiercely. The Muslims had dispersed, believing they had won. There was no resistance to this attack by the enemy. Only the Prophet[sa] with a handful of guards stood against the entire enemy and all of them fell down fighting."

"If this is true," said Anas[ra], "what use is sitting here and crying? Where our beloved Master has gone, there must we go too."

Anas[ra] had the last date in his hand. This he was about to put in his mouth but, instead, he threw it away saying, "O date, except thee, is there anything which stands between Anas[ra] and Paradise?"

Saying this, he unsheathed his sword and flung himself into the enemy forces, one against three thousand. He could not do much, but one believing spirit is superior to many. Fighting valiantly, Anas[ra] at last fell wounded, but he continued to fight. Upon this the enemy horde sprang barbarously upon him. It is said that when the battle was over, and the dead were identified, Anas's[ra] body could not be identified. It had been cut into seventy pieces. At last a sister of Anas[ra] identifying it by a mutilated finger said, "This is my brother's body" (*Bukhārī*).

Those Muslims who made a ring round the Prophet[sa] but were driven back, ran forward again as soon as they saw the enemy withdrawing. They lifted the Prophet's[sa] body from among the dead. Abū 'Ubaida bin al-Jarrāḥ[ra] caught between his teeth the rings which had sunk into the Prophet's[sa] cheeks and pulled them out, losing two teeth in the attempt.

After a little while, the Prophet[sa] returned to consciousness. The guards who surrounded him sent out messengers to tell Muslims to assemble again. A disrupted force began to assemble. They escorted the Prophet[sa] to the foot of the hill. Abū Sufyān[ra], the enemy commander, seeing these Muslim remnants, cried aloud, "We have killed Muḥammad[sa]." The Prophet[sa] heard the boastful cry but forbade the Muslims to answer, lest the enemy should know the truth and attack again and the exhausted and badly-wounded Muslims should have again to fight this savage horde. Not receiving a reply from the Muslims, Abū Ṣufyān[ra] became certain the Prophet[sa] was dead. He followed his first cry by a second and said, "We have also killed Abū Bakr[ra]." The Prophet[sa] forbade Abū Bakr[ra] to make any reply. Abū Sufyā[ra]n followed by a third, and said, "We have also killed 'Umar[ra]." The Prophet[sa] forbade 'Umar[ra] also to reply. Upon this Abū Sufyān[ra] cried that they had killed all three. Now 'Umar[ra] could not contain himself and cried, "We are all alive and, with God's grace, ready to fight you and break your heads." Abū Sufyān[ra] raised the national cry, "Glory to Hubal. Glory to Hubal. For Hubal has put an end to Islam." (Hubal was the Meccans' national idol.) The Prophet[sa] could not bear this boast against the One and Only God, Allah, for Whom he and the Muslims were prepared to sacrifice their all. He had refused to correct a declaration of his own death. He had refused to correct a declaration of the death of Abū Bakr[ra] and of 'Umar[ra] for strategic reasons. Only the remnants of his small force had been left. The enemy forces were large and buoyant. But now the enemy had insulted Allah. The Prophet[sa] could not stand such an insult. His spirit was fired. He looked angrily at the Muslims who surrounded him and said, "Why stand silent and make no reply to this insult to Allah, the Only God?"

The Muslims asked, "What shall we say, O Prophet[sa]?" "Say, 'Allah alone is Great and Mighty. Allah alone is Great and Mighty. He alone is High and Honoured. He alone is High and Honoured.' "

The Muslims shouted accordingly. This cry stupefied the enemy. They stood chagrined at the thought that the Prophet[sa] after all had not died. Before them stood a handful of Muslims, wounded and exhausted. To finish them was easy enough. But they dared not attack again. Content with the sort of victory they had won, they returned making a great show of rejoicing.

In the Battle of Uḥud, Muslim victory became converted into a defeat. Nevertheless, the battle affords evidence of the truth of the Prophet[sa]. For in this battle were fulfilled the prophecies the Prophet[sa] had made before going into battle. Muslims were victorious in the beginning. The Prophet's[sa] beloved uncle, Ḥamza[ra], died fighting. The commander of the enemy was killed early in the action. The Prophet[sa] himself was wounded and many Muslims were killed. All this happened as it had been foretold in the Prophet's[sa] vision.

Besides the fulfilment of the incidents told beforehand this battle afforded many proofs of the sincerity and devotion of Muslims. So exemplary was their behaviour that history fails to provide a parallel to it. Some incidents in proof of this we have already narrated. One more seems worth narrating. It shows the certainty of conviction and devotion displayed by the Prophet's[sa] Companions. When the Prophet[sa] retired to the foot of the hill with a handful of Muslims, he sent out some of his Companions to look after the wounded lying on the field. A Companion after long search found a wounded Muslim of Medina. He was near death. The Companion bent over him and said, "Peace on you." The wounded Muslim raised a trembling hand, and holding the visitor's hand in his own, said, "I was waiting for someone to come."

"You are in a critical state," said the visitor to the soldier. "Have you anything to communicate to your relations?"

"Yes, yes," said the dying Muslim. "Say peace to my relations and tell them that while I die here, I leave behind a precious trust to be taken care of by them. That trust is the Prophet of God[sa]. I hope my relations will guard his person with their lives and remember this my only dying wish" (*Mu'aṭṭā* and *Zurqānī*).

Dying persons have much to say to their relations, but these early Muslims, even in their dying moments, thought not of their relations, sons, daughters or wives, nor of their property, but only of the Prophet[sa]. They faced death in the certainty that the Prophet[sa] was the saviour of the world. Their children if they survived, would achieve but little. If they died guarding the Prophet's[sa] person, they would have served both God and man. They believed that in sacrificing their families they served mankind and they served their God. In inviting death for them they secured life everlasting for mankind at large.

The Prophet[sa] collected the wounded and the dead. The wounded were given first-aid and the dead were buried. The Prophet[sa] then learnt that the enemy had treated the Muslims most savagely, that they had mutilated the bodies of the dead Muslims and cut off a nose here and an ear there. One of the mutilated bodies was that of Ḥamza[ra], the Prophet's[sa] uncle. The Prophet[sa] was moved, and said, "The actions of disbelievers now justify the treatment which we so far thought was unjustified." As he said this, he was commanded by God to let the disbelievers alone and to continue to show them compassion.

RUMOUR OF PROPHET'S[sa] DEATH REACHES MEDINA

The rumour of the Prophet's[sa] death and the news of the dispersal of the Muslim army reached Medina, before the remnants of the Muslim force could return to the town. Women and children ran madly towards Uḥud. Many of them learnt the truth from the returning soldiers and went back. One woman of the tribe of Banū Dīnār went on until she reached Uḥud. This woman had lost her husband, father and brother in the battle. According to some narrators, she had also lost a son. A returning soldier met her and told her that her father had died. She said in reply, "I do not care for my father; tell me about the Prophet[sa]." The soldier knew the Prophet[sa] was alive, so he did not answer her query at once, but went on to tell her of her brother and husband who had also died. At each report she remained unmoved and asked again and again, "What has the

Prophet[sa] of God done?" It was a strange expression to use, but when we remember it was a woman who used it, it no longer seems so strange. A woman's emotions are strong. She often addresses a dead person as though he were alive. If that person is nearly related, she tends to make a complaint to him and ask why he is abandoning her and leaving her behind uncared for and unlooked after. It is common for women to mourn the loss of their dear ones in this way. The expression used by this woman, therefore, is appropriate to a woman grieving over the Prophet's[sa] death. This woman held the Prophet[sa] dear and refused to believe he was dead even after she had heard that he was. At the same time she did not deny the news but continued to say in true womanly grief, "What has the Prophet[sa] of God done?" By saying this she pretended the Prophet[sa] was alive, and complained that a loyal leader like him had chosen to give them all the pain of separation.

When the returning soldier found that this woman did not care about the death of her father, brother and husband, he understood the depth of her love for the Prophet[sa] and told her, "As for the Prophet[sa], he is as you wish, fully alive." The woman asked the soldier to show her the Prophet[sa]. He pointed to one part of the field. The woman rushed to that part and reaching the Prophet[sa], held his mantle in her hand, kissed it and said, "My father and mother be sacrificed to thee, O Prophet of God[sa], if thou livest, I care not who else dies" (*Hishām*).

We can see, therefore, what fortitude and devotion did Muslims—both men and women—display in this battle. Christian writers narrate proudly the story of Mary Magdalene and her companions and tell us of their devotion and bravery. It is said that in the small hours of the morning they stole through the Jews and made for the tomb of Jesus[as]. But what is this compared with the devotion of this Muslim woman of the tribe of Dīnār?

One more example is recorded in history. After the dead had been buried and the Prophet[sa] was returning to Medina, he saw women and children who had come out of Medina to receive him. The cord of his dromedary was held by Sa'd bin Mu'ādh[ra], a chief of Medina. Sa'd[ra] was leading the dromedary pompously. He seemed to proclaim to the world that Muslims had after all succeeded in leading the Prophet[sa] back to Medina hale and hearty. As he was advancing he saw his own aged mother advancing to meet the returning party of Muslims. This aged woman was very weak-sighted. Sa'd[ra] recognized her and, turning to the Prophet[sa], said, "Here, O Prophet[sa], is my mother."

"Let her come forward," replied the Prophet[sa].

The woman came forward and with a vacant look tried to spot the Prophet's[sa] face. At last she was able to spot it and was glad. The Prophet[sa] seeing her said, "Woman, I grieve over the loss of thy son."

"But," replied the devoted woman, "after I have seen you alive, I have swallowed all my misfortunes." The Arabic expression she used was "I have roasted my misfortune and swallowed it" (*Halbiyya*, Vol. 2, p. 210). What depth of emotion does this expression indicate. Normally, grief eats up a human being, and here was an aged woman who had lost her son, a staff for her old age. But she said that, instead of letting her grief eat her up, she had eaten up her grief. The fact that her son had died for the Prophet[sa] would sustain her during the rest of her days.

The Prophet[sa] reached Medina. In this battle, many Muslims were killed and many wounded. Still the battle cannot be said to have ended in defeat for Muslims. The incidents which we have related above prove the reverse. They prove that Uḥud was as great a victory for Muslims as any other. Muslims who turn to the pages of their early history can derive sustenance and inspiration from Uḥud.

Back in Medina, the Prophet[sa] returned to his mission. He engaged himself again in training and teaching his followers. But as before, his work did not go on uninterruptedly. After Uḥud, the Jews became more daring, and the hypocrites began to raise their heads again. They began to think that the extirpation of Islam was within their means and their competence. Only, they had to make a concerted effort. Accordingly, the Jews put to use new methods of vexation. They would publish foul abuse in verse, and in this way they would insult the Prophet[sa] and his family. Once the Prophet[sa] was called to decide a dispute and he had to go to a Jewish fortress. The Jews planned to drop a stone slab on him and thus put an end to his life. The Prophet[sa] had a forewarning of this from God. It was his wont to receive such timely warnings. The Prophet[sa] left his seat without saying anything. The Jews later admitted their foul intrigue. Muslim women were insulted in the streets. In one such incident a Muslim lost his life. On another occasion the Jews stoned a Muslim girl and she died in great pain. This behaviour of the Jews strained their relations with Muslims and forced them to fight against the Jews. But Muslims only turned them out of Medina. One of the two Jewish tribes migrated to Syria. Of the other, some went to Syria and some settled in Khaibar, a well-fortified Jewish stronghold, to the north of Medina.

In the interval of peace between Uḥud and the next battle, the world witnessed an outstanding example of the influence of Islam on its followers. We refer to the prohibition of drink. In describing the condition of Arab society before Islam, we pointed out that the Arabs were confirmed drunkards. To drink five times a day was in fashion in every Arab home. To lose oneself under the effect of drink was a common practice and of this the Arabs were not in the least ashamed. Rather they thought it was a virtue. When a guest arrived, it was the duty of the house-wife to send drinks round. To wean such a people from this deadly habit was no easy matter. But in the fourth year after the Hijra the Prophet[sa] received the command that drinking had been forbidden. With the promulgation of this command, drinking disappeared from Muslim society. It is recorded that when the revelation making drink unlawful was received, the Prophet[sa] sent for a Companion and ordered him to proclaim the new command in the streets of Medina. In the house of an Anṣārī (a Muslim of Medina) a drinking party was going on. Many persons had been invited and cups of wine were being served. One large pot had been drunk and a second one was going to be broached. Many had lost their senses, and many more were on the way to lose them. In this condition they heard some one proclaim that drinking had been forbidden by the Prophet[sa] under a command of God. One of the party stood up and said, "It looks like a proclamation against drinking; let us find out if this is so." Another stood up, struck the earthen pot full of wine with his staff, broke it to pieces and said, "First obey, then inquire. It is enough that we have heard of such a proclamation. It is not meet that we should go on drinking while we make inquiries. It is rather our duty to let the wine flow in the street and then inquire about the proclamation" (*Bukhārī* and *Muslim, Kitāb al-Ashriba*). This Muslim was right. For, if drinking had been forbidden, they would have been guilty of an offence, had they gone on drinking on the other hand, if drinking had not been forbidden, they would not lose much if for once they should let the wine in their pots flow into the streets. Drinking disappeared from the entire Muslim society after this proclamation. No special effort or campaign was needed to bring about this revolutionary change. Muslims who heard this command and witnessed the ready response with which it was received lived up to seventy or eighty years. No case is known of any Muslim who, having heard of this prohibition, showed the weakness of offending against it. If there was any such case, it must have been of one who did not have the chance to come under the direct influence of the Prophet[sa]. Compare with this the prohibition movement of America and of the efforts to promote temperance which have been made for so many years in Europe. In the one case a simple proclamation by the Prophet[sa] was enough to obliterate a social evil rooted deep in Arab society. In the other, prohibition was enacted by special laws. Police and the army, custom officials and excise inspectors, all exerted themselves as a team and tried to put down the evil of drink but failed and had to confess their failure. The drunkards won and the drink evil could not be defeated. Ours is said to be an age of social progress. But when we compare our age with the age of early Islam, we wonder which of the two deserves this title—this age of ours or the age in which Islam brought about this great social revolution?

What happened at Uḥud was not liable to be easily forgotten. The Meccans thought Uḥud was their first victory against Islam. They published the news all over Arabia and used it to excite the Arab tribes against Islam and to persuade them that Muslims were not invincible. If they continued to prosper, it was not because of any strength of their own but because of the weakness of Arab orthodoxy. It was due to the weakness of Arab idolaters. If the Arab idolaters made a concerted effort, to overpower the Muslims was not a difficult business. The result of this propaganda was that hostility against Muslims began to gather strength. The other Arab tribes began to outstrip the Meccans in harassing the Muslims. Some began to attack them openly. Some began to inflict losses upon them surreptitiously. In the fourth year after the Hijra, two Arab tribes, the ‘Aḍl and the Qāra, sent their representatives to the Holy Prophet[sa] to submit that many of their men were inclined towards Islam. They requested the Prophet[sa] to send to them some Muslims well-versed in the teaching of Islam, to live among them and teach them the New Religion. Actually this was an intrigue hatched by the Banū Liḥyān, arch-enemy of Islam. They sent these delegates to the Prophet[sa] under promise of a rich reward. The Prophet[sa] received the request unsuspectingly and sent ten Muslims to teach the tribes the tenets and principles of Islam. When this party reached the territory of the Banū Liḥyān, their escorts had the news delivered to the tribesmen and invited them to arrest the party or to put them to death. On this vicious suggestion, two hundred armed men of the Banū Liḥyān set out in pursuit of the Muslim party and overtook them at last at a spot called Rajī'. An encounter took place between ten Muslims and two hundred of the enemy. The Muslims were full of faith. The enemy was without any. The ten Muslims climbed up an eminence and challenged the two hundred. The enemy tried to overpower the Muslims by vile intrigue. They offered to spare them if only they would come down. But the party chief replied that they had seen enough of the promises made by disbelievers. So saying, they turned to God and prayed. God was well aware of their plight. Was it not meet that He should inform their Prophet[sa] of this? When the disbelievers found the small party of Muslims adamant, they launched their attack upon them. The party fought without thought of defeat. Seven of the ten fell fighting. To the three who remained the disbelievers renewed their promise to spare their lives, on condition that they should come down from the eminence. These three believed the disbelievers and surrendered. As soon as they did so, the disbelievers tied them up. One of the three said, "This is the first breach of your plighted word. God only knows what you will do next." Saying this, he refused to go with them. The disbelievers started belabouring the victim and dragging him down the way. But they were so overawed by the resistance and determination shown by this one man that they murdered him on the spot. The other two they took with them and sold them as slaves to the Quraish of Mecca. One of the two was Khubaib[ra], the other Zaid[ra]. The purchaser of Khubaib[ra] wanted to murder him so as to avenge his own father, who had been killed at Badr. One day, Khubaib[ra] asked for a razor to complete his toilet. Khubaib[ra] was holding the razor when a child of the household approached him out of curiosity. Khubaib[ra] took the child and put him on his knee. The child's mother saw this and became terrified. Her mind was full of guilty feelings, and here was a man whom they were going to murder in a few days holding a razor so dangerously near their child. She was convinced that Khubaib[ra] was going to murder the child. Khubaib[ra] saw the consternation on the face of the woman and said, "Do you imagine I am going to murder your child. Do not think so for a moment. I cannot do such a foul thing. Muslims do not play false."

The woman was impressed by the honest and straightforward bearing and behaviour of Khubaib[ra]. She remembered this ever afterwards and used to say she had never seen a prisoner like Khubaib[ra]. At last the Meccans led Khubaib[ra] to an open field to celebrate his murder in public. When the appointed moment came, Khubaib[ra] asked for leave to say two *rak'ats* of prayer. The Quraish agreed and Khubaib[ra] addressed in public view his last prayers to God in this world. When he had finished praying, he said he wanted to continue, but did not do so lest they should think he was afraid of dying. Then he quietly submitted his neck to the executioner. As he did so, he hummed the verses:

> **While I die a Muslim, I care not whether my headless body drops to the right or to the left. And why should I? My death is in the way of God; if He wills, He can bless every part of my dismembered body (*Bukhārī*).**

Khubaib[ra] had hardly finished murmuring these verses when the executioner's sword fell on his neck and his head fell to one side. Those who had assembled to celebrate this public murder included one Sa'īd bin 'Āmir[ra] who later became a Muslim. It is said that whenever the murder of Khubaib[ra] was related in Sa'īd's[ra] presence, he would go into a fit (*Hishām*). The second prisoner, Zaid[ra], was also taken out to be murdered. Among the spectators was Abū Sufyān[ra], chief of Mecca. Abū Sufyān[ra] turned to Zaid[ra] and asked, "Would you not rather have Muḥammad[sa] in your place?

Would you not prefer to be safe at home while Muḥammad[sa] was in our hands?"

Zaid[ra] replied proudly, "What, Abū Sufyān[ra]? What do you say? By God, I would rather die, than that the Prophet[sa] should tread on a thorn in a street in Medina." Abū Sufyān[ra] could not help being impressed by such devotion. He looked at Zaid[ra] in amazement and declared unhesitatingly, but in measured tones, "God is my witness, I have not known any one love another as much as the Companions of Muḥammad[sa] love Muḥammad[sa]" (*Hishām*, Vol. 2).

About this time some people of Najd also approached the Prophet[sa] for Muslims to teach them Islam. The Prophet[sa] did not trust them. But Abū Barā', chief of the 'Āmir tribe, happened to be in Medina at the time. He offered to act as surety for the tribe and assured the Prophet[sa] that they would commit no mischief. The Prophet[sa] selected seventy Muslims who knew the Qur'an by heart. When this party reached Bi'r Ma'ūna one of them, Ḥarām bin Malḥān[ra] went to the chief of the 'Āmir tribe (a nephew of Barā') to give him the message of Islam. Apparently Ḥarām[ra] was well received by the tribesmen. But while he was addressing the chief, a man stole up from behind and attacked Ḥarām[ra] with a lance. Ḥarām[ra] died on the spot. As the lance pierced through Ḥarām's[ra] neck, he was heard saying, "God is great. The Lord of the Ka'ba is my witness, I have attained my goal" (*Bukhārī*). Having murdered Ḥarām[ra] in this foul manner, the tribal leaders provoked the tribe into an attack upon the rest of this party of Muslim teachers. "But," said the tribesmen, "Our chief, Abū Barā', offered to act as surety; we cannot attack this party." Then the tribal chiefs, with the assistance of the two tribes who had gone to the Prophet[sa] to ask for Muslim teachers and some other tribes, attacked the Muslim party. The simple appeal, "We have come to preach and to teach, not to fight," had no effect. They started murdering the party. All but three of the seventy were murdered. One of the survivors was lame and had climbed a hill before the encounter began. Two others had gone to a wood to feed their camels. On returning from the wood they found sixty-six of their companions lying dead on the field. The two counselled together. Said one, "We should go and make a report of this to the Holy Prophet[sa]."

Said the other, "I cannot leave a spot where the chief of our party, whom our Prophet[sa] appointed our leader, has been murdered." So saying, he sprang single-handed upon the disbelievers and died fighting. The other was taken prisoner but was later released in fulfilment of a vow which the tribal chief had taken. The murdered party included 'Āmir bin Fuhaira[ra], a freedman of Abū Bakr[ra]. His murderer was one Jabbār[ra] who later became a Muslim. Jabbār[ra] attributed his conversion to this mass massacre of Muslims.

"When I started murdering 'Āmir[ra]," says Jabbār[ra], "I heard 'Āmir[ra] say, 'By God I have met my goal' I asked someone why a Muslim said this sort of thing when he was meeting his death. That person explained that Muslims regarded death in the path of God as a blessing and a victory." Jabbār[ra] was so impressed by this reply, that he started making a systematic study of Islam, and ultimately became a Muslim (*Hishām* and *Usud al-Ghāba*).

The news of the two sad events, in which about eighty Muslims lost their lives as the result of a mischievous intrigue, reached Medina simultaneously. These were no ordinary men who were murdered. They were bearers of the Qur'an. They had committed no crime and had harmed nobody. They were taking part in no battle. They had been decoyed into enemy hands by a lie told in the name of God and religion. These facts proved conclusively that enmity to Islam was determined and deep. On the other hand the zeal of Muslims for Islam was equally determined and deep.

ENCOUNTER WITH BANŪ MUṢṬALIQ

After the Battle of Uḥud, there was a severe famine at Mecca. Disregarding all enmity which the Meccans bore against him, and disregarding all machinations which they had been employing to spread disaffection against him throughout the country, the Prophet[sa] raised a fund to help the poor of Mecca in their dire need. The Meccans remained unimpressed even by this expression of goodwill. Their hostility went on unabated. In fact it became worse. Tribes which had so far been sympathetic towards Muslims also became hostile. One such tribe was Banū Muṣṭaliq. They had good relations with Muslims. But now they had started preparing for an attack on Medina. When the Prophet[sa] heard of their preparations he sent men to find out the truth. The men returned and confirmed the reports. The Prophet[sa] decided to go and meet this new attack. Accordingly, he raised a force and led it to the territory of Banū Muṣṭaliq. When the Muslim force met the enemy, the Prophet[sa] tried to persuade the enemy to withdraw without fighting. They refused. Battle was joined and in a few hours the enemy was defeated.

Because the Meccan disbelievers were bent upon mischief and friendly tribes were turning hostile, the hypocrites among Muslims had also ventured on this occasion to take part in the battle on the Muslim side. They probably thought they might have a chance to do some mischief. The encounter with Banū Muṣṭaliq was over in a few hours. The hypocrites, therefore, did not have any chance to do any mischief during the battle. The Holy Prophet[sa], however, decided to stay in the town of Banū Muṣṭaliq for a few days. During his stay a quarrel arose between a Meccan and a Medinite Muslim over drawing water from a well. The Meccan happened to be an ex-slave. He struck the Medinite, who raised an alarm, crying out for fellow-Medinites—known as the Anṣār or Helpers. The Meccan also raised an alarm and cried out for fellow-Meccans—known as the Muhājirīn or

Refugees. Excitement prevailed. Nobody inquired what had happened. Young men on both sides drew their swords. 'Abdullāh bin Ubayy ibn Salūl thought it a God-send. He decided to add fuel to the fire. "You have gone too far in your indulgence to the Refugees. Your good treatment of them has turned their heads, and now they are trying to dominate you in every way." The speech might have had the effect which 'Abdullāh desired. The quarrel might have assumed serious proportions. But it did not. 'Abdullāh was wrong in assessing the effect of his mischievous speech. Believing, however, that the Anṣār were being persuaded, he went so far as to say:

> **Let us return to Medina. Then will the most honoured among its citizens turn out the most despised (*Bukhārī*).**

By the most honoured citizen, he meant himself and by the most despised he meant the Prophet[sa] As soon as he said this, believing Muslims were able to see through the mischief. It was not an innocent speech they had listened to, they said, but the speech of Satan who had come to lead them astray. A young man stood up and reported to the Prophet[sa] through his uncle. The Prophet[sa] sent for 'Abdullāh bin Ubayy ibn Salūl and his friends and asked them what had happened. 'Abdullāh and his friends denied that they had taken any such part as had been attributed to them in this incident. The Prophet[sa] said nothing. But the truth began to spread. In the course of time 'Abdullāh bin Ubayy ibn Salūl's own son, 'Abdullāh[ra], also heard about it. Young 'Abdullāh[ra] at once saw the Prophet[sa], and said, "O Prophet[sa], my father has insulted you. Death is his punishment. If you decide so, I would rather have you command me to kill my father. If you command someone else, and my father dies at his hands, I may be led to avenge my father by killing that man. Maybe I incur the displeasure of God in this way."

"But," said the Prophet[sa], "I have no such intention. I will treat your father with compassion and consideration." When young 'Abdullāh[ra] compared the disloyalty and discourtesy of his father with the compassion and kindness of the Prophet[sa], he made for Medina full of suppressed anger against his father. He stopped his father on the way and said he would not let him go any farther on the road to Medina until he had withdrawn the words he had used against the Prophet[sa]. "The lips which said, 'The Prophet[sa] is despised and you are honoured,' must now say, 'The Prophet[sa] is honoured and you are despised.' Until you say this I will not let you go." 'Abdullāh bin Ubayy ibn Salūl was astonished and frightened and said, "I agree, my son, that Muḥammad[sa] is honoured and that I am despised." Young 'Abdullāh[ra] then let his father go (*Hishām*, Vol. 2).

We have mentioned before two Jewish tribes who had to be banished out of Medina on account of their mischievous machinations and murderous intrigues. Banū Naḍīr, one of the two, migrated partly to Syria, partly to a town called Khaibar in the north of Medina. Khaibar was a well-fortified Jewish centre in Arabia. The Jews, who had migrated there, began to excite the Arabs against Muslims. The Meccans were already sworn enemies of Islam. No fresh provocation was needed to excite the Meccans against Muslims. Similarly the Ghaṭafān of Najd, because of their friendly relations with the Meccans, were hostile to Muslims. The Jews settled in Khaibar already counted on the Quraish of Mecca and the Ghaṭafān of Najd. Besides these, they planned to turn Banū Sulaim and Banū Asad against Islam. They also persuaded Banū Sa'd, a tribe in alliance with the Jews, to join the Meccans in an alliance against Islam. After a long intrigue a confederacy of Arab tribes was organized to fight the Muslims. This included the Meccans, the tribes living in territories around Mecca, the tribes of Najd, and those living in territories to the north of Medina.

BATTLE OF THE DITCH

A large army was raised in the fifth year of the Hijra. The strength of this army has been estimated by historians as between ten and twenty-four thousand men. But a confederated army raised out of the different tribes of Arabia could not be an army of ten thousand. Twenty-four thousand seems nearer the truth. It could easily have been eighteen or twenty thousand. The town of Medina which this horde wished to attack was a modest one, quite unable to resist a concerted attack by all Arabia. Its population at this time was little more than three thousand males (including old men, young men and children). Against this population the enemy had raised an army of twenty to twenty-four thousand able-bodied men, experienced in warfare; and (having been assembled from different parts of the country) they were an army with a well-selected personnel. The population of Medina, on the other hand, which could be called upon to resist this huge army included males of all ages. One can judge the odds against which the Muslim population of Medina had to contend. It was a most unequal encounter. The enemy was twenty to twenty-four thousand strong, and Muslims hardly three thousand including, as we have said, all the males of the town, the old and the young. When the Prophet[sa] heard of the huge enemy preparations, he held a council and asked for advice. Among those who were consulted was Salmān[ra] the Persian, being the first Muslim convert from Persia. The Prophet[sa] asked Salmān[ra] what they did in Persia if they had to defend a town against a huge army. "If a town is unfortified, and the home force very small," said Salmān[ra], "the custom in our country is to dig a ditch round the town and to defend from inside." The Prophet[sa] approved of the idea. Medina has hills on one side. These provided a natural protection on that side. Another side with a concentration of lanes had a compact population. On this side the town could not be attacked unawares. The third side had houses and palm-groves and, at some distance, the fortresses of the Jewish tribe, Banū Quraiẓa. The Banū Quraiẓa had signed a pact of peace with the Muslims. Therefore this side was also considered safe from enemy attack. The fourth side was an open plain and it was from this side that the enemy attack was most likely and most feared. The Prophet[sa], therefore, decided to dig a ditch on this open side so as to prevent the enemy from attacking unawares. The task was shared among Muslims—ten men were to dig ten yards of the ditch. Altogether a mile long ditch, of sufficient width and depth, had to be dug.

When the digging was going on, they came upon a rock which Muslim sappers found hard to tackle. A report was sent to the Prophet[sa] who made for the spot at once. Taking a pickaxe he struck the rock hard. Sparks came out and the Prophet[sa] cried aloud "*Allāhu Akbar*". He struck again. Again a light came out and again the Prophet[sa] cried out, "*Allāhu Akbar*". He struck a third time. Light came out again, the Prophet[sa] said, "*Allāhu Akbar*" and the rock was in fragments. The Companions asked the Prophet[sa] about all this. Why did he say, "*Allāhu Akbar*" again and again?

"I struck this rock three times with this pickaxe, and three times did I see scenes of the future glory of Islam revealed to me. In the first sparks I saw the Syrian palaces of the Roman Empire. I had the keys of those palaces given to me. The second time I saw the illumined palaces of Persia at Madā'in, and had the keys of the Persian Empire given to me. The third time, I saw the gates of San'ā and I had the keys of the Kingdom of Yemen given to me. These are the promises of God and I trust you will put reliance in them. The enemy can do you no harm" (*Zurqānī*, Vol. 2).

With their limited man-power, the ditch which the Muslims were able to dig could not be a perfect one from the point of view of military strategy, but it at least seemed to ensure against the sudden entry of the enemy into the town. That it was not impassable, subsequent events in the battle amply proved. No other side suited the enemy from which to attack the town.

From the side of the ditch, therefore, the huge army of Arabian tribesmen began to approach Medina. As soon as the Prophet[sa] got to know of this, he came out to defend it with twelve hundred men, having posted other men to defend other parts of the town.

Historians estimate differently the number which defended the ditch. Some put it at three thousand, others at twelve to thirteen hundred, still others at seven hundred. These estimates are very difficult and apparently difficult to reconcile. But, after weighing the evidence, we have come to the conclusion that all the three estimates of the Muslim numbers engaged in defending the ditch are correct. They relate to different stages of the battle.

FIGHT AGAINST HEAVY ODDS

We have already agreed that, after the withdrawal of the hypocrites at Uḥud, the number of Muslims left in the field was seven hundred. The Battle of the Ditch took place only two years after the Battle of Uhud. During these two years, no large accessions to Islam are recorded in history. An increase during this time in the number of combatant Muslims from seven hundred to three thousand is not to be expected. At the same time, it does not stand to reason that between Uḥud and the Ditch there was no rise in the number of combatant Muslims. Islam continued to add to its numbers and we should expect some increase between the Battle of Uḥud and the Battle of the Ditch. From these two considerations, it seems to follow that the estimate which puts the number of Muslim combatants in the Battle of the Ditch at one thousand two hundred is correct. The only question to be answered is, why some authorities put the number at three thousand and some at seven hundred. Our answer to this question is that the two figures relate to two different stages of the battle. The Battle of the Ditch was fought in three stages. We had the first stage before the enemy had come near to Medina, and Muslims were engaged in digging the ditch. During this time, we may well assume that in removing the excavated earth to a distance, children and, to some extent even women must have come in to assist. In the digging of the trench we may, therefore, assume that there were altogether three thousand souls employed on the Muslim side. The number included children and some women. The children were able to help in carrying the earth, and women who always vied with the men in helping all Muslim campaigns, must have been useful in doing many ancillary jobs connected with the digging. There is evidence to support this assumption. When the digging started, even children were asked to come. Practically the whole population took part in the digging. But as soon as the enemy arrived and the battle began, the Prophet[sa] ordered boys under fifteen to withdraw from the scene of operations. Those above fifteen were allowed to take part if they were so minded (*Ḥalbiyya*, Vol. 2). From this it appears that at the time of digging, Muslim numbers were much larger than when the battle began. At the time of the battle the very young boys had all withdrawn. Estimates which put the Muslim numbers in the battle at three thousand relate only to the digging, and those which put the figure at one thousand two hundred relate to the actual battle in which only grown-up males took part. The only estimate we have not accounted for is that which puts the figure at seven hundred. Even this estimate, according to us, is correct. It has been proposed by as reliable an authority as Ibn Isḥāq, who is supported in this estimate by no less a person than Ibn Ḥazm. It is difficult to question this estimate. Fortunately, when we turn to the other details of the battle, even this estimate turns out to be correct. There is evidence to show that when the Banū Quraiẓa, against their plighted word, joined the enemy, and decided to attack Medina in the rear, the Holy Prophetsa, having been apprised of their evil intention, decided to post guards in the part of the town exposed to the attack of Banū Quraiẓa. This part of Medina had originally been left undefended because the Banū Quraiẓa were in alliance with Muslims. And it was assumed that they would not let the enemy attack the town from their side. It is known that when the defection of the Banū Quraiẓa was reported to the Prophetsa and it became evident that Muslim women, considered safe in this part of the town because of the alliance, were no longer safe, the Prophetsa decided to send two forces, of two and three hundred men, to guard two different parts of the now exposed town. The Prophetsa ordered them to raise occasional cries of "*Allāhu Akbar*", so that the main Muslim forces should know that the Muslim women were safe. The estimate of Ibn Isḥāq, therefore, which puts the number of combatants in the Battle of the Ditch at seven hundred, is also correct. If five hundred men out of one thousand two hundred were sent to guard the rear of the town, only seven hundred could remain. Thus all the three estimates of the number of the Muslim army in the Battle of the Ditch turn out to be correct.

To defend the ditch, therefore, the Holy Prophetsa had only seven hundred men. True, the ditch had been dug. But to face and to repel an army as large as the enemy had, even with the help of the ditch seemed well-nigh impossible. But as usual Muslims trusted their God and relied on His help. Their small force waited for the enemy host, while the women and children had been sent to two apparently safe parts of the town. When the enemy reached the ditch, they were amazed because this stratagem had never been used before in any Arab battle. So they decided to camp on their side of the ditch and to deliberate over methods of attacking and entering Medina. One side was protected by the ditch. A second side had hills with their natural protection. A third side had stone houses and groves of trees. It was impossible for the enemy to make any sudden attack on any part of the town. The enemy commanders took counsel together and decided that it was necessary to try to wean the Banū Quraiẓa, the Jewish tribe, still living in Medina, from their alliance with the Muslims and ask them to join the Arab confederates in this critical onslaught against Medina. Only the Banū Quraiẓa could give them a way to the town. At last Abū Sufyān[ra] selected Ḥuyaī bin Akhṭab, chief of the banished tribe of Banū Naḍīr and principal instigator of Arab tribes against Medina, and appointed him to negotiate with the Banū Quraiẓa for facilities to attack the town from the rear. Ḥuyaī bin Akhṭab went to the Jewish fortress to see the leader of the Banū Quraiẓa. At first they refused to see him. But when he explained that this was a very opportune moment to defeat the Muslims, he succeeded in winning over one of the Quraiẓites, Ka'b. He explained that all Arabia had turned out to attack and destroy the Muslims. The army which stood at the other side of the ditch was not an army, but an ocean of able-bodied men whom the Muslims could not possibly resist. Ultimately it was agreed that as soon as the army of disbelievers succeeded in forcing the ditch the Banū Quraiẓa would attack that part of Medina to which the Holy Prophet[sa] had sent all the women and children for safety. This plan, it was believed, would smash the Muslim resistance, and prove a death-trap for their entire population—men, women and children. If this plan had met with even partial success, it would have cost the Muslims dear and made things very difficult for them. They would have had no escape from this death-trap.

TREACHERY OF BANŪ QURAIẒA

The Banū Quraiẓa, as we have said, were in alliance with the Muslims. Even if they had not joined the battle on the Muslim side, it was expected that they would at least bar the way of the enemy on their side. The

Prophet[sa], therefore, had left that part of the town entirely unguarded. The Banū Quraiẓa knew that the Muslims trusted their good faith. So when they decided to join the Arabs, it was agreed that they would not join them openly lest the Muslims should become alert and take steps to guard the part of the town on the side of the Banū Quraiẓa. It was a very dangerous plot.

When it was agreed that Muslims were to be attacked from two sides, the Arab army started assailing the ditch. A few days passed, however, and nothing happened. Then they hit upon the idea of posting their archers on an eminence and ordering them to attack parties of Muslims defending the ditch. These stood on the edge separated by short intervals. As soon as the Muslim defence showed any signs of breaking, the disbelievers would try to cross the ditch with the help of their first-rate horsemen. They believed that when such attacks were repeated, they would obtain possession of a point on the Muslim side of the ditch at which they would be able to land their forces for a full-fledged attack on the town. Attack after attack was therefore made. Muslim defenders had to fight ceaselessly. One day they were kept so engaged in repelling these attacks that some of the daily prayers could not be said at the appointed time. The Prophet[sa] was grieved over this and said, "God punish the infidels, they have upset our prayers." The incident shows the intensity of the enemy attack. But it also shows that the Prophet's[sa] first and last concern was the worship of God. Medina had been beleaguered on all sides. Not only men, but also women and children were faced with certain death. The whole of the town was in the grip of anxiety. But the Prophet[sa] still thought of holding the daily prayers at their appointed hours. Muslims do not worship God only once a week, as do Christians and Hindus. Muslims are required to worship five times a day. During a battle, to hold even one public prayer is difficult, not to speak of holding five prayers a day in congregation. But the Prophet[sa] convened the five daily prayers even during battle. If one of these prayers was upset by enemy attack, it pained him.

To return to the battle, the enemy was attacking from the front, the Banū Quraiẓa were planning to attack from the rear but not in such a way as to make the Muslim population alert. They wanted to enter the town from behind and to kill the women and children sheltered there. One day the Banū Quraiẓa sent a spy to find out whether guards had been posted for the protection of women and children and, if so, in what strength. There was a special enclosure for families which the enemy regarded as their special target. The spy came and began to hover round this enclosure and to look about suspiciously. While he was doing so, Ṣafiyya[ra], an aunt of the Prophet[sa], spotted him. Only one male adult happened to be on guard duty at the time and even he was ill. Ṣafiyya[ra] reported to him what she had seen and suggested he should lay hand on this spy before he was able to inform the enemy how unprotected the women and children were in that part of the town. The sick Muslim refused to do anything upon which Ṣafiyya[ra] herself picked up a staff and began to fight this undesirable visitor. With the help of other women she succeeded in over-powering and killing him. Later it was proved that this man was really an agent of the Banū Quraiẓa. Muslims became nervous and began to apprehend other attacks from this side which they had so far thought quite safe. But the attack from the front was so heavy that the whole of the Muslim force was needed to resist it. Nevertheless, the Prophet[sa] decided to spare a part of the force for the protection of women and children. As we have said in our discussion of the Muslim numbers in this battle, out of twelve hundred men, the Prophet[sa] sent five hundred for the protection of women in the town. For the defence of the ditch, therefore, only seven hundred men were left to fight an army of between eighteen and twenty thousand. Many Muslims were unnerved at the odds which they had to face. They went to the Prophet[sa] and said how critical the situation was, and how impossible it seemed to save the town. They requested the Prophet[sa] to pray. They also requested him to teach them a special prayer for this occasion. The Prophet[sa] replied, "Have no fear. Only pray to God that He should protect you from your weaknesses, strengthen your hearts, and relieve your anxiety." The Prophet[sa] prayed himself in the following words:

> **God, Thou hast sent to me the Qur'an. Thou waitest not to call anyone to account. These hordes which have come to attack us, give them defeat. God, I beseech thee again: Defeat them, make us dominate over them, and upset all their evil intentions (*Bukhārī*).**

And again:

> **God, Thou hearest those who cry to Thee in misery and in affliction. Thou repliest to those who are stricken with anxiety. Relieve me of my pain, my anxiety, and my fear. Thou knowest what odds I and my Companions are up against (*Zurqānī*).**

The hypocrites became more nervous than others in the Muslim force. All regard for the honour of their side and the safety of their town, their women and children, disappeared from their hearts. But they did not want to be disgraced in the presence of their own side. Therefore, they began to desert the Muslims one by one on slender excuses. The Qur'an refers to this in 33: 14

> **And a section of them even asked leave of the Prophet[sa], saying, 'Our houses are exposed and defenceless.' And they were not exposed. They only sought to flee away.**

The state of battle at the moment, and the condition in which the Muslims stood at the time is described in the Qur'an in the following verses:

> **When they came upon you from above you and from below you, and when your eyes became distracted, and the hearts reached to the throats, and you thought diverse thoughts about Allah. Then were the believers sorely tried, and they were shaken with a violent shaking. And when**

the hypocrites, and those in whose hearts was a disease said, 'Allah and His Messenger promised us nothing but delusion'. And when a party of them said, 'O people of Yathrib, you have possibly no stand against the enemy, therefore turn back' (33: 11-14).

Here Muslims are reminded how they were attacked from the front by a confederacy of Arab tribes, and in the rear by the Jews. They are reminded how miserable they were at that time. Their eyes flinched and their hearts were in their mouths. They even began to entertain doubts about God. The believers were then on trial. They were all given a shaking. The hypocrites and the spiritually diseased began to say, 'We have all been fooled by false promises made to us by God and His Prophet[sa]!' A party of them even began to unnerve the Muslim force saying, 'There is no fighting now. There is nothing to do but to go back.'

How true believers behaved on this occasion is also described in the Qur'an:

And when the believers saw the confederates, they said, 'This is what Allah and His Messenger[sa] promised us; and Allah and His Messenger[ra] spoke the truth.' And it only increased them in faith and submission. Among the believers are men who have been true to the covenant they had made with Allah. There are some of them who have fulfilled their vow, and some who still wait, and they have not changed their condition in the least (33: 23, 24).

The true believers, that is to say, were unlike the hypocrites and the weak. When they saw the huge numbers of the enemy, they were reminded of what God and His Prophet[sa] had told them already. This concerted attack by the tribes of Arabia was proof only of the truth of God and the Prophet[sa]. The true believers remained unshaken. Rather they increased in the spirit of obedience and in the fervour of faith. The true believers stood by their compact with God. Some of them had already attained to the goal of their lives by meeting their death. Some were only waiting to die in the path of God and reach their goal.

The enemy attacked the ditch fiercely and uninterruptedly. Sometimes he succeeded in clearing it. One day, important generals of the enemy succeeded in going across. But they were attacked so bravely by the Muslims that they had to fall back. In this encounter, Naufal, a big leader of the disbelievers, lost his life. So big was this leader that the disbelievers thought they would not be able to stand any insult to his dead body. They, therefore, sent word to the Prophet[sa], that if he would return the body of this chief, they would pay ten thousand dirhams. It was a high price for the return of the dead body. The offer was made out of a sense of guilt. The disbelievers had mutilated the Muslim dead at Uḥud and were afraid that Muslims would do the same. But the teaching of Islam was different. Islam forbade outright the mutilation of the dead. When the Prophet[sa] received the message and the offer, he said, "What use have we for this body? We want nothing in return for this. If it please you, take away the body" (*Zurqānī*, Vol. 2, p. 114).

A passage in Muir's *Life of Mohammad* (London-1878, p.322) describes eloquently the fierceness of the attack on Muslims. We need not apologize for quoting it here:

> **Next morning, Mahomed found the whole force of the Allies drawn out against him. It required the utmost activity and an unceasing vigilance on his side to frustrate the manoeuvres of the enemy. Now they would threaten a general assault; then breaking up into divisions they would attack various posts in rapid and distracting succession; and at last, watching their opportunity, they would mass their troops on the least protected point, and, under cover of a sustained and galling discharge of arrows, attempt to force the trench. Over and again a gallant dash was made at the city, and at the tent of Mahomed[sa], by such leaders of renown as Khālid[ra] and 'Amr[ra]; and these were only repelled by constant counter-marches and unremitting**

archery. This continued throughout the day; and, as the army of Mahomed[sa] was but just sufficient to guard the long line, there could be no relief. Even at night Khālid[ra], with a strong party of horses, kept up the alarm, and still threatening the line of defence, rendered outposts at frequent intervals necessary. But all the endeavours of the enemy were without effect. The trench was not crossed.

The battle had gone on for two days. Still there had been no hand-to-hand fighting, no great bloodshed. Twenty-four hours of fighting had resulted in only three deaths on the enemy side and five on the Muslim side. Sa'd bin Mu'ādh[ra], a chief of the Aus tribe and a devotee of the Prophet[sa], was wounded. Repeated attacks on the ditch, however, resulted in some damage, and this made further attack easier. Great scenes of valour and of loyalty were witnessed. It was a cold night, perhaps the coldest in Arabia. We have on the authority of 'Ā'isha[ra], the Prophet's[sa] holy consort, that the Prophet[sa] rose from his sleep again and again to guard the damaged part of the ditch. He became exhausted. He returned to bed but then, having warmed himself a little, went again to guard the ditch. One day he was so exhausted that he seemed quite unable to move. Then he said he wished some devoted Muslim would come and relieve him of the physical labour of guarding the ditch in the cold of the night. Soon he heard a voice. It was Sa'd bin Waqqāṣ[ra]. The Prophet[sa] asked him why he had come.

"To guard your person," said Sa'd[ra].

"There is no need to guard my person," said the Prophet[sa] "A part of the ditch is damaged. Go and guard it that Muslims may be safe." Sa'd[ra] went, and the Prophet[sa] was able to sleep. (There was some coincidence. For when the Prophet[sa] arrived at Medina and danger to his person was very great, even then it was Sa'd[ra] who offered himself for a guard.) On another occasion during these difficult days, the Prophet[sa] heard the sound of arms. "Who is it?" asked the Prophet[sa]. " 'Ibād bin Bishr[ra]," was the reply.

"Have you anyone else with you?" asked the Prophetsa. "Yes," said 'Ibādra, "A party of Companions. We will guard your tent."

"Leave my tent alone. The disbelievers are trying to cross the ditch. Go and fight them" (*Ḥalbiyya*, Vol. 2).

As we said before, the Jews tried to enter the town surreptitiously. A Jewish spy lost his life in the effort. When they found that their intrigue had become known, they began to help the Arab confederates more openly. A concerted attack in the rear, however, was not attempted, because the field on this side was narrow and with the posting of the Muslim guards a large-scale attack had become impossible. But a few days later, the Jews and pagan confederates decided to make a simultaneous and sudden attack upon the Muslims.

THE CONFEDERATES DISPERSE

This dangerous plan, however, was foiled by God in a miraculous manner. It happened in this way'. One Nu'aimra, who belonged to the tribe of Ghaṭafān, became inclined towards Islam. He had come with the pagan armies but looked for an opportunity to help the Muslims. Alone, he could not do much. But when he saw that Jews had made common cause with the Arabs and Muslims seemed faced with certain death and destruction, Nu'aimra made up his mind to do what he could to save the Muslims. He went to the Banū Quraiẓa, and talked to their chiefs. If the Arab armies ran away, what did they expect Muslims would do? The Jews being in compact with the Muslims, should they not be ready for punishment due to those who prove false to a compact? The interrogation frightened the Jewish leaders. They asked him what they should do. Nu'aimra advised them to ask for seventy pagans as hostages. If the pagans were honest about a concerted attack they would not refuse the request. They should say that these seventy would guard their strategic points, while they themselves attacked the Muslims from the rear. After his talks with the Jews he went to the pagan leaders. He asked them what they would do if the Jews went back on their compact; if, to conciliate the Muslims they asked for pagan hostages and then handed them over to the Muslims. Was it not important for them to test the honesty of the Jews and ask them to participate in the common attack at once? The pagan chiefs were impressed by this advice. Acting upon it, they sent word to the Jews asking them whether they would not attack the town from the rear now that they (the confederates) were ready for the planned attack. The Jews replied that the following day was their sabbath and they could not fight on that day. Secondly, they said, they belonged to Medina, and the Arab confederates were all outsiders. Should the Arabs flee from the battle, what were the Jews going to do? The Arabs should, therefore, give seventy men as hostages. The Jews would then be ready to carry out their part of the attack. Suspicion was already at work. The Arabs refused to entertain the Jewish request. If the Jews were honest in their compact with the Arabs, there was no meaning in the sort of proposal which they had made. Suspicion being subversive of courage, the Arab armies lost their zeal, and when night came, went to sleep burdened with doubts and difficulties. Both officers and men repaired to their tents in depressed mood. Then a miracle happened, help coming from heaven to the Muslims. A keen wind began to blow. Tent walls were swept away. Cooking pots toppled over fires. Some fires were extinguished. The pagans believed in keeping alive a fire throughout the night. A blazing camp-fire was a good omen, an extinguished one a bad omen. When a fire in front of a tent became extinguished, the occupants thinking it a bad augury, would withdraw from the battle for the day, and join again. The pagan leaders were already stricken with doubts. When some campers packed away, others thought that the Muslims had made a night attack. The suggestion became contagious. They all started packing and withdrawing from the field. It is said that Abū Ṣufyān[ra] was asleep in his tent. News of the sudden withdrawal of the pagan divisions reached his ears. He got up agitated and, in excitement, mounted a tethered camel. He spurred the animal, but the animal would not move. His friends pointed to what he was doing, untied the animal, and Abū Sufyān[ra] with his friends was able to leave the field.

Two-thirds of the night had passed. The battle-field had cleared already. An army of between twenty and twenty-five thousand soldiers and followers disappeared, leaving a complete wilderness behind. Just at that time the Prophet[sa] had a revelation that the enemy had fled as the result of an act of God. To find out what had happened the Prophet[sa] wanted to send one of his followers to scan the battlefield and make a report. The weather was icy cold. Little wonder, the ill-clad Muslims were freezing. Some heard the Prophet's[sa] voice when he called out in the night. They wanted to reply, but could not. The cold was forbidding. Only Ḥudhaifa[ra] was able to say aloud, "Yes, Prophet[sa] of God, what do you want us to do?"

The Prophet[sa] called out again. Again nobody could answer because of the cold. Only Ḥudhaifa[ra] answered again. The Prophet[sa] asked Ḥudhaifa[ra] to go and survey the battle-field, for God had informed him that the enemy had fled. Ḥudhaifa[ra] went near the ditch, and from there saw that the enemy had vacated the field. There were no soldiers and no men. Ḥudhaifa[ra] returned to the Prophet[sa], recited the Kalima and said the enemy had fled. On the morrow Muslims also unpegged their tents and started packing for the city. A severe trial lasting for about twenty days had ended.

BANŪ QURAIẒA PUNISHED

Muslims were able to breathe again in peace. But they still had the Banū Quraiẓa to settle with. The Banū

Quraiẓa had dishonoured their pact with the Muslims and this could not be passed over. The Prophet[sa] collected his exhausted force and told them that there was no rest for them yet. Before the sun went down, they must fall upon the Banū Quraiẓa in their fortifications. Then he sent 'Alī[ra] to the Banū Quraiẓa to ask them why they had gone back on their solemn word. The Banū Quraiẓa showed no regret and no inclination to ask for forgiveness. Instead, they insulted 'Alī[ra] and the other Muslim delegates and started hurling vile abuse at the Prophet[sa] and the women of his family. They said they did not care for Muḥammad[sa] and had never had any kind of pact with him. When 'Alī[ra] returned to report the reply of the Jews, he found the Prophet[sa] and the Companions advancing towards the Jewish fortifications. The Jews had been abusing the Prophet[sa], his wives and daughters. Fearing lest this should pain the Prophet[sa], 'Alī[ra] suggested there was no need for the Prophet[sa] to take part as the Muslims themselves could deal with the Jews. The Prophet[sa] understood 'Alī[ra] and said, "You want me not to hear their abuse, 'Alī[ra]?"

"Exactly," said 'Alī[ra].

"But why?" said the Prophet[sa]. "Moses[as] was of their kith and kin. Yet they inflicted more suffering on him than they have on me." The Prophet[sa] continued to advance. The Jews put up their defences and started fighting. Their women also joined them. Some Muslims were sitting at the foot of a wall. A Jewish woman, seeing this, dropped a stone on them, killing one named Khallad[ra]. The siege went on for some days. At the end of this period, the Jews felt they would not be able to hold out for long. Then their chiefs sent word to the Prophet[sa] requesting him to send Abū Lubāba[ra], an Anṣārī chief of the Aus, a tribe friendly to the Jews. They wanted to consult him about a possible settlement. The Prophet[sa] sent Abū Lubāba[ra] to the Jews, who asked him if they should lay down their arms and accept the award of the Prophet[sa]. Abū Lubāba[ra] said they should. But at the same time he passed a finger over his neck, making the sign of death. The Prophet[sa] had said nothing on this subject to anybody. But Abū Lubāba[ra], fearing that the crime of the Jews merited nothing but death, unwittingly made this sign, which proved fateful for the Jews. The latter declined Abū Lubāba's[ra] advice and refused to accept the Prophet's[sa] award. Had they accepted it, the utmost punishment they would have had was expulsion from Medina. But as ill-luck would have it, they refused to accept the Prophet's[sa] award. Instead of the Prophet's[sa], they said, they would accept the award of Sa'd bin Mu'ādh[ra], chief of their allies, the Aus. They would agree to any punishment proposed by him. A dispute also arose among the Jews. Some of them began to say that their people had really gone back on their agreement with the Muslims. The behaviour of the Muslims, on the other hand, showed that they were true and honest and that their religion also was true. Those who thought in this way joined Islam. 'Amr bin Ma'dī[ra], one of the Jewish chiefs, reproved his people and said, "You have committed a breach of faith and gone back on your plighted word. The only course now open to you is either to join Islam or give *jizya.*"

They said, "We will neither join Islam nor give *jizya,* for dying is better than giving *jizya.*" 'Amr replied that in that case he stood absolved, and saying this left the fort. He was sighted by Muḥammad bin Maslama[ra], commander of a Muslim column, who asked him who he was. On learning of his identity he told him to depart in peace and himself prayed loudly:

"God, give me ever the power to screen the mistakes of the decent."

What he meant was that this Jew had shown remorse and regret over the conduct of his people. It was the moral duty of Muslims, therefore, to forgive men like him. In letting him go he had done a good thing, and he prayed that God should give him the chance to do such good deeds again and again. When the Prophet[sa] got to know of what Muḥammad bin Maslama[ra] had done, he did not reprove him for letting go this Jewish leader. Rather, he approved of what had been done.

The disposition to make peace and to accept the award of the Prophet[sa] had been expressed only by individual Jews. As a people, they remained adamant and refused to accept the award of the Prophet[sa] and asked, instead, for the award of Sa‘d[ra] bin Mu‘ādh (*Bukhārī*, *Ṭabarī* and *Khamis*). The Prophet[sa] accepted their demand and sent word to Sa‘d[ra], who was lying wounded, to come and give his award on the Jewish breach of faith. As soon as the Prophet's[sa] decision was announced, the Ausites who had been allies of the Banū Quraiẓa for a long time ran to Sa‘d[ra] and began to press him to give his award in favour of the Banū Quraiẓa. The Khazraj, they said, had always tried to save Jews allied to them. It was up to Sa‘d[ra] to save the Jews allied to his tribe. Sa‘d[ra] went mounted to the Banū Quraiẓa. Men of his tribe ran with him on both sides, pressing him not to punish the Banū Quraiẓa. All that Sa‘d[ra] said in reply was that the person who had to make an award held a trust. He had to discharge the trust with integrity. "I will therefore give my award, taking everything into consideration, and without fear or favour," he said. When Sa‘d[ra] reached the Jewish fortress, he saw the Banū Quraiẓa lined up against the wall of the fort, waiting for him. On the other side were Muslims. When Sa‘d[ra] got near them he asked, "Will you accept my award?" They said, "Yes."

SA‘D'S[ra] AWARD IN HARMONY WITH THE BIBLE

Turning to the Banū Quraiẓa he asked the same question,and they also agreed. Then shyly he pointed to the side where the Prophet[sa] was sitting and asked if the people on that side also agreed to abide by his award. On hearing this, the Prophet[sa] replied, "Yes" (*Ṭabarī* and *Hishām*). Then Sa‘d[ra] gave his award in accordance with the following commandment of the Bible. Says the Bible:

When thou comest nigh unto a city to fight against it, then proclaim peace unto it. And it shall be, if it make thee answer of peace, and open unto thee, then it shall be, that all the people that is found therein shall be tributaries unto thee, and they shall serve thee. And if it will make no peace with thee, but will make war against thee, then thou shalt besiege it: And when the Lord thy God hath delivered it into thine hands, thou shalt smite every male thereof with the edge of the sword: But the women, and the little ones, and the cattle, and all that is in the city, even all the spoil thereof, shalt thou take unto thyself; and thou shalt eat the spoil of thine enemies, which the Lord thy God hath given thee. Thus shalt thou do unto all the cities which the Lord thy God doth give thee for an inheritance, thou shalt save alive nothing that breatheth: But thou shalt utterly destroy them; namely, the Hittites, and the Amoiites, the Canaanites, and the Perizzites, the Hivites, and the Jebusites; as the Lord thy God hath commanded thee: That they teach you not to do after all their abominations, which they have done unto their gods; so should ye sin against the Lord your God (*Deut.* 20: 10-18).

According to the teaching of the Bible, if the Jews had won and the Prophet[sa] had lost, all Muslims—men, women and children—would have been put to death. We know from history that this was the very intention of the Jews. The least the Jews would have done was to put to death the men, to enslave the women and children and make away with the belongings of the Muslims, this being the treatment laid down in Deuteronomy for enemy nations living in distant parts of the world. Sa'd[ra] was friendly to the Banū Quraiẓa. His tribe was in alliance with theirs. When he saw that the Jews had refused to accept the award of the Prophet[sa] and refused thus to have the lighter punishment prescribed for such an offence in Islam, he decided to award to the Jews the punishment which Moses[as] had laid down. The responsibility for this award does not rest with the Prophet[sa] or the Muslims, but with Moses[as] and his teaching and with the Jews who had treated the

Muslims so cruelly. They were offered what would have been a compassionate award. But, instead of accepting this, they insisted on an award by Sa'd[ra]. Sa'd[ra] decided to punish the Jews in accordance with the Law of Moses[as]. Yet Christians to this day continue to defame the Prophet[sa] of Islam and say that he was cruel to the Jews. If the Prophet[sa] was cruel to the Jews, why was he not cruel to other people or on other occasions? There were many occasions on which the Prophet's[sa] enemies threw themselves at his mercy, and never did they ask in vain for his forgiveness. On this occasion the enemy insisted on a person other than the Prophet[sa] making the award. This nominee of the Jews, acting as umpire between them and the Muslims, asked the Prophet[sa] and the Jews in public whether they would accept his award. It was after the parties had agreed, that he proceeded to announce it. And what was his award? It was nothing but the application of the Law of Moses[as] to the offence of the Jews. Why then should they not have accepted it? Did they not count themselves among the followers of Moses[as]? If any cruelty was perpetrated, it was by the Jews on the Jews. The Jews refused to accept the Prophet's[sa] award and invited instead the application of their own religious law to their offence. If any cruelty was perpetrated it was by Moses[as], who laid down this penalty for a beleaguered enemy and laid this down in his book under the command of God. Christian writers should not pour out the vials of their wrath on the Prophet[sa] of Islam. They should condemn Moses[as] who prescribed this cruel penalty or the God of Moses[as], Who commanded him to do so.

The Battle of the Ditch over, the Prophet[sa] declared that from that day onwards pagans would not attack Muslims; instead, Muslims would now attack pagans. The tide was going to turn. Muslims were going to take the offensive against tribes and parties which had so far been gratuitously attacking and harassing them. What the Prophet[sa] said was no empty threat. In the Battle of the Ditch the Arab confederates had not suffered any considerable losses. They had lost only a few men. In less than a year's time they could have come and attacked Medina again and with even better preparations. Instead of any army of twenty thousand they could have raised for a new attack an army of forty, or even fifty, thousand. An army numbering a hundred or a hundred and fifty thousand was not beyond their capacity. But now for twenty-one years, the enemies of Islam had done their utmost to extirpate Islam and Muslims. Continued failure of their plans had shaken their confidence. They had begun to fear that what the Prophet[sa] taught was true, and that their national idols and gods were false, that the Creator was the One Invisible God taught by the Prophet[sa]. The fear that the Prophet[sa] was right and they wrong had begun to creep upon them. There was no outward sign of this fear, however. Physically, the disbelievers went about as they had always done. They went to their idols and prayed to them as national custom required. But their spirit was broken. Outwardly they lived the lives of pagans and disbelievers; inwardly their hearts seemed to echo the Muslim slogan, 'There is no God but Allah.'

After the Battle of the Ditch the Prophet[sa], as we have observed already, declared that henceforward disbelievers would not attack Muslims but that, instead, Muslims would attack disbelievers. Muslim endurance had reached its limit. The tide was going to turn (*Bukhārī, Kitābal Maghāzī*).

DID THE PROPHET[sa] SEEK TO CONTINUE WARFARE?

In the battles which had so far been fought, Muslims had either remained in Medina or gone some distance out of it to fight the aggression of disbelievers. Muslims did not initiate these encounters, and showed no disposition to continue them after they had started. Normally hostilities once begun, can be ended in only two ways—an agreed peace or the submission of one side to the other. In the encounters between Muslims and disbelievers so far there had been no hint of a peace nor had either side offered to submit. True, there had been pauses in the fighting, but nobody could say that war between Muslims and disbelievers had ended. According to ordinary canons, Muslims could have attacked the enemy tribes and compelled them to surrender. But Muslims did not do this. When the enemy stopped fighting, Muslims stopped also. They stopped because they believed there might be a talk of peace. But when it became evident that there was no talk of peace by the disbelievers, nor was there any disposition on their part to surrender, the Prophet[sa] thought that the time had come to end the war either by a peace or by the surrender of one side to the other. War had to be ended if there was to be peace. After the Battle of the Ditch, therefore, the Prophet[sa] seemed determined to secure one of two things; peace or surrender. That Muslims should surrender to disbelievers was out of question. The victory of Islam over its persecutors had been promised by God. Declarations to this effect had been made by the Prophet[sa] during his stay at Mecca. Could Muslims then have sued for peace? A movement for peace can be initiated either by the stronger or by the weaker side. When the weaker side sues for peace it has to surrender, temporarily or permanently, a part of its territory or part of its revenues; or it has to accept other conditions imposed upon it by the enemy. When the stronger side proposes peace it is understood that it does not aim at the total destruction of the weaker side but is willing to let it retain complete or partial independence in return for certain conditions. In the battles which had so far been fought between Muslims and disbelievers the latter had suffered defeat after defeat. Yet their power had not been broken. They had only failed in their attempts to destroy Muslims. Failure to destroy another does not mean defeat. It only means that aggression has not yet succeeded; attacks which have failed may be repeated. The Meccans, therefore, had not been beaten; only their aggression against Muslims had failed. Militarily speaking, Muslims were decidedly the weaker side. True, their defence was still maintained, but they constituted a miserable minority and a minority which, though it had been able to resist the aggression of the majority, had been unable to take the offensive. Muslims, therefore, had not yet established their independence. If they had sued for peace, it would have meant that their defence had broken, and that they were now ready to accept the terms of the disbelievers. An offer of peace by them would have been disastrous for Islam. It would have meant self-annihilation. It would have brought new life to an enemy demoralized by repeated defeats. A growing sense of defeat would have given place to renewed hope and ambition. Disbelievers would have thought that though Muslims had saved Medina they were still pessimistic about their ultimate victory over disbelievers. A suggestion of peace, therefore, could not have proceeded from the Muslim side. It could have proceeded from the Meccan side, or from a third side, if a third side could have been found. No third side could, however, be found. In the conflict which had arisen Medina was set against all Arabia. It was the disbelievers, therefore, who could have sued the Muslims for peace, and there was no sign of this. Thus warfare between Muslims and Arabs might have gone on for ever. The Muslims could not, and the Arabs would not, sue for peace. Civil strife in Arabia, therefore, seemed to have no end, at least not for another hundred years.

There was only one way open to Muslims if they wanted to put an end to this strife. They were not prepared to surrender their conscience to the Arabs, to renounce, that is to say, their right to profess, practise and preach what they liked; and there was no movement for peace from the side of disbelievers. Muslims had been able to repel repeated aggression. It was for them, therefore, to force the Arabs either to surrender or to accept peace. The Prophet[sa] decided to do so.

Was it war which the Prophet[sa] sought? No, it was not war but peace that he wanted to bring about. If he had done nothing at this time, Arabia would have remained in the grip of civil warfare. The step which he took was the only way to peace. There have been some long wars in history. Some have lasted for a hundred, some for thirty years or so. Long wars have always resulted from lack of decisive action by either side. Decisive action, as we have said, can take only one of two forms—complete surrender or a negotiated peace.

Could the Prophet[sa] have remained passive? Could he have withdrawn himself and his small force of Muslims behind the walls of Medina and left everything else to take care of itself ? This was impossible. The disbelievers had started the aggression. Passivity would not have meant the end of war but, rather, its continuation. It would have meant that the disbelievers could attack Medina whenever they liked. They could stop when they liked and attack when they liked. A pause in warfare did not mean the end of war. It meant only a strategic move.

TEACHINGS OF JUDAISM AND CHRISTIANITY ABOUT WAR

But the question now arises—Can it ever be right to fight for a faith? Let us, therefore, turn to this question.

The teaching of religion on the subject of war takes different forms. The teaching of the Old Testament, we have cited above. Moses[as] is commanded to enter the land of Canaan by force, to defeat its population and to settle his own people in it (Deut. 20: 10-18). In spite of this teaching in the Book of Moses[as], and in spite of its reinforcement by practical example of the Prophets Joshua[as], David[as] and others, Jews and Christians continue to hold their Prophets in reverence and to regard their books as the Books of God.

At the end of the Mosaic tradition, we had Jesus[as] who taught;

> **But I say unto you, That ye resist not evil: but whosoever shall smite thee on thy right cheek, turn to him the other also (*Matthew* 5: 39).**

Christians have often cited this teaching of Jesus[as] and argued that Jesus[as] preached against war. But in the New Testament, we have passages which purport to teach quite the opposite. One passage, for instance, says:

> **Think not that I am come to send peace on earth: I came not to send peace, but a sword (*Matthew* 10: 34).**

And another passage says:

> **Then said he unto them. But now, he that hath a purse, let him take it, and likewise his scrip: and he that hath no sword, let him sell his garment, and buy one (*Luke* 22: 36).**

Of the three verses the last two contradict the first. If Jesus[as] came for war, why did he teach about turning the other cheek? It seems we have either to admit a contradiction in the New Testament, or we have to explain one of the contradictory teachings in a suitable manner. We are not concerned here with the question whether turning the other cheek can ever be practicable. We are concerned only to point out that, throughout their long history, no Christian people have ever hesitated to make war. When Christians first attained to power in Rome, they took part in wars both defensive and aggressive. They are dominant powers in the world today, and they continue to take part in wars both defensive and aggressive. Only now the side which wins is canonized by the rest of the Christian world. Their victory is said to be the victory of Christian civilization. Christian civilization has come to mean whatever tends to be dominant and successful. When two Christian powers go to war, each claims to be the protector of

Christian ideals. The power which wins is canonized as the true Christian power. It is true, however, that from the time of Jesus[as] to our time, Christendom has been involved—and indications are that it will continue to remain involved—in war. The practical verdict of the Christian peoples, therefore, is that war is the real teaching of the New Testament, and that turning the other cheek was either an opportunist teaching dictated by the helplessness of early Christians, or it is meant to apply only to individuals, not to States and peoples.

Secondly, even if we assume that Jesus[as] taught peace and not war, it does not follow that those who do not act upon this teaching are not holy and honoured. For Christendom has ever revered exponents of war such as Moses[as], Joshua[as] and David[as]. Not only this, the Church itself has canonized national heroes who suffered in wars. They were made saints by the Popes.

THE QUR'AN ON WAR AND PEACE

The teaching of Islam is different from both these teachings. It strikes a mean between the two. Islam does not teach aggression as did Moses[as]. Nor does it, like present-day (and presumably corrupt) Christianity, preach a contradiction. It does not ask us to turn the other cheek and at the same time to sell our clothes to buy a sword. The teaching of Islam fits into the natural instincts of man, and promotes peace in the only possible way.

Islam forbids aggression, but it urges us to fight if failure to fight jeopardizes peace and promotes war. If failure to fight means the extirpation of free belief and of the search of truth, it is our duty to fight. This is the teaching on which peace can ultimately be built, and this is the teaching on which the Prophet[sa] based his own policies and his practice. The Prophet[sa] suffered continuously and consistently at Mecca but did not fight the aggression of which he was an innocent victim.

When he escaped to Medina, the enemy was out to extirpate Islam; it was, therefore, necessary to fight the enemy in defence of truth and freedom of belief.

We quote below the passages in the Qur'an which bear on the subject of war.

(1) In 22: 40–42 we have:

> **Permission to fight is given to those against whom war is made, because they have been wronged—and Allah indeed has power to help them—Those who have been driven out from their homes unjustly only because they said, "Our Lord is Allah"—And if Allah did not repel some men by means of others, there would surely have been pulled down cloisters and churches and synagogues and mosques, wherein the name of Allah is oft commemorated. And Allah will surely help one who helps Him. Allah is indeed Powerful, Mighty.—Those who, if We establish them in the earth, will observe Prayer and pay the Zakat and enjoin good and forbid evil. And with Allah rests the final issue of all affairs.**

The verse purports to say that permission to fight is given to the victims of aggression. God is well able to help the victims—those who have been driven out of their homes because of their beliefs. The permission is wise because, if God were not to repel the cruel with the help of the righteous, there would be no freedom of faith and worship in the world. God must help those who help to establish freedom and worship. It follows that fighting is permitted when a people have suffered long from wanton aggression—when the aggressor has had no cause for aggression and he seeks to interfere with the religion of his victim. The duty of the victim, if and when he attains to power, is to establish religious freedom and to protect all religions and all religious places. His power is to be used not for his own glorification, but for the care of the poor, the progress of the country and the general promotion of peace. This teaching is as unexceptionable as it is clear and precise. It proclaims the fact that early Muslims took to war because they were constrained to do so. Aggressive wars were forbidden by Islam. Muslims are promised political power, but are warned that this power must be used not for self-aggrandizement, but for the amelioration of the poor and the promotion of peace and progress.

(2) In (2: 191–194) we have:

And fight in the cause of Allah against those who fight against you, but do not transgress. Surely, Allah loves not transgressors. And kill them wherever you meet them and drive them out from where they have driven you out; for persecution is worse than killing. And fight them not in, and near, the Sacred Mosque until they fight you, then fight them: such is the requital for the disbelievers. But if they desist, then surely Allah is Most Forgiving, Merciful. And fight them until there is no persecution, and religion is professed for Allah. But if they desist, then remember that no hostility is allowed except against the aggressors.

Fighting is to be for the sake of God, not for our own sake or out of anger or aggrandizement, and even fighting is to be free from excesses, for excesses are displeasing to God. Fighting is between parties of combatants. Assaults on individuals are forbidden. Aggression against a religion is to be met by active resistance, for such aggression is worse than bloodshed. Muslims are not to fight near the Sacred Mosque, unless an attack is first made by the enemy. Fighting near the Sacred Mosque interferes with the public right of pilgrimage. But if the enemy attacks, Muslims are free to reply, this being the just reward of aggression. But if the enemy desists, Muslims must desist also, and forgive and forget the past. Fighting is to continue so long as religious persecution lasts and religious freedom is not established. Religion is for God. The use of force or pressure in religion is wrong. If the Kafirs desist from it and make religion free, Muslims are to desist from fighting the Kafirs. Arms are to be taken up against those who commit excesses. When excesses cease, fighting must cease also.

Categorically, we may say, the verses teach the following rules:

(i) War is to be resorted to only for the sake of God and not for the sake of any selfish motives, not for aggrandizement or for the advancement of any other interests.

(ii) We can go to war only against one who attacks us first.

(iii) We can fight only those who fight against us. We cannot fight against those who take no part in warfare.

(iv) Even after the enemy has initiated the attack, it is our duty to keep warfare within limits. To extend the war, either territorially or in respect of weapons used, is wrong.

(v) We are to fight only a regular army charged by the enemy to fight on his side. We are not to fight others on the enemy side.

(vi) In warfare immunity is to be afforded to all religious rites and observances. If the enemy spares the places where religious ceremonies are held, then Muslims also must desist from fighting in such places.

(vii) If the enemy uses a place of worship as a base for attack, then Muslims may return the attack. No blame will attach to them if they do so. No fighting is allowed even in the neighbourhood of religious places. To attack religious places and to destroy them or to do any kind of harm to them is absolutely forbidden. A religious place used as a base of, operations may invite a counter-attack. The responsibility for any harm done to the place will then rest with the enemy, not with Muslims.

(viii) If the enemy realizes the danger and the mistake of using a religious place as a base, and changes the battle-front, then Muslims must conform to the change. The fact that the enemy started the attack from a religious place is not to be used as an excuse for attacking that place. Out of reverence Muslims must change their battle-front as soon as the enemy does so.

(ix) Fighting is to continue only so long as interference with religion and religious freedom lasts. When religion becomes free and interference with it is no longer permitted and the enemy declares and begins to act accordingly, then there is to be no war, even if it is the enemy who starts it.

(3) In 8: 39–41 we have:

> **Say to those who disbelieve, if they desist, that which is past will be forgiven them; and if they return thereto, then verily the example of the former people has already gone before them.**
>
> **And fight them until there is no persecution and religion is wholly for Allah. But if they desist, then surely Allah is Watchful of what they do. And if they turn their backs, then know that Allah is your Protector. What an excellent Protector and what an excellent Helper.**

That is to say, wars have been forced upon Muslims. But if the enemy desists, it is the duty of Muslims to desist also, and forgive the past. But if the enemy does not desist and attacks Muslims again and again, then he should remember the fate of the enemies of earlier Prophets. Muslims are to fight, while religious persecution lasts, and so long as religion is not for God and interference in religious matters is not abandoned. When the aggressor desists, Muslims are to desist also. They are not to continue the war because the enemy believes in a false religion. The value of beliefs and actions is well known to God and He will reward them as He pleases. Muslims have no right to meddle with another people's religion even if that religion seems to them to be false. If after an offer of peace the enemy continues to make war, then Muslims may be sure of victory even though their numbers are small. For God will help them and who can help better than God?

These verses were revealed in connection with the Battle of Badr. This battle was the first regular fight between Muslims and disbelievers. In it Muslims were the victims of unprovoked aggression. The enemy had chosen to disturb the peace of Medina and of the territory around. In spite of this, victory went to the Muslims and important leaders of the enemy were killed. To retaliate against such unprovoked aggression seems natural, just and necessary. Yet Muslims are taught to stop fighting as soon as the enemy ceases it. All that the enemy is required to concede is freedom of belief and worship.

(4) In 8: 62—63 we have:

> **And if they incline towards peace, incline thou also towards it, and put thy trust in Allah. Surely, it is He Who is All-Hearing, All-Knowing. And if they intend to deceive thee, then surely Allah is sufficient for thee. He it is Who has strengthened thee with His help and with the believers.**

That is to say, if in the course of a battle the disbelievers at any time incline towards peace, Muslims are to accept the offer at once and to make peace. Muslims are to do so even at the risk of being deceived. They are to put their trust in God. Cheating will not avail against Muslims, who rely on the help of God. Their victories are due not to themselves but to God. In the darkest and most difficult times, God has stood by the Prophet[sa] and his followers. So will He stand by them against cheats. An offer of peace is to be accepted. It is not to be rejected on the plea that it may only be a ruse with which the enemy seeks to gain time for a fresh attack.

The stress on peace in the verses is not without significance. It anticipates the peace which the Prophet[sa] signed at Ḥudaibiya. The Prophet[sa] is warned that a time will come when the enemy will sue for peace. The offer is not to be turned down on the ground that the enemy was the aggressor and had committed excesses, or that he cannot be trusted. The straight path inculcated by Islam requires a Muslim to accept an offer of peace. Both piety and policy make the acceptance desirable.

(5) In 4: 95 we have:

O ye who believe! when you go forth in the cause of Allah, make proper investigation and say not to anyone who greets you with the greeting of peace, "Thou art not a believer." You seek the goods of this life, but with Allah are good things in plenty. Such were you before this, but Allah conferred His favour on you; so do make proper investigation. Surely, Allah is well aware of what you do.

That is to say, when Muslims go out for war, they are to make sure that the unreasonableness of war has been explained to the enemy and that he still wants war. Even so, if a proposal of peace is received from an individual or a group, Muslims are not to turn it down on the plea that it is not honest. If Muslims turn down proposals of peace, they will not be fighting for God, but for self-aggrandizement and worldly gain. Just as religion comes from God, worldly gain and glory also come from Him. Killing is not to be the aim. One whom we wish to kill today may be guided tomorrow. Could Muslims have become Muslims if they had not been spared? Muslims are to abstain from killing because lives spared may turn out to be lives guided. God is well aware of what men do and to what ends and with what motives they do it.

The verse teaches that even after war has begun, it is the duty of Muslims to satisfy themselves that the enemy is bent upon aggression. It often happens that no aggression is intended but that out of excitement and fear the enemy has started preparations for war. Unless Muslims are satisfied that an aggressive attack has been planned by the enemy, they are not to go to war. If it turns out, or if the enemy claims, that his preparations are for self-defence, Muslims are to accept the claim and desist from war. They are not to argue that the enemy preparations point to nothing but aggression; maybe he intended aggression, but his intention has changed. Are not intentions and motives continually changing? Did not enemies of Islam become friends?

(6) On the inviolability of treaties the Qur'an says clearly:

Excepting those of the idolaters with whom you have entered into a treaty and who have not subsequently failed you in anything nor aided anyone against you. So fulfil to these the treaty you have made with them till their term. Surely, Allah loves those who are righteous (9: 4).

Pagans, who enter into a pact with Muslims, keep the pact and do not help the enemy against Muslims, are to have reciprocal treatment from Muslims. Piety requires that Muslims should fulfil their part of a pact in the letter as well as the spirit.

(7) Of an enemy at war with Muslims who wishes to study the Message of Islam, the Qur'an orders:

And if anyone of the idolaters ask protection of thee, grant him protection, so that he may hear the word of Allah: then convey him to his place of security. That is because they are a people who have no knowledge (9: 6).

That is to say, if any of those at war with Muslims seek refuge with Muslims in order to study Islam and ponder over its Message, they are to have refuge with Muslims for such time as may be reasonably necessary for such a purpose.

(8) Of prisoners of war, the Qur'an teaches:

It does not behove a Prophet that he should have captives until he engages in a regular fighting in the land. You desire the goods of the world, while Allah desires for you the Hereafter. And Allah is Mighty, Wise (8: 68).

That is to say, it does not become a Prophet to make prisoners of his enemy save as a result of regular war involving much bloodshed. The system of making prisoners of enemy tribes without war and bloodshed practised until—and even after—the advent of Islam, is here made unlawful. Prisoners can be taken only from combatants and after a battle.

(9) Rules for the release of prisoners are also laid down. Thus we have:

Then afterwards either release them as a favour or by taking ransom—until the war lays down its burdens (47:5).

The best thing, according to Islam, is to let off prisoners without asking for ransom. As this is not always possible, release by ransom is also provided for.

(10) There is provision for prisoners of war who are unable themselves to pay, and who have none who can or will pay, for their release. Often, relations are able to pay, but do not, because they prefer to let their relations remain prisoners—possibly with the intention of misappropriating their property in their absence. This provision is contained in the Qur'an:

> **And such as desire a deed of manumission from among those whom your right hands possess, write it for them, if you know any good in them; and give them out of the wealth of Allah which He has bestowed upon you (24: 34).**

That is, those who do not deserve to be released without ransom but who have no one to pay ransom for them—if they still ask for their freedom—can obtain it by signing an undertaking that, if allowed to work and earn, they will pay their ransom. They are to be allowed to do so, however, only if their competence to work and earn is reasonably certain. If their competence is proved, they should even have financial help from Muslims in their effort to work and earn. Individual Muslims who can afford to do so should pay; or, public subscription should be raised to put these unfortunates on their feet.

The passages from the Qur'an which we have quoted above contain the teaching of Islam on the subject of war and peace. They tell us in what circumstances, according to Islam, is it right to go to war and what limits have to be observed by Muslims when they make war.

THE PROPHET'S[sa] PRECEPTS ABOUT WAR

Muslim teaching, however, does not consist only of precepts laid down in the Qur'an. It also includes the precepts and example of the Prophet[sa]. What he did or what he taught in concrete situations is also an essential part of the Islamic teaching. We append here some sayings of the Prophet[sa] on the subject of war and peace.

(i) Muslims are forbidden altogether to mutilate the dead (*Muslim*).

(ii) Muslims are forbidden to resort to cheating (*Muslim*).

(iii) Children are not to be killed, nor women (*Muslim*).

(iv) Priests and religious functionaries and religious leaders are not to be interfered with (*Ṭaḥāvī*).

(v) The old and decrepit and women and children are not to be killed. The possibility of peace should always be kept in view (*Abū Dāwūd*).

(vi) When Muslims enter enemy territory, they should not strike terror into the general population. They should permit no ill-treatment of common folk (*Muslim*).

(vii) A Muslim army should not camp in a place where it causes inconvenience to the general public. When it marches it should take care not to block the road nor cause discomfort to other wayfarers.

(viii) No disfigurement of face is to be permitted (*Bukhārī* and *Muslim*).

(ix) The least possible losses should be inflicted upon the enemy (*Abū Dāwūd*).

(x) When prisoners of war are put under guard, those closely related should be placed together (*Abū Dāwūd*).

(xi) Prisoners should live in comfort. Muslims should care more for the comfort of their prisoners than for their own (*Tirmidhī*).

(xii) Emissaries and delegates from other countries should be held in great respect. Any mistakes or discourtesies they commit should be ignored (*Abū Dāwūd, Kitāb al jihād*).

(xiii) If a Muslim commits the sin of ill-treating a prisoner of war, atonement is to be made by releasing the prisoner without ransom.

(xiv) When a Muslim takes charge of a prisoner of war, the latter is to be fed and clothed in the same way as the Muslim himself (*Bukhārī*).

The Holy Prophet[sa] was so insistent on these rules for a fighting army that he declared that whoever did not observe these rules, would fight not for God but for his own mean self (*Abū Dāwūd*).

Abū Bakr[ra], the First Khalifah of Islam, supplemented these commands of the Prophet[sa] by some of his own. One of these commands appended here also constitutes part of the Muslim teaching:

(xv) Public buildings and fruit-bearing trees (and food crops) are not to be damaged (*Mu'aṭṭā*).

From the sayings of the Prophet[sa] and the commands of the First Khalifah of Islam it is evident that Islam has instituted steps which have the effect of preventing or stopping a war or reducing its evil. As we have said before, the principles which Islam teaches are not pious precepts only; they have their practical illustration in the example of the Prophet[sa] and the early Khalifahs of Islam. As all the world knows, the Prophet[sa] not only taught these principles; he practised them and insisted on their observance.

Turning to our own time we must say that no other teaching seems able to solve the problem of war and peace. The teaching of Moses[as] is far from our conceptions of justice and fair-play. Nor is it possible to act upon that teaching today. The teaching of Jesus[as] is impracticable and has ever been so. Never in their history have Christians tried to put this teaching into practice. Only the teaching of Islam is practicable; one which has been both preached and practised by its exponents, and the practice of which can create and maintain peace in the world.

In our time, Mr. Gāndhī apparently taught that even when war is forced on us we should not go to war. We should not fight. But this teaching has not been put into practice at any time in the history of the world. It has never been put in the crucible and tested. It is impossible, therefore, to say what value this teaching may have in terms of war and peace. Mr. Gāndhī lived long enough to see the Indian Congress attain to political independence. Yet the Congress Government has not disbanded either the army or the other armed forces of India. It is only making plans for their Indianization. It also has plans for the reinstatement of those Indian officers who constituted themselves into the Indian National Army (and who were dismissed by the British authorities) during the Japanese attack on Burma and India in the last stages of the recent World War. Mr. Gāndhī has himself, on many occasions, raised his voice in extenuation of crimes of violence, and urged the release of those who committed such crimes. This shows at least that Mr. Gāndhī's teaching cannot be put into practice and that Mr. Gāndhī knows it as well as all his followers. No practical example at least has been offered to show the world how non-violence can be applied when armed disputes arise between nation and nation and State and State, or how non-violence can prevent or stop a war. To preach a method of stopping wars, but never to be able to afford a practical illustration of that method indicates that the method is impracticable. It would, therefore, seem that human experience and human wisdom point to only one method of preventing or stopping war; and that method was taught and practised by the Prophet[sa] of Islam.

SPORADIC ATTACKS BY DISBELIEVERS

The Arab confederates returned from the Battle of the Ditch defeated and depressed, but far from realizing that their power to harass the Muslims was over. Though defeated, they knew they were still a dominant majority. They could easily maltreat individual Muslims, beat and even kill them. By assaults on individuals they hoped to wipe away their feeling of defeat. Not long after the battle, therefore, they began to attack Muslims around Medina. Some men of the Fazāra tribe mounted on camels attacked Muslims near Medina. They made away with the camels found in that part, took a woman as prisoner and escaped with the loot. The woman made good her escape, but the party of Fazāra succeeded in taking away a number of animals. A month later, a party of the Ghaṭafān tribe attacked from the north in an attempt to dispossess Muslims of their herds of camels. The Prophet[sa] sent Muḥammad bin Maslama[ra] with ten mounted Companions for a reconnaissance, and for the protection of the Muslim herds. But the enemy waylaid the Muslim party and murderously attacking them, left them all for dead. Muḥammad bin Maslama[ra], however, was only lying unconscious. Recovering consciousness he pulled himself together, returned to Medina and made a report. A few days later, an envoy of the Prophet[sa] on his way to the Roman capital was attacked and robbed by men of the Jurham tribe. A month later, the Banū Fazāra attacked a Muslim caravan and made away with much loot. It is possible that this attack was not prompted by religious antagonism. The Banū Fazāra were a tribe of marauders given to looting and killing. The Jews of Khaibar, the main factor in the Battle of the Ditch, were also determined to avenge the crushing defeat which they suffered in that battle. They went about inciting tribal settlements and officers of State on the Roman frontier. Arab leaders, therefore, unable to make a straightforward attack on Medina, were intriguing with the Jews to make life impossible for Muslims. The Prophet[sa], however, had yet to make up his mind for a decisive fight. Arab leaders might make an offer of peace, he thought, and civil strife might end.

THE PROPHET[sa] LEAVES FOR MECCA WITH ONE THOUSAND FIVE HUNDRED COMPANIONS

During this time the Prophet[sa] saw a vision which is mentioned thus in the Qur'an:

> **You will certainly enter the Sacred Mosque, if God will, in security, some having their heads shaven, and others having their hair cut short; and you will not fear. But He knew what you knew not. He has in fact ordained for you, besides that, a victory near at hand (48: z8).**

That is to say, God had decided to let Muslims enter the precincts of the Ka'ba in peace, with heads shaven and hair cut (these being the external signs of pilgrims to the Ka'ba), and without fear. But Muslims did not know exactly how God was to let this happen. Moreover, before Muslims performed their pilgrimage in peace, they were to have another victory, a precursor of the victory promised in the vision.

In this vision God foretold the ultimate victory of Muslims, their peaceful march into Mecca and the conquest of Mecca without the use of arms. But the Prophet[sa] understood it to mean that Muslims had been commanded by God immediately to attempt a circuit of the Ka'ba. The Prophet[sa]'s error in interpreting the vision was to become the occasion of the victory 'near at hand' promised in the vision. In error, therefore, the Prophet[sa] planned a march towards the Ka'ba. He announced his vision and his interpretation of it to Muslims and asked them to prepare. "You will go," he said, "only to perform a circuit of the Ka'ba. There were, therefore, to be no demonstrations against the enemy." Late in February 628, fifteen hundred[1] pilgrims, headed by the Prophet[sa],

---

1 In this pilgrimage planned a year after the Battle of the Ditch, only one thousand five hundred men accompanied the Prophet[sa]. The number of Muslim combatants in the Battle of the Ditch could have been less but not more than this number. Historians who put the number of the Muslim combatants in the Battle of the Ditch at three thousand, therefore, are

set out on their journey to Mecca. A mounted guard of twenty went some distance ahead to warn the Muslims in case the enemy showed signs of attacking.

The Meccans soon had reports of this caravan. Tradition had established the circuit of the Ka'ba as a universal right. It could not very well be denied to Muslims. They had announced in unambiguous terms that the purpose of their march was to perform the circuit, nothing else. The Prophet[sa] had forbidden demonstrations of every kind. There were to be no disputes, no questionings or claims. In spite of this, the Meccans started preparing as for an armed conflict. They put up defences on all sides, called the surrounding tribes to their aid and seemed determined to fight. When the Prophet[sa] reached near Mecca, he was informed that the Quraish were ready to fight. They were clad in tiger skins, had their wives and children with them and had sworn solemnly not to let the Muslims pass. The tiger skins were a sign of a savage determination to fight. Soon after, a column of Meccans marching in the van of their army confronted the Muslims. Muslims could not now advance except by drawing the sword. The Prophet[sa], however, was determined to do nothing of the kind.

He employed a guide to show the Muslim caravan an alternative route through the desert. Led by this guide, the Prophet[sa] and his Companions reached Ḥudaibiya, a spot very near Mecca.

The Prophet's[sa] dromedary stopped and refused to go any farther.

"The animal seems tired, O Prophet[sa] of God. Better change your mount," said a Companion.

"No, no," said the Prophet[sa]. "the animal is not tired. It seems rather that God wants us to stop here and to go no further. I propose, therefore, to camp here and to ask

---

wrong. The number can quite reasonably be put at one thousand two hundred.

the Meccans if they would let us perform the Pilgrimage. I, for one, will accept any conditions they may choose to impose" (*Ḥalbiyya,* Vol. 2, p. 13).

The Meccan army at this time was not in Mecca. It had gone out some distance to meet the Muslims on the main road to Medina. If the Prophet[sa] wanted, he could have led his fifteen hundred men into Mecca and taken the town without resistance. But he was determined to attempt only the circuit of the Ka'ba, and that only if the Meccans permitted. He would have resisted and fought the Meccans only if the Meccans had chosen to strike first. Therefore, he abandoned the main road and camped at Ḥudaibiya. Soon the news reached the Meccan commander, who ordered his men to withdraw and post themselves near Mecca. Then the Meccans sent a chief, Budail by name, to parley with the Prophet[sa]. The Prophet[sa] explained to Budail that he and the Muslims wanted only to perform the circuit of the Ka'ba; but if the Meccans wished to fight, the Muslims were ready. Then 'Urwa, son-in-law of Abū Ṣufyān[ra], the Meccan commander, came to the Prophet[sa]. He behaved most discourteously. He called the Muslims tramps and dregs of society and said the Meccans would not let them enter Mecca. More and more Meccans came to have talks and the last thing they said was that at least that year they would not let Muslims perform even the circuit of the Ka'ba. The Meccans would be humiliated if they permitted the circuit this year. The following year, they might do so.

Some tribes allied with the Meccans urged upon the Meccan leaders to let the Muslims perform the circuit. After all, it was only the right of circuit they wanted. Why should they be stopped even from this? But the Meccans remained adamant. Thereupon the tribal leaders said, the Meccans did not want peace and threatened to disassociate themselves from them. Out of fear, the Meccans were persuaded to try to reach a settlement with the Muslims. As soon as the Prophet[sa] got to know of this, he sent 'Uthmān[ra] (later the Third

Khalifah of Islam) to the Meccans. 'Uthmān[ra] had many relatives in Mecca. They came out and surrounded him, and offered to let him perform the circuit, but declared that they would not let the Prophet[sa] do so until the following year. "But," said 'Uthmān[ra], "I will not perform the circuit unless it is in the company of my Master." 'Uthmān's[ra] talks with the chiefs of Mecca became prolonged. A rumour was mischievously spread that he had been murdered. It reached the ears of the Prophet[sa]. Upon this the Prophet[sa] assembled the Companions and said, "The life of an envoy is held sacred among all nations. I have heard that the Meccans have murdered 'Uthmān[ra]. If this is true, we have to enter Mecca, whatever the consequences." The Prophet[sa]'s earlier intention to enter Mecca peacefully had to be changed, under the changed circumstances. The Prophet[sa] went on, "Those who promise solemnly that if they have to go further, they will not turn back save as victors, should come forward and take the oath on my hand." The Prophet[sa] had hardly finished speaking, when all the fifteen hundred Companions stood up and jumped over one another to hold the Prophet's[sa] hand and take the oath. This oath possesses a special importance in the history of early Islam. It is called the "Pledge of the Tree". When the oath was taken, the Prophet[sa] was sitting under a tree. Everyone of those who took the oath remained proud of it to the end of his days. Of the fifteen hundred present on the occasion, not one held back. They all promised that if the Muslim envoy had been murdered, they would not go back. Either they would take Mecca before dusk, or they would all die fighting. The taking of the oath was not over when 'Uthmān[ra] returned. He reported that the Meccans did not agree to let the Muslims perform the circuit until the following year. They had appointed their delegates to sign a settlement with the Muslims. Soon after, Suhail, a chief of Mecca, came to the Prophet[sa]. A settlement was reached and recorded.

TREATY OF ḤUDAIBIYA

It ran as follows:

In the name of Allah. These are the conditions of peace between Muḥammad[sa], son of 'Abdullāh, and Suhail ibn 'Amr, the envoy of Mecca. There will be no fighting for ten years. Anyone who wishes to join Muḥammad[sa] and to enter into any agreement with him, is free to do so. Anyone who wishes to join the Quraish and to enter into an agreement with them is also free to do so. A young man, or one whose father is alive, if he goes to Muḥammad[sa] without permission from his father or guardian, will be returned to his father or guardian. But should anyone go to the Quraish, he will not be returned. This year Muḥammad[sa] will go back without entering Mecca. But next year he and his followers can enter Mecca, spend three days and perform the circuit. During these three days the Quraish will withdraw to the surrounding hills. When Muḥammad[sa] and his followers enter into Mecca, they will be unarmed except for the sheathed swords which wayfarers in Arabia always have with them (*Bukhārī*).

Two interesting things happened during the signing of this peace. After the terms had been settled the Prophet[sa] started to dictate the agreement and said, "In the name of Allah, the Gracious, the Merciful."

Suhail objected and said, "Allah we know and believe in, but what is this 'the Gracious and the Merciful?' This agreement is between two parties. Therefore the religious beliefs of both parties will have to be respected."

The Prophet[sa] agreed at once and said to his scribe, "Only write, 'In the name of Allah'." The Prophet[sa] then proceeded to dictate the terms of the agreement. The opening sentence was, 'These are the conditions of peace between the people of Mecca and Muḥammad[sa], the Prophet[sa] of God'. Suhail objected again, and said, "If we thought you a Prophet[sa] of God, we would not have fought you." The Prophet[sa] accepted this objection also.

Instead of Muḥammad[sa], the Prophet[sa] of God, he proposed Muḥammad[sa] son of 'Abdullāh. As the Prophet[sa] was agreeing to everything the Meccans proposed, the Companions felt agitated over the humiliation. Their blood began to boil, and 'Umar[ra], the most excited of them all, went to the Prophet[sa] and asked, "O Prophet[sa] of God, are we not in the right?"

"Yes," said the Prophet[sa], "we are in the right." "And were we not told by God that we would perform the circuit of the Ka'ba?" asked 'Umar[ra].

" Yes," said the Prophet[sa].

"Then why this agreement and why these humiliating terms?"

"True," said the Prophet[sa], "God did foretell that we would perform the circuit in peace but He did not say when. I did judge as though it was going to be this year. But I could be wrong. Must it be this year?"

'Umar[ra] was silenced.

Then other Companions raised their objections. Some of them asked why they had agreed to restore to his father or guardian a young man who should turn Muslim, without obtaining the same condition for a Muslim who should turn over or happen to go to the Meccans. The Prophet[sa] explained there was no harm in this. "Everybody who becomes a Muslim," he said, "does so because he accepts the beliefs and practices inculcated by Islam. He does not become a Muslim in order to join a party and to adopt its customs. Such a man will propagate the Message of Islam wherever he goes, and serve as an instrument for the spread of Islam. But a man who gives up Islam is no use to us. If he no longer believes at heart what we believe, he is no longer one of us. It is better he should go elsewhere." This reply of the Prophet[sa] satisfied those who had doubted the wisdom of the course adopted by the Prophet[sa]. It should satisfy today all those who think that in Islam the punishment of apostasy is death. Had this been so, the Prophet[sa] would have insisted on the return and punishment of those who gave up Islam.

When the agreement had been written down and the signatures of the parties affixed, there soon arose an occasion which tested the good faith of the parties. A son of Suhail, the Meccan plenipotentiary, appeared before the Prophet[sa], bound, wounded and exhausted. He fell at the Prophet's[sa] feet and said, "O Prophet[sa] of God, I am a Muslim at heart, and because of my faith I have to suffer these troubles at the hands of my father. My father was here with you. So I escaped and managed to come to you." The Prophet[sa] had not spoken when Suhail intervened and said that the agreement had been signed and he would have to go with him. Abū Jandal[ra]—this being the young man's name—stood before the Muslims, a brother of brothers, driven to desperation by the ill-treatment of his father. To have to send him back was an obligation they could not endure. They unsheathed their swords and seemed determined to die or save this brother. Abū Jandal[ra] himself entreated the Prophet[sa] to let him remain. Would he send him back to the tyrants from whose clutches he had managed to escape? But the Prophet[sa] was determined. He said to Abū Jandal[ra], "Prophets do not eat their words. We have signed this agreement now. It is for you to bear with patience and to put your trust in God. He will certainly provide for your freedom and for the freedom of other young persons like you." After the peace had been signed, the Prophet[sa] returned to Medina. Soon after, another young convert from Mecca, Abū Baṣīr[ra] by name, reached Medina. But in accord with the terms of the agreement, he also was sent back by the Prophet[sa]. On the way back, he and his guards had a fight in the course of which he killed one of the guards and thus managed to escape. The Meccans went to the Prophet[sa] again and complained. "But," said the Prophet[sa], "we handed over your man to you. He has now escaped out of your hands. It is no longer our duty to find him and hand him over to you again. A few days later, a woman escaped to Medina. Some of her relations went after her and demanded her return. The Prophet[sa] explained that the agreement had laid down an exception about men, not about women; so he refused to return this woman.

PROPHET'S[sa] LETTERS TO VARIOUS KINGS

After settling down in Medina on return from Ḥudaibiya, the Prophet[sa] instituted another plan for the spread of his Message. When he mentioned this to the Companions, some of them who were acquainted with the customs and forms observed in the courts of kings told the Prophet[sa] that kings did not entertain letters which did not bear the seals of the senders. Accordingly the Prophet[sa] had a seal made on which were engraved the words, *Muḥammad Rasūlullāh[sa]*.

Out of reverence, *Allah* was put at the top, beneath it *Rasūl* and lastly Muḥammad[sa].

In Muḥarram 628, envoys went to different capitals, each with a letter from the Prophet[sa], inviting the rulers to accept Islam. Envoys went to Heraclius, the Roman Emperor, the Kings of Iran, Egypt (the King of Egypt was then a vassal of the Kaiser) and Abyssinia. They went to other kings and rulers also. The letter addressed to the Kaiser was taken by Diḥya Kalbī[ra] who was instructed to call first on the Governor of Buṣra. When Diḥya[ra] saw the Governor, the great Kaiser himself was in Syria on a tour of the Empire. The Governor readily passed Diḥya[ra] on to the Kaiser. When Diḥya[ra] entered the court, he was told that whoever was received in audience by the Kaiser must prostrate himself before him. Diḥya[ra] refused to do this, saying that Muslims did not bow before any human being. Diḥya[ra], therefore, sat before the Kaiser without making the prescribed obeisances. The Kaiser had the letter read by an interpreter and asked if an Arab caravan was in the town. He said he desired to interrogate an Arab about this Arabian Prophet[sa] who had sent him an invitation to accept Islam. It so happened that Abū Sufyān[ra] was in the town with a commercial caravan. The court officials took him to the Kaiser. Abū Sufyān[ra] was ordered to stand in front of the other Arabs, who were told to correct him if he should tell a lie or make a wrong statement. Then Heraclius proceeded to interrogate Abū Ṣufyān[ra]. The conversation is thus recorded in history:

H: Do you know this man who claims to be a Prophet[sa] and who has sent me a letter? Can you say what sort of family he comes from?

A-S: He comes of a noble family and is one of my relations.

H: Have there been Arabs before him who have made claims similar to his?

A-S: No.

H: Did your people ever charge him with lying before he announced his claim?

A-S: No.

H: Has there been a king or a ruler among his forefathers?

A—S: No.

H: How do you judge his general ability and his capacity for judgement?

A—S: We have never found any fault in his ability and his capacity for judgement.

H: What are his followers like? Are they big and powerful persons or are they poor and humble?

A—S: Mostly poor and humble and young.

H: Do their numbers tend to increase or decrease?

A—S: To increase.

H: Do his followers ever go back to their old beliefs?

A—S: No.

H: Has he ever broken a pledge?

A—S: Not so far. But we have recently entered into a new pact with him. Let us see what he does about it.

H: Have you had any fight with him yet?

A—S: Yes.

H: With what result?

A—S: Like buckets on a wheel, victory and defeat alternate between us and him. In the Battle of Badr, for instance, in which I was not present, he was able to overpower our side. In the Battle of Uḥud, in which I commanded our side, we took his side to task. We tore their stomachs, their ears and their noses,

H: But what does he teach?

A—S: That we should worship the One God and not set up equals with Him. He preaches against the idols our forefathers worshipped. He wants us, instead, to worship the Only God, to speak the truth only and always to abjure all vicious and corrupt practices. He exhorts us to be good to one another and to keep our covenants and discharge our trusts.

This interesting conversation came to an end and then the Kaiser said:

I first asked you about his family and you said he belonged to a noble family. In truth, Prophets always come of noble families. I then asked you if anyone before him had made a similar claim and you said, No. I asked you this question because I thought that if in the recent past some one had made such a claim, then one could say that this Prophet[sa] was imitating that claim. I then asked you whether he had ever been charged with lying before his claim had been announced and you said, No. I inferred from this that a person who does not lie about men will not lie about God. I next asked you if there had been a king among his forefathers and you said, No. From this I understood that his claim could not be a subtle plan for the recovery of the kingdom. I then asked you whether the entrants into his fold were mostly big, prosperous and powerful individuals or poor and weak. And you said in reply, that they were generally poor and weak, not proud and big, and so are the early followers of a Prophet. I then asked you whether his numbers were increasing or decreasing and you said they

were increasing. At this I remembered that the followers of a Prophet go on increasing until the Prophet attains his goal. I then asked you if his followers left him out of disgust or disappointment, and you said, No. At this I remembered that the followers of Prophets are usually steadfast. They may fall away for other reasons, but not out of disgust for the faith. I then asked you if there had been fights between you and him and, if so, with what results. And you said that you and his followers were like buckets on a wheel and the Prophets are like that. In the beginning their followers suffer reverses and meet with misfortunes, but in the end they win. I then asked you about what he teaches and you said he teaches the worship of One God, truth-speaking, virtue and the importance of keeping covenants and discharging trusts. I asked you also whether he ever played false, and you said, No. And this is the way of virtuous men. It seems to me, therefore, that his claim to being a Prophet[sa] is true. I was half expecting his appearance in our time, but I did not know he was going to be an Arab. If what you have told me is true, then I think his influence and his dominion will certainly spread over these lands (*Bukhārī*).

The speech unsettled the courtiers who began to blame the King for applauding a Teacher of another community. Protests were raised. The court officials then sent away Abū Sufyān[ra] and his friends. The text of the letter which the Prophet[sa] wrote to the Kaiser is to be found in historical records. It runs as follows:

From Muḥammad[sa], the Servant of God and His Messenger. To the Chief of Rome, Heraclius. Whoever treads the path of divine guidance, on him be peace. After this, O King, I invite you to Islam. Become a Muslim. God will protect you from all afflictions, and reward you twice over. But if you deny and refuse to accept this Message, then the sin not only of your own denial, but of the denial of your subjects, will be on your head. "Say, 'O People of the Book! come to a word equal between us and you that we worship none but Allah, and that we associate no

partner with Him, and that some of us take not others for lords beside Allah.' But if they turn away, then say, 'Bear witness that we have submitted to God' " (*Zurqānī*).

The invitation to Islam was an invitation to believe that God is One and that Muḥammad[sa] is His Messenger. Where the letter says that if Heraclius becomes a Muslim, he will be rewarded twice over, the reference is to the fact that Islam teaches belief in both Jesus[as] and Muḥammad[sa].

It is said that when the letter was presented to the Emperor, some courtiers suggested it should be torn up and thrown away. The letter, they said, was an insult to the Emperor. It did not describe the Emperor as Emperor but only as Ṣaḥibul Rūm, i.e., the Chief of Rome. The Emperor, however, said that it was unwise to tear up the letter without reading it. He also said that the address, 'Chief of Rome', was not wrong. After all, the Master of everything was God. An Emperor was only a chief.

When the Prophet[sa] was told how his letter had been received by Heraclius, he seemed satisfied and pleased and said that because of the reception which the Roman Emperor had given his letter, his Empire would be saved. The descendants of the Emperor would continue long to rule over the Empire. That is in fact what happened. In the wars which took place later, a large part of the Roman Empire, in accordance with another prophecy of the Prophet[sa] of Islam, passed out of the possession of Rome; yet for six hundred years after this, the dynasty of Heraclius remained established in Constantinople. The Prophet's[sa] letter remained preserved in the State archives for a long time. Ambassadors of the Muslim King, Manṣūr Qalāwūn, visited the court of Rome, and were shown the letter deposited in a case. The then Roman Emperor showing the letter said it had been received by a forefather of his from their Prophet[sa] and had been carefully preserved.

LETTER TO THE KING OF IRAN

The letter to the King of Iran was sent through 'Abdullāh bin Ḥudhāfa[ra]. The text of this letter was as follows:

> **In the name of Allah, the Gracious, the Merciful.. This letter is from Muḥammad[sa], the Messenger of God, to Chosroes, the Chief of Iran. Whoever submits to a perfect guidance, and believes in Allah, and bears witness that Allah is One, and has no equal or partner, and that Muḥammad[sa] is His Servant and Messenger, on him be peace. O King, under the command of God, I invite you to Islam. For I have been sent by God as His Messenger[sa] to all mankind, so that I may warn all living men and complete my Message for all unbelievers. Accept Islam and protect yourself from all afflictions. If you reject this invitation, then the sin of the denial of all your people will rest on your head (*Zurqani* and *Khamīs*).**

'Abdullāh bin Ḥudhāfa[ra] says that when he reached the court of Chosroes he applied for admission to the royal presence. He handed over the letter to the Emperor and the Emperor ordered an interpreter to read it and explain its contents. On listening to the contents, the Chosroes was enraged. He took back the letter and tore it to pieces. 'Abdullāh bin Ḥudhāfa[ra] reported the incident to the Prophet[sa]. On hearing the report, the Prophet[sa] said:

What the Chosroes has done to our letter even that will God do to his Empire (i.e., rend it to pieces).

The fit of temper which the Chosroes showed on this occasion was the result of the pernicious propaganda carried on against Islam by Jews who had migrated from Roman territory to Iran. These Jewish refugees took a leading part in anti-Roman intrigues sponsored in Iran, and had, therefore, become favourites at the Iranian court. The Chosroes was full of rage against the Prophet[sa]. The reports about the Prophet[sa] which the Jews had taken to Iran, it seemed to him, were confirmed by this letter. He thought the Prophet[sa] was an aggressive adventurer with designs on Iran. Soon after, the Chosroes wrote to the Governor of Yemen, saying that one of the Quraish in Arabia had announced himself a Prophet[sa]. His claims were becoming excessive. The Governor was asked to send two men charged with the duty of arresting this Quraishite and bringing him to the court of Iran. Bādhān, the Governor of Yemen under the Chosroes, sent an army chief with a mounted companion to the Prophet[sa]. He also gave them a letter addressed to the Prophet[sa], in which he said that on receipt of the letter the Prophet[sa] should at once accompany the two messengers to the court of Iran. The two planned to go first to Mecca. When somewhere near Ṭā'if, they were told that the Prophet[sa] lived in Medina. So they went to Medina. On arrival this army chief told the Prophet[sa] that Bādhān, the Governor of Yemen, had been ordered by the Chosroes to arrange for the Prophet's[sa] arrest and despatch to Iran. If the Prophet[sa] refused to obey, he and his people were to be destroyed and their country made desolate. Out of compassion for the Prophet[sa], this delegate from Yemen insisted that the Prophet[sa] should obey and agree to be led to Iran. Having listened to this, the Prophet[sa] suggested that the delegates should see him again the following day. Overnight the Prophet[sa] prayed to God Who informed him that the insolence of the Chosroes had cost him his life. "We have set his own son against him, and this son will murder his father on Monday the 10th Jumād al-'Ūlā of this year." According to some reports, the revelation said, "The son has murdered the father this very night." It is possible that that very night was the 10th Jumād al-'Ūlā In the morning, the Prophet[sa] sent for the Yemen delegates and told them of what had been revealed to him overnight. Then he prepared a letter for Bādhān saying that the Chosroes was due to be murdered on a certain day of a certain month. When the Governor of Yemen received the letter he said, "If this man be a true Prophet[sa], it will be even as he says. If he be not true, then God help him and his country." Soon after, a boat from Iran anchored at the port of Yemen. It brought a letter from the Emperor of Iran to the Governor of Yemen. The letter bore a new seal, from which the Governor concluded that the prophecy of the Arabian Prophet[sa] had proved true. A new seal meant a new king. He opened the letter. It said:

> **From Chosroes Siroes to Bādhān, the Governor of Yemen. I have murdered my father because his rule had become corrupt and unjust. He murdered the nobles and treated his subjects with cruelty. As soon as you receive this letter, collect all officers and ask them to affirm their loyalty to me. As for my father's orders for the arrest of an Arabian Prophet[sa], you should regard those orders as cancelled (*Ṭabarī*, Vol. 3, pp. 1572–1574 and *Hishām* p. 46).**

Bādhān was so impressed by these events that he and many of his friends at once declared their faith in Islam and informed the Prophet[sa] accordingly.

THE LETTER TO THE NEGUS

The letter to the Negus, King of Abyssinia, was carried by 'Amr bin Umayya Damrī[ra]. It ran as follows:

> **In the name of Allah, the Gracious, the Merciful, Muḥammad[sa], the Messenger of God, writes to the Negus, King of Abyssinia. O King, peace of God be upon you. I praise before you the One and Only God. None else is worthy of worship. He is the King of kings, the source of all excellences, free from all defects, He provides peace to all His servants and protects His creatures. I bear witness that Jesus, son of Mary[as] was a Messenger of God, who came in fulfilment of promises made to Mary by God. Mary had consecrated her life to God. I invite you to join with me in attaching ourselves to the One and Only God and in obeying Him. I invite you also to follow me and believe in the God Who hath sent me. I am His Messenger. I invite you and your armies to join the Faith of the Almighty God. I discharge my duty hereby. I have delivered to you the Message of God, and made clear to**

you the meaning of this Message. I have done so in all sincerity and I trust you will value the sincerity which has prompted this message. He who obeys the guidance of God becomes heir to the blessings of God (*Zurqānī*).

When this letter reached the Negus, he showed very great regard and respect for it. He held it up to his eyes, descended from the throne and ordered an ivory box for it. Then he deposited it in the box and said, "While this letter is safe, my kingdom is safe." What he said proved true. For one thousand years Muslim armies were out on their career of conquest. They went in all directions, and passed by Abyssinia on all sides, but they did not touch this small kingdom of the Negus—; and this, out of regard for two memorable acts of the Negus the protection he afforded the refugees of early Islam and the reverence he showed to the Prophet's[sa] letter. The Empire of Rome became dismembered. The Chosroes lost his dominions. The kingdoms of China and India disappeared but this small kingdom of the Negus remained inviolate, because its ruler received and protected the first Muslim refugees and showed respect and reverence for the Prophet's[sa] letter.

Muslims returned the magnanimity of the Negus in this way. Compare with this the treatment which a Christian people, in this age of civilization meted out to this Christian kingdom of the Negus. They bombarded from the air the open cities of Abyssinia and destroyed them. The royal family had to take refuge elsewhere and to stay away from their country for several years. The same people have been treated in two different ways by two different peoples. Muslims held Abyssinia sacred and inviolate because of the magnanimity of one of its rulers. A Christian nation attacked and plundered it in the name of civilization. It shows how wholesome and lasting in their effects are the Prophet's[sa] teaching and example. Muslim gratitude to a Christian kingdom made the kingdom sacred to Muslims. Christian greed attacked the same kingdom, not caring it was Christian.

LETTER TO THE RULER OF EGYPT

The letter to Muqauqis was carried by Ḥāṭib ibn Abī Balta'ara. The text of this letter was exactly the same as that to the Roman Emperor. The letter to the Roman Emperor said that the sin of the denial of the Roman subjects would be on his head. The letter to the Muqauqis said that the sin of the denial of the Copts would be on the head of the ruler. It ran as follows:

> **In the name of Allah, the Gracious, the Merciful. This letter is from Muḥammadsa, the Messenger of Allah, to Muqauqis, the Chief of the Copts. Peace be upon him who follows the path of rectitude. I invite you to accept the Message of Islam. Believe and you will be saved and your reward will be twofold. If you disbelieved, the sin of the denial of the Copts will also be on your head. Say, "O People of the Book! come to a word equal between us and you that we worship none but Allah, and that we associate no partner with Him, and that some of us take not others for lords beside Allah. But if they turn away, then say, 'Bear witness that we have submitted to God.'" (*Ḥalbiyya*, Vol. 3, p. 275).**

When Ḥāṭibra reached Egypt, he did not find the Muqauqisin the capital. Ilatib followed him to Alexandria, where he was holding court near the sea. Ḥāṭibra went by boat. The court was strongly guarded. Therefore Ḥāṭibra showed the letter from a distance and began to speak aloud. The Muqauqis ordered Ḥāṭibra to be brought to him. The Muqauqis read the letter and said, "If this man be a true Prophetsa, why does he not pray for the destruction of his enemies?" Ḥāṭibra replied, "You believe in Jesusas. He was ill-treated by his people, yet he did not pray for their destruction." The King paid a tribute to Ḥāṭibra and said he was a wise envoy of a wise man. He had answered well the questions put to him. Upon this Ḥātibra spoke again. "Before you," he said, "there was a king who was proud, arrogant and cruel. He was the Pharaoh who persecuted Mosesas. At last he was overtaken by divine punishment. Show no pride therefore. Believe in this Prophet[sa] of God. By God Moses[as] did not foretell about Jesus[as] as clearly as did Jesus[as] foretell about Muḥammad[sa]. We invite you to Muḥammad the Prophet[sa], just as you Christians invite the Jews to Jesus[as]. Every Prophet has his followers. The followers must obey their Prophet. Now that a Prophet[sa] has appeared in your time it is your duty to believe in him and follow him. And remember our religion does not ask you to deny or disobey Jesus[as]. Our religion requires everyone to believe in Jesus[as]."

Hearing this, Muqauqis revealed that he had heard of the teaching of this Prophet[sa] and he felt that he did not teach anything evil nor forbid anything good. He had also made inquiries and found that he was no sorcerer or soothsayer. He had heard of some of his prophecies which had come true. Then he sent for an ivory box and placed the letter of the Prophet[sa] in it, sealed it and handed it over to a servant girl for safe deposit. He also wrote a letter in reply to the Prophet[sa]. The text of this letter is recorded in history. It runs as follows:

> **In the name of Allah, the Gracious, the Merciful. From Muqauqis, King of the Copts, to Muḥammad[sa], son of 'Abdullāh. Peace be on you. After this, I say that I have read your letter and pondered over its contents and over the beliefs to which you invite me. I am aware that the Hebrew Prophets have foretold the advent of a Prophet[sa] in our time. But I thought he was going to appear in Syria. I have received your envoy, and made a present of one thousand *dinars* and five *khil'ats* to him and I send two Egyptian girls as a present to you. My people, the Copts, hold these girls in great esteem. One of them is Mary[ra] and the other Sīrīn[ra]. I also send you twenty garments made of Egyptian linen of high quality. I also send you a mule for riding. In the end I pray again that you may have peace from God (*Zurqānī* and *Ṭabarī*).**

From this letter it is clear that, though Muqauqis treated the letter with respect he did not accept Islam.

LETTER TO CHIEF OF BAḤRAIN

The Prophet[sa] also sent a letter to Mundhir Taimī, Chief of Baḥrain. This letter was carried by 'Alā' ibn Ḥaḍramī[ra]. The text of this letter has been lost. When it reached this Chief, he believed, and wrote back to the Prophet[sa] saying that he and many of his friends and followers had decided to join Islam. Some, however, had decided to stay outside. He also said that there were some Jews and Magians living under him. What was he to do about them?

The Prophet[sa] wrote again to this Chief thus:

I am glad at your acceptance of Islam. Your duty is to obey the delegates and messengers whom I should send to you. Whoever obeys them, obeys me. The messenger who took my letter to you praised you to me, and assured me of the sincerity of your belief. I have prayed to God for your people. Try, therefore, to teach them the ways and practices of Islam. Protect their property. Do not let anyone have more than four wives. The sins of the past are forgiven. As long as you are good and virtuous you will continue to rule over your people. As for Jews and Magians, they have only to pay a tax. Do not, therefore, make any other demands on them. As for the general population, those who do not have land enough to maintain them should have four dirhams each, and some cloth to wear (*Zurqānī* and *Khamīs*).

The Prophet[sa] also wrote to the King of 'Umān, the Chief of Yamāma, the King of Ghassān, the Chief of Banī Nahd, a tribe of Yemen, the Chief of Hamdān, another tribe of Yemen, the Chief of Banī 'Alīm and the Chief of the Ḥaḍramī tribe. Most of them became Muslims.

These letters show how perfect was the Prophet's[sa] faith in God. They also show that from the very beginning the Prophet[sa] believed that he had been sent by God not to any one people or territory, but to all the peoples of the world. It is true that these letters were received by their addressees in different ways. Some of them accepted Islam at once. Others treated the letters with consideration, but did not accept Islam. Still others treated them with ordinary courtesy. Still others showed contempt and pride. But it is true also—and history is witness to the fact—that the recipients of these letters or their peoples met with a fate in accordance with their treatment of these letters.

FALL OF KHAIBAR

As we have said above, the Jews and other opponents of Islam were now busy inflaming the tribes against the Muslims. They were now convinced that Arabia was unable to withstand the rising influence of Islam and that Arab tribes were unable to attack Medina. The Jews, therefore, began to intrigue with the Christian tribes settled on the southern frontier of the Roman Empire. At the same time they started writing against the Prophet[sa] to their co-religionists in Iraq. By malicious propaganda carried on through correspondence they sought to excite the Chosroes of Iran against Islam. As a result of Jewish machinations the Chosroes turned against Islam, and even sent orders to the Governor of Yemen to arrest the Prophet[sa]. It was by special divine intervention and divine grace that the Prophet[sa] remained safe, and the foul plan of the Emperor of Iran was brought to nought. It should be obvious that, but for the divine help which attended the Prophet[sa] throughout his career, the tender movement of early Islam would have been nipped in the bud under the hostility and opposition of the Emperors of Rome and Iran. When the Chosroes ordered the arrest of the Prophet[sa], it so happened that before the orders could be carried out the Emperor was deposed and put to death by his own son and his orders for the arrest of the Prophet[sa] cancelled by the new ruler. The officials of Yemen were impressed by this miracle; so the province of Yemen readily became part of the Muslim Empire. The intrigues which the Jews kept on hatching against

Muslims and their town of Medina made it necessary that they should be driven farther away from Medina. If they had been allowed to continue to live nearby their intrigues were almost certain to give rise to more and more bloodshed and violence. On returning from Hudaibiya the Prophetsa waited for five months and then decided to banish them from Khaibar. Khaibar was only a little distance from Medina and from here the Jews found it very easy to carry on their intrigues. With this intent, the Prophetsa (some time in August 628 A.D.) marched to Khaibar. He had one thousand six hundred men with him. Khaibar, as we have said, was a well-fortified town. It was surrounded on all sides by rocks on which were perched little fortresses. To conquer such a place with so small a force was no easy task. The small posts lying on the outskirts of Khaibar fell after a little fighting. But when the Jews collected themselves into the central fort of the town, all attacks on it and all forms of strategy employed against it seemed to fail. One day the Prophetsa had a revelation that Khaibar would fall at the hands of 'Alīra. The following morning the Prophetsa announced this to his followers and said, "Today, I will hand over the black flag of Islam to him who is dear to God, His Prophetsa and all the Muslims. God has ordained that our victory at Khaibar should take place at his hands." The following day he sent for 'Alīra and handed to him the flag. 'Alīra did not wait. He took his men and attacked the central fort. In spite of the fact that the Jews had collected in force inside this fort, 'Alīra and his division were able to conquer it before dark. A peace was signed. The conditions were that all Jews, their wives and their children would quit Khaibar and settle in some place far away from Medina. Their property and their belongings would pass into the hands of Muslims. Anyone who tried to conceal any of his property or stores, or made a wrong statement, would not be protected by the peace. He would have to pay the penalty laid down for breach of faith.

Three interesting incidents took place in this siege of Khaibar. One of them constitutes a Sign of God and two afford insight into the high moral character of the Prophet[sa].

A widow of Kināna, a chief of Khaibar, was married to the Prophet[sa]. The Prophet[sa] saw that her face bore some marks, the impression of a hand. "What is this on your face, Ṣafiyya[ra]?" asked the Prophet[sa].

"It was like this," replied Ṣafiyya[ra]. "I saw the moon fall in my lap in a dream. I related the dream to my husband. No sooner had I related the dream than my husband gave a heavy slap on my face and said, 'You desire to marry the King of Arabia'" (*Hishām*). The moon was the national emblem of Arabia. The moon in the lap denoted some intimate connection with the King of Arabia. A split moon or a dropping moon meant dissensions in the Arab State or its destruction.

The dream of Ṣafiyya[ra] is a sign of the truth of the Holy Prophet[sa]. It is also a sign of the fact that God reveals the future to His servants through dreams. Believers have more of this grace than unbelievers. Ṣafiyya[ra] was a Jewess when she saw this dream. It so happened that her husband was killed in the siege of Khaibar. This siege was a punishment for the Jewish breach of faith. Ṣafiyya[ra] was made a prisoner and, in the distribution of prisoners, was given to a Companion. It was then found that she was the widow of a chief. It was, therefore, felt that it would be more in accord with her rank if she were to live with the Prophet[sa]. The Prophet[sa], however, chose to give her the status of a wife and she agreed. In this way was her dream fulfilled.

There were two other incidents. One relates to a shepherd who looked after the sheep of a Jewish chief. This shepherd became a Muslim. After his conversion he said to the Prophet[sa], "I cannot go back to my people now, O Prophet of God[sa]. What shall I do with the sheep and goats of my old master?"

"Set the faces of the animals towards Khaibar and give them a push. God will lead them back to their master" said the Prophetsa. The shepherd did as he was told, and the herd reached the Jewish fort. The guards at the fort received them (*Hishām*, Vol 2, p.191). The incident shows how seriously the Prophetsa regarded the question of individual rights and how important in his view it was for a trustee to discharge his trust. In war the property and belongings of the losers are rightfully appropriated by the victors. Ours is an age of civilization and culture, but can we show anything equal to this? Has it ever happened that a retreating enemy left behind stores which the victors sent back to their owners? In the present case the goats belonged to one of the combatants of the enemy side. The return of the goats meant making over to the enemy food which would last them for several months. With it the enemy could resist the siege for a long time. Yet the Prophetsa had the goats returned, and this in order to impress upon a new convert the importance of discharging a trust.

The third incident relates to a Jewish woman who tried to poison the Prophetsa. She asked the Companions what part of an animal the Prophetsa relished for a dish. She was told that he preferred the shoulder of lamb or goat. The woman slaughtered a goat and made cutlets on hot stones. Then she mixed with them a deadly poison, especially in pieces cut from the shoulder, believing the Prophetsa would prefer them.

The Prophetsa was returning to his tent, having said the evening prayers in congregation. He saw this woman waiting for him near his tent and asked, "Is there anything I can do for you, woman?"

"Yes, Abu'l Qāsimsa, you can accept a present from me." The Prophetsa asked a Companion to take whatever the woman had brought. When the Prophetsa sat down to his meal this present of roasted meat was also laid before him. The Prophetsa took a morsel. A Companion Bishr ibn al-Barā' ibn al-Ma'rūrra also took a morsel. The other Companions present at the meal stretched their hands to eat the meat. But the Prophetsa stopped them saying, he thought the meat was poisoned. Upon this Bishr[ra] said that he also thought the same. He wanted to throw away the meat but was afraid it might disturb the Prophet[sa]. "Seeing you take a morsel," he said, "I also took one, but I soon began to wish you had not taken yours at all." Soon afterwards Bishr[ra] became ill and, according to some reports, died there and then. According to other reports he died after remaining ill for some time. The Prophet[sa] then sent for the woman and asked her if she had poisoned the meat. The woman asked the Prophet[sa] how he ever got to know about it. The Prophet[sa] was holding a piece in his hand, and said,"My hand told me this," meaning he was able to judge from its taste. The woman admitted what she had done. "What made you do this? " asked the Prophet[sa].

"My people were at war with you and my relations were killed in this battle, I decided to poison you, believing that if you were an impostor you would die and we should be safe, but if you were a Prophet[sa], God would save you."

Hearing this explanation the Prophet[sa] forgave the woman, although she had earned, the penalty of death (*Muslim*). The Prophet[sa] was ever ready to forgive, and punished only when punishment was necessary, when it was feared the guilty one would continue to commit mischief.

THE PROPHET'S[sa] VISION FULFILLED

In the seventh year after the Hijra, in February 629 to be exact, the Prophet[sa] was due to go to Mecca for the circuit of the Ka'ba. This had been agreed to by the Meccan leaders. When the time came for the Prophet[sa] to depart, he collected two thousand followers and set out in the direction of Mecca. When he reached Marraẓẓuhrān, a halting place near Mecca, he ordered his followers to shed their armours. These were collected in one place. In strict conformity with the terms of the agreement signed at Hudaibiya, the Prophet[sa] and his followers entered the Sacred Enclosure, wearing only sheathed swords; Returning to Mecca after seven years' externment, it was no ordinary thing for two thousand persons to enter Mecca. They remembered the tortures to which they had been subjected during their days at Mecca. At the same time, they saw how gracious God had been to them in letting them come back and make a circuit of the Ka'ba in peace. Their anger was only equal to their joy. The people of Mecca had come out of their houses and perched themselves on the hill-tops to see the Muslims. The Muslims were full of zeal and enthusiasm and pride. They wanted to tell the Meccans that the promises which God had made to them had all come true. 'Abdullāh bin Rawāha[ra] started singing songs of war, but the Prophet[sa] stopped him saying, "No war songs. Only say, There is none to be worshipped except the One God. It is God Who helped the Prophet[sa] and raised the believers from degradation to dignity and Who drove off the enemy" (*Ḥalbiyya*, Vol. 3, p. 73).

After circuiting the Ka'ba and running between the hills of Ṣafā and Marwā, the Prophet[sa] and his Companions stopped in Mecca for three days. 'Abbās[ra] had a widowed sister-in-law, Maimūna[ra], and he proposed that the Prophet[sa] should marry her. The Prophet[sa] agreed. On the fourth day the Meccans demanded the withdrawal of the Muslims. The Prophet[sa] ordered the withdrawal and asked his followers to start back for Medina. So religiously did he carry out the agreement and so careful was he to respect Meccan sentiments that he left his newly-wed wife behind in Mecca. He arranged that she should join him with the part of the caravan carrying the personal effects of the pilgrims. The Prophet[sa] mounted his camel and was soon out of the limits of the sacred precincts. For the night the Prophet[sa] camped at a place called Sarif, and there in his tent Maimūna[ra] joined him.

We might have omitted this insignificant detail from a short account of the Life of the Prophet[sa], but the incident has one important interest, and it is this. The

Prophet[sa] has been attacked by European writers because he had several wives. They think a plurality of wives is evidence of personal laxity and love of pleasure. This impression of the Prophet's[sa] marriages, however, is belied by the devotion and self-consuming love which the Prophet's[sa] wives had for him. Their devotion and love proved that the Prophet's[sa] married life was pure, unselfish and spiritual. It was so singular in this respect that no man can be said to have treated his one wife so well as the Prophet[sa] treated his many. If the Prophet's[sa] married life had been motivated by pleasure, it would most certainly have resulted in making his wives indifferent and even antagonistic to him. But the facts are quite otherwise. All the Prophet's[sa] wives were devoted to him, and their devotion was due to his unselfish and high-minded example. To his unselfish example they reacted by unsparing devotion. This is proved by many incidents recorded in history. One relates to Maimūna[ra] herself. She met the Prophet[sa] for the first time in a tent in the desert. If their marital relations had been coarse, if the Prophet[sa] had preferred some wives to others because of their physical charms, Maimūna[ra] would not have cherished her first meeting with the Prophet[sa] as a great memory. If her marriage with the Prophet[sa] had been associated with unpleasant or indifferent memories, she would have forgotten everything about it. Maimūna[ra] lived long after the Prophet's[sa] death. She died full of years but could not forget what her marriage with the Prophet[sa] had meant for her. On the eve of her death at eighty, when the delights of the flesh are forgotten, when things only of lasting value and virtue move the heart, she asked to be buried at one day's journey from Mecca, at the very spot where the Prophet[sa] had camped on his return to Medina, and where after his marriage she had first met him. The world knows of many stories of love both real and imaginary, but not of many which are more moving than this.

Soon after this historic circuit of the Ka'ba, two renowned generals of the enemy joined Islam. They proved renowned generals of Islam. One was Khālid bin Walīd[ra] whose genius and courage shook the Roman Empire to its foundations and under whose generalship country after country was added by Muslims to their Empire. The other was 'Amr bin al-'Āṣ[ra], the conqueror of Egypt.

BATTLE OF MAUTA

On return from the Ka'ba, the Prophet[sa] began to receive reports that Christian tribes on the Syrian border, instigated by Jews and pagans, were preparing for an attack upon Medina. He, therefore, despatched a party of fifteen to find out the truth. They saw an army massing on the Syrian border. Instead of returning at once with the report they tarried. Their zeal for expounding Islam got the better of them, but the effect of their well-meaning zeal proved to be the very opposite of what they had wished and expected.

Reviewing events now, we can see that those who, under enemy provocation, were planning to attack the Prophet's[sa] homeland could be expected to behave in no other way. Instead of listening to the exposition, they took out their bows and started raining arrows on this party of fifteen. The party, however, remained unmoved. They received arrows in reply to arguments, but they did not turn back. They stood firm, fifteen against thousands, and fell fighting.

The Prophet[sa] planned an expedition to punish the Syrians for this wanton cruelty, but in the meantime he had reports that the forces which had been concentrating on the border had dispersed. He, therefore, postponed his plans.

The Prophet[sa], however, wrote a letter to the Emperor of Rome (or to the Chief of the Ghassān tribe who ruled Buṣra in the name of Rome). In this letter, we may presume, the Prophet[sa] complained of the preparations which had been visible on the Syrian border and of the foul and entirely unjust murder of the fifteen Muslims whom he had sent to report on the border situation. This letter was carried by al-Ḥarth[ra], a Companion of the Prophet[sa]. He stopped en route at Mauta where he met Shurahbil, a Ghassān chief acting as a Roman official. "Are you a messenger of Muḥammad[sa]?" asked this chief. On being told "Yes," he arrested him, tied him up and belaboured him to death. It may quite reasonably be assumed that this Ghassān chief was a leader of the army which had engaged and put to death the fifteen Muslims who had tried only to preach. The fact that he said to al-Ḥarth[ra], "Perhaps you are carrying a message from Muḥammad[sa]" shows he was afraid lest the Prophet's[sa] complaint that tribesmen under the Kaiser had attacked the Muslims should reach the Kaiser. He was afraid lest he should have to account for what had happened. There was safety, he thought, in murdering the Prophet's[sa] envoy. The expectation was not realized. The Prophet[sa] got to know of the murder. To avenge this and the earlier murders, he raised a force of three thousand and despatched it to Syria under the command of Zaid bin Hāritha[ra], freed slave of the Prophet[sa], whom we mentioned in our account of his life in Mecca. The Prophet[sa] nominated Ja'far ibn Abī Tālib as the successor of Zaid[ra], should Zaid[ra] die, and 'Abdullāh bin Rawaḥā[ra], should Ja'far die. Should 'Abdullāh bin Rawaḥā[ra] also die, Muslims were to choose their own commander. A Jew who heard this exclaimed, "O Abu'l Qāsim[sa], if thou art a true Prophet[sa], these three officers whom thou hast named are sure to die; for God fulfils the words of a Prophet[sa]." Turning to Zaid[ra], he said,"Take it from me, if Muḥammad[sa] is true you will not return alive." Zaid[ra], a true believer that he was, said in reply, "I may return alive or not, but Muḥammad[sa] is a true Prophet of God" (*Ḥalbiyya,* Vol. 3, p. 75).

The following morning the Muslim army set out on its long march. The Prophet[sa] and the Companions went some distance with it. A large and important expedition such as this had never before gone without the Prophet[sa] commanding in person. As the Prophet[sa] walked along to bid the expedition farewell, he counselled and instructed. When they reached the spot where the people of Medina generally bade farewell to friends and relations going to Syria, the Prophet[sa] stopped and said:

> **I urge you to fear God and to deal justly with Muslims who go with you. Go to war in the name of Allah and fight the enemy in Syria, who is your enemy, as well as Allah's. When you are in Syria, you will meet those who remember God much in their houses of worship. You should have no dispute with them, and give no trouble to them. In the enemy country do not kill any women or children, nor the blind or the old; do not cut down any tree, nor pull down any building (*Ḥalbiyya,* Vol. 3).**

Having said this, the Prophet[sa] returned and the Muslim army marched forward. It was the first Muslim army sent to fight the Christians. When Muslims reached the Syrian border, they heard that the Kaiser himself had taken the field with one hundred thousand of his own soldiers and another hundred thousand recruited from the Christian tribes of Arabia. Confronted by such large enemy numbers, the Muslims half wanted to stop on the way and send word to the Prophet[sa] at Medina. For he might be able to reinforce their numbers or wish to send fresh instructions. When the army leaders took counsel, 'Abdullāh bin Rawāḥa[ra] stood up, full of fire, and said, "My people, you set out from your homes to die as martyrs in the way of God, and now when martyrdom is in sight you seem to flinch. We have not fought so far because we were better equipped than the enemy in men or material. Our mainstay was our faith. If the enemy is so many times superior to us in numbers or equipment, what does it matter? One reward out of two we must have. We either win, or die as martyrs in the way of God." The army heard ibn Rawāḥa[ra] and was much impressed. He was right, they said, with one voice. The army marched on. As they marched, they saw the Roman army advancing towards them. So at Mauta the Muslims took up their positions and the battle began. Soon Zaid[ra], the Muslim commander, was killed and the Prophet's cousin Ja'far ibn Abī Ṭālib[ra] received the standard and the command of the army. When he saw that enemy pressure was increasing and Muslims, because of utter physical inferiority, were not holding their own he dismounted from his horse and cut its legs. The action meant that at least he was not going to flee; he would prefer death to flight.

To cut the legs of one's mount was an Arab custom to prevent stampede and panic. Ja'far[ra] lost his right hand, but held the standard in his left. He lost his left hand also and then held the standard between the two stumps pressed to his chest. True to his promise, he fell down fighting. Then 'Abdullāh bin Rawāḥa[ra], as the Prophet[sa] had ordered, grasped the standard and took over the command. He also fell fighting. The order of the Prophet[sa] now was for Muslims to take counsel together and elect a commander. But there was no time to hold an election. The Muslims might well have yielded to the vastly superior numbers of the enemy. But Khālid bin Walīd[ra], accepting the suggestion of a friend, took the standard and went on fighting until evening came. The following day Khālid[ra] took the field again with his crippled and tired force but employed a stratagem. He changed the positions of his men—those in front changed with those in the rear and those on the right flank changed with those on the left. They also raised some slogans. The enemy thought Muslims had received reinforcements overnight and withdrew in fear. Khālid[ra] saved his remnants and returned. The Prophet[sa] had been informed of these events through a revelation. He collected the Muslims in the mosque. As he rose to address them his eyes were wet with tears. He said:

I wish to tell you about the army which left here for the Syrian border. It stood against the enemy and fought. First Zaid[ra], then Ja'far[ra] and then 'Abdullāh bin Rawāḥa[ra] held the standard. All three fell, one after the other, fighting bravely. Pray for them all. After them the standard was held by Khālid bin Walīd[ra]. He appointed himself. He is a sword among the swords of God. So he saved the Muslim army and returned (*Zād al-Ma'ād,* Vol. 1, and *Zurqānī*).

The Prophet's[sa] description of Khālid[ra] became popular. Khālid[ra] came to be known as 'the sword of God'.

Being one of the later converts, Khālid[ra] was often taunted by other Muslims. Once he and 'Abdur Raḥmān bin 'Auf[ra] quarrelled over something. 'Abdur Raḥmān bin 'Auf[ra] reported against Khālid[ra] to the Prophet[sa]. The Prophet[sa] chid Khālid[ra] and said, "Khālid[ra], you annoy one who has been serving Islam from the time of Badr. I say to you that even if you give away gold of the weight of Uḥud in the service of Islam, you will not become as deserving of divine reward as "'Abdur Raḥmān[ra]

"But they taunt me," said Khālid[ra], "and I have to reply."

Upon this the Prophet[sa] turned to others and said, "You must not taunt Khālid[ra]. He is a sword among the swords of God which remains drawn against disbelievers."

The Prophet's[sa] description came to literal fulfilment a few years later.

On Khālid's[ra] return with the Muslim army, some Muslims of Medina described the returning soldiers as defeatist and lacking in spirit. The general criticism was that they should all have died fighting. The Prophet[sa] chid the critics. Khālid[ra] and his soldiers were not defeatist or lacking in spirit, he said. They were soldiers who returned again and again to attack. The words meant more than appeared on the surface. They foretold battles which Muslims were to fight with Syria.

THE PROPHET[sa] MARCHES ON MECCA WITH TEN THOUSAND FOLLOWERS

In the eighth year of the Hijra in the month of Ramadan (December, 629 A.D.) the Prophet[sa] set out on that last expedition which definitely established Islam in Arabia.

At Ḥudaibiya it was agreed between Muslims and disbelievers that Arab tribes should be allowed to join the disbelievers as well as the Prophet[sa]. It was also agreed that for ten years the parties would not go to war against each other unless one party should violate the pact by attacking the other. Under this agreement, the Banū Bakr joined the Meccans, while the Khuzā'a entered into an alliance with Muslims. The Arab disbelievers had scant regard for treaties, especially for treaties with Muslims. It so happened that the Banū Bakr and the Khuzā'a had some outstanding differences. The Banū Bakr consulted the Meccans about settling their old scores with the Khuzā'a. They argued that the Hudaibiya treaty had been signed. The Khuzā'a felt secure because of their pact with the Prophet[sa]. Now, therefore, was the time for them to attack the Khuzā'a. The Meccans agreed. They and the Banū Bakr, accordingly, joined in a night attack on the Khuzā'a and put to death many of their men. The Khuzā'a sent forty of their men mounted on fleet camels to Medina to report this breach of agreement to the Prophet[sa]. They said it was up to Muslims now to march on Mecca to avenge this attack. The delegation met the Prophet[sa] and the Prophet[sa] told them unambiguously that he regarded their misfortunes as his own. He pointed to a rising cloud in the sky and said, "Like the rain drops which you see yonder, Muslim soldiers will drop down to your aid." The Meccans were perturbed over the news of the Khuzā'a delegation to Medina. They sent Abū Sufyān[ra] posthaste to Medina to restrain Muslims from the attack. Abū Sufyān[ra] reached Medina and began to urge that as he was not present at Ḥudaibiya, a new peace will have to be signed by Muslims. The Prophet[sa] thought it unwise to answer this plea. Abū Sufyān[ra] became excited, went to the mosque and announced:

"O People, I renew, on behalf of the Meccans, our assurance of peace to you" (*Zurqānī*).

The people of Medina did not understand this speech. So, they only laughed. The Prophet[sa] said to Abū Sufyān[ra], "Your statement is one sided and we cannot agree to it." In the meantime, the Prophet[sa] had sent word to all the tribes. Assured that they were ready and on the march, he asked the Muslims of Medina to arm themselves and prepare. On the 1st January, the Muslim army set out on its march. At different points on their way, they were joined by other Muslim tribes. Only a few days' journey had been covered, when the army entered the wilderness of Fārān, Its number—exactly as the Prophet[as] Solomon had foretold long before—had now swelled to ten thousand. As this army marched towards Mecca, the silence all around seemed more and more ominous to the Meccans. They persuaded Abū Sufyān[ra] to move out again and find out what the Muslim design was. He was less than one day's journey out of Mecca when he saw at night the entire wilderness lit up with camp-fires. The Prophet[sa] had ordered a fire in front of every camp. The effect of these roaring fires in the silence and darkness of the night was awful. "What could this be?" Abū Sufyān[ra] asked his companions, "Has an army dropped from the heavens? I know of no Arab army so large." They named some tribes and at every name Abū Sufyān[ra] said, "No Arab tribe or people could have an army as large." Abū Sufyān[ra] and his friends were still speculating when a voice from the dark shouted, "Abu Ḥanzala[ra]"! (Ḥanẓala was a son of Abū Sufyān[ra].)

"'Abbās, are you here?" said Abū Sufyān[ra].

"Yes, the Prophet's[sa] army is near. Act quickly or humility and defeat await you," replied 'Abbās[ra].

'Abbās[ra] and Abū Sufyān[ra] were old friends. 'Abbās[ra] insisted that Abū Sufyān[ra] should accompany him on the same mule and go to the Prophet[sa]. He gripped Abū Sufyān's[ra] hand, pulled him up and made him mount. Spurring the mule, they soon reached the Prophet's[sa] camp. 'Abbās[ra] was afraid lest 'Umar[ra], who was guarding the Prophet's[sa] tent, should fall upon Abū Sufyān[ra] and kill him. But the Prophet[sa] had taken precautions, announcing that if anybody should meet Abū Sufyān[ra] he should make no attempt to kill him. The meeting impressed Abū Sufyān[ra] deeply. He was struck by the rise which had taken place in the fortunes of Islam. Here was the Prophet[sa] whom Meccans had banished from Mecca with but one friend in his company. Hardly seven years had passed since then, and now he was knocking at the gates of Mecca with ten thousand devotees. The tables had been completely turned. The fugitive Prophet[sa] who, seven years before, had escaped from Mecca for fear of life, had now returned to Mecca, and Mecca was unable to resist him.

FALL OF MECCA

Abū Sufyān[ra] must have been thinking furiously. Had not an incredibly great change taken place in seven years? And now as leader of the Meccans, what was he going to do? Was he going to resist, or was he going to submit? Troubled by such thoughts, he appeared stupefied to outside observers. The Prophet[sa] saw this agitated Meccan leader. He told 'Abbās[ra] to take him away and entertain him for the night, promising to see him in the morning. Abū Sufyān[ra] spent the night with 'Abbas. In the morning they called on the Prophet[sa]. It was time for the early morning prayers. The bustle and activity which Abū Sufyān[ra] saw at this early hour was quite unusual in his experience. He had not known—no Meccan had known—such early risers as Muslims had become under the discipline of Islam. He saw all the

Muslim campers turned out for their morning prayers. Some went to and fro in quest of water for ablutions, others to supervise the lining up of worshippers for the service. Abū Sufyān[ra] could not understand this activity early in the morning. He was frightened. Was a new plan afoot to overawe him?

"What can they all be doing?" he asked in sheer consternation.

"Nothing to be afraid of," replied 'Abbās[ra]. "They are only preparing for the morning prayers."

Abū Sufyān[ra] then saw thousands of Muslims lined up behind the Prophet[sa], making the prescribed movements and devotions at the bidding of the Prophet[sa]—half prostrations, full prostrations, standing up again, and so on. 'Abbās[ra] was on guard duty, so he was free to engage Abū Sufyān[ra] in conversation.

"What could they be doing now?" asked Abū Sufyān[ra]. "Everything the Prophet[sa] does, is done by the rest."

"What are you thinking about? It is only the Muslim prayer, Abū Sufyān[ra]. Muslims would do anything at the bidding of the Prophet[sa]—give up food and drink for instance."

"True," said Abū Sufyān[ra], "I have seen great courts. I have seen the court of the Chosroes and the court of the Kaiser, but I have never seen any people as devoted to their leader as Muslims are to their Prophet[sa]" (*Ḥalbiyya*, Vol. 2, p. 90).

Filled with fear and guilt, Abū Sufyān[ra] went on to ask 'Abbās[ra] if he would not request the Prophet[sa] to forgive his own people —meaning the Meccans.

The morning prayers over, 'Abbās[ra] led Abū Sufyān[ra] to the Prophet[sa].

Said the Prophet[sa] to Abū Sufyān[ra]. "Has it not yet dawned upon you that there is no one worthy of worship except Allah?"

"My father and my mother be a sacrifice to you. You have ever been kind, gentle and considerate to your kith and kin. I am certain now that if there were anyone else worthy of worship, we might have had some help against you from him."

"Has it not also dawned upon you that I am a Messenger of Allah[sa]?"

"My father and my mother be a sacrifice to you, on this I still have some doubts."

While Abū Sufyān[ra] hesitated to acknowledge the Prophet[sa] as Messenger of God, two of his companions who had marched out of Mecca with him to do reconnoitring duty for the Meccans, became Muslims. One of them was Ḥakīm bin Ḥizām[ra]. A little later, Abū Sufyān[ra] also joined, but his inner conversion seems to have been deferred until after the conquest of Mecca. Ḥakīm bin Ḥizām[ra] asked the Prophet[sa] if the Muslims would destroy their own kith and kin.

"These people," said the Prophet[sa], "have been very cruel. They have committed excesses and proved themselves of bad faith. They have gone back on the peace they signed at Ḥudaibiya and attacked the Khuzā'a savagely. They have made war in a place which had been made inviolate by God."

"It is quite true, O Prophet[sa] of God, our people have done exactly as you say, but instead of marching upon Mecca you should have attacked the Hawāzin," suggested Ḥakīm[ra].

"The Hawāzin also have been cruel and savage. I hope God will enable me to realize all the three ends: the conquest of Mecca, the ascendancy of Islam and the defeat of the Hawāzin."

Abū Sufyān[ra], who had been listening, now asked the Prophet[sa]: "If the Meccans draw not the sword, will they have peace?"

"Yes," replied the Prophet[sa], "everyone who stays indoors will have peace."

"But O Prophet[sa]," intervened 'Abbās[ra], "Abū Sufyān[ra] is much concerned about himself. He wishes to know if his rank and position among the Meccans will be respected."

"Very good," said the Prophet[sa]: "Whoever take shelter in the house of Abū Sufyān[ra] will have peace. Whoever enters the Sacred Mosque will-have peace. Those who lay down their arms will have peace. Those who close their doors and stay in will have peace. Those who stay in the house of Ḥakīm bin Ḥizām[ra] will have peace."

Saying this, he called Abū Ruwaiḥa[ra] and handed over to him the standard of Islam. Abū Ruwaiḥa[ra] had entered into a pact of brotherhood with Bilāl[ra], the negro slave. Handing over the standard, the Prophet[sa] said, "Whoever stands under this standard will have peace." At the same time, he ordered Bilāl[ra] to march in front of Abū Ruwaiḥa[ra] and announce to all concerned that there was peace under the standard held by Abū Ruwaiḥa[ra].

THE PROPHET[sa] ENTERS MECCA

The arrangement was full of wisdom. When Muslims were persecuted in Mecca, Bilāl[ra], one of their targets, was dragged about the streets by ropes tied to his legs. Mecca gave no peace to Bilāl[ra], but only physical pain, humiliation and disgrace. How revengeful Bilāl[ra] must have felt on this day of his deliverance. To let him avenge the savage cruelties suffered by him in Mecca was necessary, but it had to be within the limits laid down by Islam. Accordingly, the Prophet[sa] did not let Bilāl[ra] draw the sword and smite the necks of his former persecutors. That would have been un-Islamic. Instead, the Prophet[sa] handed to Bilāl's[ra] brother the standard of Islam, and charged Bilāl[ra] with the duty of offering peace to all his former persecutors under the standard borne by his brother. There was beauty and appeal in this revenge. We have to picture Bilāl[ra] marching in front of his brother and inviting his enemies to peace. His passion for revenge could not have lasted. It must have dissolved as he advanced inviting Meccans to peace under a standard held aloft by his brother.

While the Muslims marched towards Mecca, the Prophet[sa] had ordered 'Abbās[ra] to take Abū Sufyān[ra] and his friends to a spot from where they could easily view the Muslim army, its behaviour and bearing. 'Abbās[ra] did so and from a vantage-point Abū Sufyān[ra] and his friends watched the Arab tribes go past on whose power the Meccans had banked all these years for their plots against Islam. They marched that day not as soldiers of disbelief but as soldiers of belief. They raised now the slogans of Islam, not the slogans of their pagan days. They marched in formation, not to put an end to the Prophet's[sa] life, but to lay down their lives to save his; not to shed his blood, but their own for his sake. Their ambition that day was not to resist the Prophet's[sa] Message and save the superficial solidarity of their own people. It was to carry to all parts of the world the very Message they had so far resisted. It was to establish the unity and solidarity of man. Column after column marched past until the Ashja' tribe came in Abū Sufyān's[ra] view. Their devotion to Islam and their self-sacrificing zeal could be seen in their faces, and heard in their songs and slogans.

"Who can they be?" asked Abū Sufyān[ra].

"They are the Ashja' tribe."

Abū Sufyān[ra] looked astonished and said, "In all Arabia, no one bore greater enmity to Muḥammad[sa]."

"We owe it to the grace of God. He changed the hearts of the enemy of Islam as soon as He deemed fit," said 'Abbās[ra].

Last of all came the Prophet[sa], surrounded by the columns of Anṣār and Muhājirīn. They must have been about two thousand strong, dressed in suits of armour. The valiant 'Umar[ra] directed their marching. The sight proved the most impressive of all. The devotion of these Muslims, their determination and their zeal seemed overflowing. When Abū Sufyān's[ra] eyes fell on them, he was completely overpowered.

"Who can they be?" he asked.

"They are the Anṣār[ra] and the Muhājirīn surrounding the Prophet[sa]," replied 'Abbās[ra].

"No power on earth could resist this army," said Abū Sufyān[ra], and then, addressing 'Abbās more specifically, "'Abbās[ra], your nephew has become the most powerful king in the world."

"You are still far from the truth, Abū Sufyān[ra]. He is no king; he is a Prophet[sa], a Messenger of God," replied 'Abbās[ra].

"Yes, yes, let it be as you say, a Prophet[sa], not a king," added Abū Sufyān[ra].

As the Muslim army marched past Abū Sufyān[ra], the commander of the Anṣār, Sa'd bin 'Ubāda[ra] happened to eye Abū Sufyān[ra] and could not resist saying that God that day had made it lawful for them to enter Mecca by force and that the Quraish would be humiliated.

As the Prophet[sa] was passing, Abū Sufyān[ra] raised his voice and addressing the Prophet[sa] said, "Have you allowed the massacre of your own kith and kin? I heard the commander of the Anṣār, Sa'd[ra] and his companions say so. They said it was a day of slaughter. The sacredness of Mecca will not avert bloodshed and the Quraish will be humiliated. Prophet[sa] of God, you are the best, the most forgiving, the most considerate of men. Will you not forgive and forget whatever was done by your own people?"

Abū Sufyān's[ra] appeal went home. Those very Muslims who used to be insulted and beaten in the streets of Mecca, who had been dispossessed and driven out of their homes, began to entertain feelings of mercy for their old persecutors. "Prophet[sa] of God," they said, "the accounts which the Anṣār have heard of the excesses and cruelties committed by Meccans against us, may lead them to seek revenge. We know not what they may do."

The Prophet[sa] understood this. Turning to Abū Sufyān[ra], he said, "What Sa'd[ra] has said is quite wrong.

It is not the day of slaughter. It is the day of forgiveness. The Quraish and the Ka'ba will be honoured by God."

Then he sent for Sa'd[ra], and ordered him to hand over the Anṣār flag to his son, Qais[ra] (*Hishām*, Vol. 2). The command of the Anṣār thus passed from Sa'd[ra] to Qais[ra]. It was a wise step. It placated the Meccans and saved the Anṣār disappointment. Qais[ra], a pious young man, was fully trusted by the Prophet[sa].

An incident of his last days illustrates the piety of his character. Lying on his death-bed, Qais[ra] received his friends. Some came and some did not. He could not understand this and asked why some of his friends had not come to see him. "Your charity is abundant," explained one.

You have been helping the needy by your loans. There are many in the town who are in debt to you. Some may have hesitated to come lest you should ask them for the return of the loans."

"Then I have been the cause of keeping my friends away. Please announce that no one now owes anything to Qais[ra]." After this announcement Qais[ra] had so many visitors during his last days that the steps to his house gave way.

When the Muslim army had marched past, 'Abbās[ra] told Abū Sufyān[ra] to hasten for Mecca and announce to the Meccans that the Prophet[sa] had come and explain to them how they could all have peace. Abū Sufyān[ra] reached Mecca with this message of peace for his town, but his wife, Hind, notorious for her hostility towards Muslims, met him. A confirmed disbeliever, she was yet a brave woman. She caught Abū Sufyān[ra] by the beard and called on Meccans to come and kill her cowardly husband. Instead of moving his townsmen to sacrifice their lives for the defence and honour of their town, he was inviting them to peace.

But Abū Sufyān[ra] could see that Hind was behaving foolishly "That time is gone," said he. "You had better go home and sit behind closed doors. I have seen the Muslim army. Not all Arabia could withstand it now."

He then explained the conditions under which the Prophet[sa] had promised peace to the Meccans. On hearing these conditions the people of Mecca ran for protection to the places which had been named in the Prophet's[sa] proclamation. From this proclamation eleven men and four women had been excepted. The offences which they had committed were very grave. Their guilt was not that they had not believed nor that they had taken part in wars against Islam; it was that they had committed inhumanities which could not be passed over. Actually, however, only four persons were put to death.

The Prophet[sa] had ordered Khālid bin Walīd[ra] not to permit any fighting unless they were fought against and unless the Meccans first started fighting. The part of the town which Khālid[ra] entered had not heard the conditions of peace. The Meccans posted in that part challenged Khālid[ra] and invited him to fight. An encounter ensued in which twelve or thirteen men were killed (*Hishām*, Vol. 2, p. 217). Khālid[ra] was a man of fiery temper. Somebody, warned by this incident, ran to the Prophet[sa] to request him to stop Khālid[ra] from fighting. If Khālid[ra] did not stop, said this man, all Mecca would be massacred.

The Prophet[sa] sent for Khālid[ra] at once and said, "Did I not stop you from fighting?"

"Yes, you did, O Prophet[sa] of God, but these people attacked us first and began to shoot arrows at us. For a time I did nothing and told them we did not want to fight. But they did not listen, and did not stop. So I replied to them, and dispersed them."

This was the only untoward incident which took place on this occasion. The conquest of Mecca was thus brought about practically without bloodshed.

The Prophet[sa] entered Mecca. They asked him where he would stop.

"Has 'Aqīl left any house for me to live in?" asked the Prophet[sa]. 'Aqīl was the Prophet's[sa] cousin, a son of his uncle. During the years of the Prophet's[sa] refuge at

Medina, his relations had sold all his property. There was no house left which the Prophet[sa] could call his own. Accordingly the Prophet[sa] said, "I will stop at Ḥanīf Banī Kināna." This was an open space. The Quraish and the Kināna once assembled there and swore that unless the Banū Hāshim and the Banū 'Abdul Muṭṭalib handed over the Prophet[sa] to them to deal with him as they liked, they would have no dealings with the two tribes. They would neither sell anything to them nor buy anything from them. It was after this solemn declaration that the Prophet[sa], his uncle Abū Ṭālib, his family and followers, had to take refuge in the valley of Abū Ṭālib and suffer a severe blockade and boycott lasting for three years.

The place which the Prophet[sa] chose for his stay was, therefore, full of significance. The Meccans had once assembled there and taken the oath that unless the Prophet[sa] was made over to them, they would not be at peace with his tribe. Now the Prophet[sa] had come to the same spot. It was as though he had come to tell the Meccans: "You wanted me here, so here I am. But not in the way you wanted. You wanted me as your victim, one completely at your mercy. But I am here in power. Not only my own people, but the whole of Arabia is now with me. You wanted my people to hand me over to you. Instead of that, they have handed you over to me." This day of victory was a Monday. The day on which the Prophet[sa] and Abū Bakr[ra] left the cave of Thaur for their journey to Medina was also a Monday. On that day, standing on the hill of Thaur, the Prophet[sa] turned to Mecca and said, 'Mecca! you are dearer to me than any other place but your people would not let me live here.'

When the Prophet[sa] entered Mecca, mounted on his camel, Abū Bakr[ra] walked with him holding a stirrup. As he walked along, Abū Bakr[ra] recited verses from the Sūrah, Al-Fath in which the conquest of Mecca had been foretold years before.

KA'BA CLEARED OF IDOLS

The Prophet[sa] made straight for the Ka'ba and performed the circuit of the holy precincts seven times, mounted on his camel. Staff in hand, he went round the house which had been built by the Patriarch Abraham[as] and his son Ishmael[as] for the worship of the One and Only God, but which by their misguided children had been allowed to degenerate into a sanctuary for idols. The Prophet[sa] smote one by one the three hundred and sixty idols in the house. As an idol fell, the Prophet[sa] would recite the verse, "Truth has come and falsehood has vanished away. Falsehood does indeed vanish away fast." This verse was revealed before the Prophet[sa] left Mecca for Medina and is part of the Chapter, Banī Isrā'īl. In this Chapter was foretold the flight of the Prophet[sa] and the conquest of Mecca. The Chapter is a Meccan Chapter, a fact admitted even by European writers. The verses which contain the prophecy of the Prophet's[sa] flight from Mecca, and the subsequent conquest of Mecca are as follows:

> **And say 'O my Lord, make my entry a good entry, and make my going out a good outgoing. And grant me from Thyself a power that may help me.' And, 'Truth has come and falsehood has vanished away. Falsehood does indeed vanish away fast!' (17: 81-82).**

The conquest of Mecca is foretold here in the form of a prayer taught to the Prophet[sa]. The Prophet[sa] is taught to pray for entering Mecca and for departing from it under good auspices; and for the help of God in assuring an ultimate victory of truth over falsehood. The prophecy had literally come true. The recitation of these verses by Abū Bakr[ra] was appropriate. It braced up the Muslims, and reminded the Meccans of the futility of their fight against God and of the truth of the promises made by God to the Prophet[sa].

With the conquest of Mecca, the Ka'ba was restored to the functions for which it had been consecrated many thousands of years before by the Patriarch Abraham[as].

The Ka'ba was again devoted to the worship of the One and Only God. The idols were broken. One of these was Hubal. When the Prophet[sa] smote it with his staff, and it fell down in fragments, Zubair[ra] looked at Abū Sufyān[ra] and with a half-suppressed smile reminded him of Uḥud. "Do you remember the day when Muslims wounded and exhausted stood by and you wounded them further by shouting, 'Glory to Hubal, Glory to Hubal'? Was it Hubal who gave you victory on that day? If it was Hubal, you can see the end it has come to today."

Abū Sufyān[ra] was impressed, and admitted it was quite true that if there had been a God other than the God of Muḥammad[sa], they might have been spared the disgrace and defeat they had met with that day.

The Prophet[sa] then ordered the wiping out of the pictures which had been drawn on the walls of the Ka'ba. Having ordered this the Prophet[sa] said two rak'ats of prayer as thanks-giving to God. He then withdrew to the open court and said another two rak'ats of prayer. The duty of wiping out the pictures had been entrusted to 'Umar[ra]. He had all the pictures obliterated except that of Abraham[as]. When the Prophet[sa] returned to inspect and found this picture intact, he asked 'Umar[ra] why he had spared this one. Did he not remember the testimony of the Qur'an that Abraham[as] was neither Jew nor Christian, but a single-minded and obedient Muslim? (3: 68).

It was an insult to the memory of Abraham[as], a great exponent of the Oneness of God to have his picture on the walls of the Ka'ba. It was as though Abraham[as] could be worshipped equally with God.

It was a memorable day, a day full of the Signs of God.

Promises made by God to the Prophet[sa], at a time when their fulfilment seemed impossible, had been fulfilled at last. The Prophet[sa] was the centre of devotion and faith. In and through his person, God had manifested Himself, and shown His face, as it were, again. The Prophet[sa] sent for water of the Zamzam. He drank some of it and with the rest performed ablutions. So devoted were Muslims to the Prophet's[sa] person, that they would not let a drop of this water fall on the ground. They received the water in the hollows of their hands to wet their bodies with it; in such reverence did they hold it. The pagans who witnessed these scenes of devotion said again and again that they had never seen an earthly king to whom his people were so devoted (*Ḥalbiyya*, Vol. 3, p. 99).

THE PROPHET[sa] FORGIVES HIS ENEMIES

All rites and duties over, the Prophet[sa] addressed the Meccans and said: "You have seen how true the promises of God have proved. Now tell me what punishment you should have for the cruelties and enormities you committed against those whose only fault was that they invited you to the worship of the One and Only God."

To this the Meccans replied, "We expect you to treat us as Joseph[as] treated his erring brothers."

By significant coincidence, the Meccans used in their plea for forgiveness the very words which God had used in the Sūrah Yūsuf, revealed ten years before the conquest of Mecca. In this the Prophet[sa] was told that he would treat his Meccan persecutors as Joseph[as] had treated his brothers. By asking for the treatment which Joseph[as] had meted out to his brothers, the Meccans admitted that the Prophet[sa] of Islam was the like of Joseph[as] and as Joseph[as] was granted victory over his brothers the Prophet[sa] had been granted victory over the Meccans. Hearing the Meccans' plea, the Prophet[sa] declared at once: "By God, you will have no punishment today and no reproof" (*Hishām*).

While the Prophet[sa] was engaged in expressing his gratitude to God and in carrying out other devotions at the Ka'ba, and while he was addressing the Meccans announcing his decision to forgive and forget, misgivings arose in the minds of the Anṣār, the Medinite Muslims. Some of them were upset over the scenes of home-coming and of reconciliation which they witnessed on the return of Meccan Muslims to Mecca. Was the Prophet[sa] parting company with them, his friends in adversity who provided the first home to Islam? Was the Prophet[sa] going to settle down at Mecca, the town from which he had to flee for his life? Such fears did not seem too remote now that Mecca had been conquered and his own tribe had joined Islam. The Prophet[sa] might want to settle down in it. God informed the Prophet[sa] of these misgivings of the Anṣār. He raised his head, looked at the Anṣār and said "You seem to think Muḥammad[sa] is perturbed by the love of his town, and by the ties which bind him to his tribe." "It is true," said the Anṣār., "we did think of this."

"Do you know," said the Prophet[sa], "Who I am? I am a Servant of God and His Messenger. How can I give you up? You stood by me, and sacrificed your lives when the Faith of God had no earthly help. How can I give you up and settle elsewhere? No, Anṣār., this is impossible. I left Mecca for the sake of God and I cannot return to it. I will live and die with you."

The Anṣār were moved by this singular expression of love and loyalty. They regretted their distrust of God and His Prophet[sa], wept and asked to be forgiven. They explained that they would not have any peace if the Prophet[sa] left their town and went elsewhere. The Prophet[sa] replied that their fear was understandable and that, after their explanation, God and His Prophet[sa] were satisfied about their innocence and acknowledge their sincerity and loyalty.

How must the Meccans have felt at this time? True they did not shed the tears of devotion but their hearts must have been full of regret and remorse. For, had they not cast away with their own hands the gem which had been found in their own town? They had all the more reason to regret this because the Prophet[sa], having come back to Mecca, had decided to leave it again for Medina.

‘IKRIMA[ra] BECOMES MUSLIM

Of those who had been excepted from the general amnesty, some were forgiven on the recommendation of the Companions. Among those who were thus forgiven was ‘Ikrima[ra], a son of Abū Jahl. ‘Ikrima's[ra] wife was a Muslim at heart. She requested the Prophet[sa] to forgive him. The Prophet[sa] forgave. At the time ‘Ikrima[ra] was trying to escape to Abyssinia. His wife pursued him and found that he was about to embark. She reproved him. "Are you running away from a man as gentle and soft as the Prophet[sa]?" she said.

‘Ikrima[ra] was astonished and asked whether she really thought the Prophet[sa] would forgive him. ‘Ikrima's[ra] wife assured him that even he would be forgiven by the Prophet[sa]. In fact she had had word from him already. ‘Ikrima[ra] gave up his plan of escaping to Abyssinia and returned to see the Prophet[sa]. "I understand from my wife that you have forgiven even one like me," he said.

"Your wife is right. I have really forgiven you," said the Prophet[sa].

‘Ikrima[ra] decided that a person capable of forgiving his deadliest enemies could not be false. He, therefore, declared his faith in Islam. "I bear witness that God is One and has no equal and I bear witness that you are His Servant and His Messenger[sa]." So saying, ‘Ikrima[ra] bent his head in shame. The Prophet[sa] consoled him. " ‘Ikrima[ra]," said he, "I have not only forgiven you, but as proof of my regard for you, I have decided to invite you to ask me for anything I can give."

‘Ikrima[ra] replied, "There is nothing more or better I can ask you for than that you should pray for me to God and ask for His forgiveness and whatever excesses and enormities I have committed against you."

Hearing this entreaty, the Prophet[sa] prayed to God at once and said: "My God, forgive the enmity which 'Ikrima[ra] has born against me. Forgive him the abuse which has issued from his lips."

The Prophet[sa] then stood up and put his mantle over 'Ikrima[ra] and said, "Whoever comes to me, believing in God, is one with me. My house is as much his as mine."

The conversion of 'Ikrima[ra] fulfilled a prophecy which the Holy Prophet[sa] had made many years before. The Prophet[sa], addressing his Companions, once had said: "I have had a vision in which I saw that I was in Paradise. I saw there a bunch of grapes. When I asked for whom the bunch was meant, someone replied saying, 'For Abū Jahl'." Referring to this vision on this occasion of the conversion of 'Ikrima[ra], the Prophet[sa] said he did not understand the vision at first. How could Abū Jahl, an enemy of believers, enter Paradise and how could he have a bunch of grapes provided for him. "But now," said the Prophet[sa], "I understand my vision; the bunch of grapes was meant for 'Ikrima[ra]. Only, instead of the son I was shown the father, a substitution common in visions and dreams" (*Ḥalbiyya*, Vol. 3, p. 104).

Of the persons who had been ordered to be executed as exceptions to the general amnesty was one who had been responsible for the cruel murder of Zainab[ra], a daughter of the Prophet[sa]. This man was Habbār[ra]. He had cut the girths of Zainab's[ra] camel, on which Zainab[ra] fell to the ground and, being with child, suffered abortion. A little later she died. This was one of the inhumanities which he had committed and for which he deserved the penalty of death. This man now came to the Prophet[sa] and said, "Prophet[sa] of God, I ran away from you and went to Iran, but the thought came to me that God had rid us of our pagan beliefs and saved us from spiritual death. Instead of going to others and seeking shelter with them why not go to the Prophet[sa] himself, acknowledge my faults and my sins and ask for his forgiveness?"

The Prophet[sa] was moved and said, "Habbār[ra], if God has planted in your heart the love of Islam, how can I refuse to forgive you? I forgive everything you have done before this."

One cannot describe in detail the enormities these men had committed against Islam and Muslims. Yet how easily the Prophet[sa] forgave them! This spirit of forgiveness converted the most stone-hearted adversaries into devotees of the Prophet[sa].

BATTLE OF ḤUNAIN

The Prophet's[sa] entry into Mecca was sudden. Tribes in the vicinity of Mecca, especially those in the south, remained unaware of the event until sometime later. On hearing of it, they began to assemble their forces and to prepare for a fight with the Muslims. There were two Arab tribes, the Hawāzin and the Thaqīf, unusually proud of their valiant traditions. They took counsel together and after some deliberation elected Malik ibn 'Auf as their leader. They then invited the tribes round about to join them. Among the tribes invited was the Banū Sa'd. The Prophet's[sa] wet-nurse, Halīma, belonged to this tribe and the Prophet[sa] as a child had lived among them. Men of this tribe collected in force and set out towards Mecca taking with them their families and their effects. Asked why they had done so, they replied it was in order that the soldiers might be reminded that, if they turned back and fled, their wives and children would be taken prisoners and their effects looted—so strong was their determination to fight and destroy the Muslims. This force descended in the valley of Rauṭās most suitable base for a battle, with its natural shelters, abundance of fodder and water, and facilities for cavalry movements. When the Prophet[sa] got to know of this, he sent 'Abdullāh bin Abī Ḥadwad[ra] to report on the situation. 'Abdullāh reported that there were military concentrations in the place and there was determination to kill and be killed. The tribe was renowned for its skill in archery, and the base they had selected afforded a very great advantage to them. The Prophet[sa] approached Ṣafwān[ra], a prosperous chief of Mecca for the loan of suits of armour and weapons. Ṣafwān[ra] replied, "You seem to put pressure on me and think I will be overawed by your growing power and make over to you whatever you ask?"

The Prophet[sa] replied, "We wish to seize nothing. We only want a loan of these things, and are ready to give a suitable surety."

Ṣafwān[ra] was satisfied and agreed to lend the material. Altogether he supplied one hundred suits of armour and a suitable number of weapons. The Prophet[sa] borrowed three thousand lances from his cousin, Naufal bin Ḥarith[ra] and about thirty thousand dirhams from ʻAbdullāh bin Rabīʻa (*Mu'aṭṭa', Musnad* and *Ḥalbiyya*). When the Muslim army set out towards the Hawāzin, the Meccans expressed a wish to join the Muslim side. They were not Muslims, but they had agreed to live under a Muslim regime. Accordingly, two thousand Meccans joined the Muslims. On the way, they came to the noted Arab shrine, Dhāt Anwaṭ. Here was an old jujube tree, sacred to the Arabs. When Arabs bought arms they first went to Dhāt Anwaṭ and hung them in the shrine to receive its blessings for their arms. When the Muslim army passed by this shrine some of the soldiers said, "Prophet[sa] of God, there should be a Dhāt Anwaṭ for us also."

The Prophet[sa] disapproved and said, "You talk like the followers of Moses[as]. When Moses[as] was going to Canaan, his followers saw on the way people worshipping idols, and said to Moses[as], 'O Moses[as], make for us a god just as they have gods'" (Qur'an 7: 139).

"THE PROPHET[sa] OF GOD CALLS YOU"

The Prophet[sa] urged Muslims to always remember that Allah was Great and to pray to Him to save them from the superstitions of earlier peoples. Before the Muslim army reached Ḥunain, the Hawāzin and their allies had already prepared a number of ambuscades from which to attack the Muslims, like the fox-holes and camouflaged artillery positions of modern warfare. They had built walls around them. Behind the walls were soldiers lying in wait for the Muslims. A narrow gorge was left for Muslims to pass through. Much the larger part of the army was posted to these ambuscades, while a small number was made to line up in front of their camels. Muslims thought enemy numbers to be no more than they could see. So they went forward and attacked. When they had advanced far and the hiding enemy was satisfied that they could be attacked very easily, the soldiers lined up in front of the camels and attacked the centre of the Muslim army while the hiding archers rained their arrows on the flanks. The Meccans, who had joined for a chance to display their valour, could not stand this double attack by the enemy. They ran back to Mecca. Muslims were accustomed to difficult situations, but when two thousand soldiers mounted on horses and camels pierced their way through the Muslim army, the animals of the Muslims also took fright. There was panic in the army. Pressure came from three sides, resulting in a general rout. In this, only the Prophet[sa], with twelve Companions, stood unmoved. Not that all the Companions had fled from the field. About a hundred of them still remained, but they were at some distance from the Prophet[sa]. Only twelve remained to surround the Prophet[sa]. One Companion reports that he and his friends did all they could to steer their animals towards the battlefield. But the animals had been put to fright by the stampede of the Meccan animals. No effort seemed to avail. They pulled at the reins but the animals refused to turn. Sometimes they would pull the heads of the animals so as almost to make them touch their tails. But when they spurred the animals towards the battlefield, they would not go. Instead, they moved back all the more. "Our hearts beat in fear—fear for the safety of the Prophet[sa]," says this Companion, "but there was nothing we could do." This was how the Companions were placed. The Prophet[sa] himself stood with a handful of men, exposed on three sides to volleys of arrows. There was only one narrow pass behind them through which only a few men could pass at a time. At that moment Abū Bakr[ra] dismounted and holding the reins of the Prophet's[sa] mule said, "Prophet[sa] of God, let us withdraw for a while and let the Muslim army collect itself."

"Release the reins of my mule, Abū Bakr[ra]," said the Prophet[sa]. Saying, this, he spurred the animal forward into the gorge on both sides of which were enemy ambuscades from where the archers were shooting. As the Prophet[sa] spurred his mount, he said, "I am a Prophet[sa]. I am no pretender. I am a son of 'Abdul Muṭṭalib" (*Bukhārī*). These words spoken at a time of extreme danger to his person are full of significance. They stressed the fact that the Prophet[sa] was really a Prophet[sa], a true Messenger of God. By stressing this, he meant that he was not afraid of death or of the failure of his cause. But if, in spite of being overwhelmed by archers he remained safe, Muslims should not attribute any divine qualities to him. For he was but a human being, a son of 'Abdul Muṭṭalib. How careful was the Prophet[sa] ever to impress upon his followers the difference between faith and superstition. After uttering these memorable words, the Prophet[sa] called for 'Abbās[ra]. 'Abbās[ra] had a powerful voice. The Prophet[sa] said to him, " 'Abbās[ra], raise your voice and remind the Muslims of the oath they took under the tree at Ḥudaibiya, and of what they were taught at the time of the revelation of the Sūrah Baqara. Tell them, the Prophet[sa] of God calls them." 'Abbās[ra] raised his powerful voice. The message of the Prophet[sa] fell like thunder, not on deaf ears but on ears agog. It had an electric effect. The very Companions who had found themselves powerless to urge their mounts towards the battlefield, began to feel they were no longer in this world but in the next, facing God on the Judgement Day. The voice of 'Abbās[ra] did not sound like his own voice but the voice of the angel beckoning them to render an account of their deeds. There was nothing then to stop them from turning to the battlefield again. Many of them dismounted and with only sword and shield rushed to the battlefield, leaving their animals to go where they liked. Others dismounted, cut off the heads of their animals and rushed back on foot to the Prophet[sa]. It is said that the Anṣār on that day ran towards the Prophet[sa] with the speed with which a mother-camel or a mother-cow runs to her young on hearing its cries. Before long the Prophet[sa] was surrounded by a large number of Companions, mostly Anṣār. The enemy again suffered a defeat.

The presence of Abū Sufyān[ra] on the side of the Prophet[sa] on this day was a mighty divine Sign, a Sign of the power of God on the one hand and of the purifying example of the Prophet[sa] on the other. Only a few days before, Abū Sufyān[ra] was a bloodthirsty enemy of the Prophet[sa], commander of a bloodthirsty army determined to destroy the Muslims. But here, on this day the same Abū Sufyān[ra] stood by the side of the Prophet[sa], a friend, follower and Companion. When the enemy camels stampeded, Abū Sufyān[ra], a wise and seasoned general, saw that his own horse was likely to run wild. Quickly he dismounted and, holding the stirrup of the Prophet's[sa] mule, started going on foot. Sword in hand, he walked by the side of the Prophet[sa] determined not to let anyone come near the Prophet's[sa] person without first attacking and killing him. The Prophet[sa] watched this change in Abū Sufyān[ra] with delight and astonishment.

He reflected on this fresh evidence of the power of God. Only ten or fifteen days before, this man was raising an army to put an end to the Movement of Islam. But a change had come. An erstwhile enemy commander now stood by the Prophet's[sa] side, as an ordinary foot-soldier, holding the stirrup of his Master's mule, and determined to die for his sake. 'Abbās[ra] saw the astonishment in the Prophet's[sa] look and said, "Prophet[sa] of God, this is Abū Sufyān[ra], son of your uncle, and so your brother. Aren't you pleased with him?"

"I am," said the Prophet[sa], "and I pray, God may forgive him all the wrongs he has done." Then turning to Abū Sufyān[ra] himself, he said, "Brother!" Abū Sufyān[ra] could not restrain the affection welling up in his heart. He bent and kissed the Prophet's[sa] foot in the stirrup he was holding (*Ḥalbiyya*).

After the battle of Ḥunain, the Prophet[sa] returned the war material he had received on loan. While returning it he compensated the lenders many times over. Those who had made the loan were touched by the care and consideration which the Prophet[sa] had shown in returning the material and in compensating the lenders. They felt the Prophet[sa] was no ordinary man, but one whose moral example stood high above others. No wonder, Ṣafwān[ra] joined Islam at once.

A SWORN ENEMY BECOMES A DEVOTED FOLLOWER

The battle of Ḥunain ever reminds historians of another interesting incident which took place while it was in progress. Shaiba[ra], a resident of Mecca and in the service of the Ka'ba, took part in the encounter on the side of the enemy. He says that he had only one aim before him in this battle—that when the two armies met, he would find an opportunity to kill the Prophet[sa]. He was determined that even if the whole world joined the Prophet[sa] (let alone the whole of Arabia), he would stand out and continue to oppose Islam. When fighting became brisk, Shaiba[ra] drew his sword and started advancing towards the Prophet[sa]. As he came very near, he became unnerved. His determination began to shake. "When I got very near the Prophet[sa]," says Shaiba[ra], "I seemed to see a flame threatening to consume me. I then heard the voice of the Prophet[sa] saying, 'Shaiba[ra], come near me.' When I got near, the Prophet[sa] moved his hand over my chest in great affection. As he did so, he said, 'God, relieve Shaiba[ra] of all satanic thought'." With this little touch of affection Shaiba[ra] changed. His hostility and enmity evaporated, and from that moment Shaiba[ra] held the Prophet[sa] dearer than anything else in the world. As Shaiba[ra] changed, the Prophet[sa] invited him to come forward and fight. "At that moment," says Shaiba[ra], "I had but one thought, and that was to die for the sake of the Prophet[sa]. Even if my father had come my way, I would have hesitated not a moment to thrust my sword in his chest" (*Ḥalbiyya*).

The Prophet[sa] then marched towards Ṭā'if, the town which had stoned him and driven him out. The Prophet[sa] besieged the town, but accepting the suggestion of some friends abandoned the siege. Later, the people of Ṭā'if joined Islam voluntarily.

THE PROPHET[sa] DISTRIBUTES BOOTY

After the conquest of Mecca and the victory of Ḥunain, the Prophet[sa] was faced with the task of distributing the money and property paid as ransom or abandoned in the battlefield by the enemy. If custom had been followed, this money and property should have been distributed among the Muslim soldiers who took part in these encounters. But on this occasion, instead of distributing it among the Muslims, the Prophet[sa] distributed it among the Meccans and the people who lived round about Mecca. These people had yet to show an inclination towards the Faith. Many were professed deniers. Those who had declared their faith were yet new to it. They had no idea how self-denying a people could become after they had accepted Islam. But, instead of benefiting by the example of self-denial and self-sacrifice which they saw, instead of reciprocating the good treatment they received from the Muslims, they became more avaricious and greedier than ever. Their demands began to mount. They mobbed the Prophet[sa], and pushed him to a spot under a tree with his mantle having been torn from his shoulders. At last the Prophet[sa] said to the crowd, "I have nothing else to give. If I had, I would have made it over to you. I am no miser, nor am I mean" (*Bukhārī*, Chap on *Faraḍūl Khums*).

Then going near his dromedary and pulling out a hair, he said to the crowd, "Out of this money and property I want nothing at all, not even as much as a hair. Only, I must have a fifth, and that for the State. That is the share which Arab custom has ever admitted as just and right. That fifth will not be spent on me. It will be spent on you and your needs. Remember that one who misappropriates or misuses public money will be humiliated in the sight of God on the Judgement Day."

It has been said by malicious critics that the Prophet[sa] longed to become a king and to have a kingdom. But imagine him confronted by a mean crowd, while he is already a king. If he had longed to become a king and to have a kingdom, would he have treated a beggarly mob as he treated this Meccan mob? Would he have agreed to be mobbed at all in the way he was? Would he have argued and explained? It is only Prophets[as] and Messengers[as] of God who can set such an example. All the booty, the money, and the valuable material that there was to distribute had been distributed among the deserving and the poor. Still there were those who remained unsatisfied, who mobbed the Prophet[sa], protested against the distribution charging the Prophet[sa] with injustice.

One Dhu'l Khuwaiṣira came near the Prophet[sa] and said, "Muḥammad[sa], I am a witness to what you are doing." "And what am I doing? " asked the Prophet[sa].

"You are committing an injustice," said he.

"Woe to you," said the Prophet[sa]. "If I can be unjust, then there is no one on the face of the earth who can be just" (*Muslim, Kitābul Zakāt*).

True believers were full of rage. When this man left the assembly some of them said, "This man deserves death. Will you let us kill him?"

"No," said the Prophet[sa]. "If he observes our laws and commits no visible offence, how can we kill him?"

"But," said the believers, "when a person says and does one thing but believes and desires quite another, would he not deserve to be treated accordingly?"

"I cannot deal with people according to what they have in their hearts. God has not charged me with this. I can deal with them according to what they say and do."

The Prophet[sa] went on to tell the believers that one day this man and others of his kin would stage a rebellion in Islam. The Prophet's[sa] words came true. In the time of 'Alī[ra], the Fourth Khalifah of Islam, this man and his friends led the rebellion against him and became the leaders of a universally condemned division of Islam, the Khawārij.

After dealing with the Hawāzin, the Prophet[sa] returned to Medina. It was another great day for its people. One great day was when the Prophet[sa] arrived at Medina, a refugee from the ill-treatment of the Meccans. On this great day, the Prophet[sa] reentered Medina, full of joy and aware of his determination and promise to make Medina his home.

MACHINATIONS OF ABŪ 'ĀMIR

We must now turn to the activities of one Abū 'Āmir Madanī. He belonged to the Khazraj tribe. Through long association with Jews and Christians he had acquired the habit of silent meditation and of repeating the names of God. Because of this habit, he was generally known as Abū 'Āmir, the Hermit. He was, however, not a Christian by faith. When the Prophet[sa] went to Medina after the Hijra, Abū 'Āmir escaped from Medina to Mecca. When at last Mecca also submitted to the growing influence of Islam, he began to hatch a new intrigue against Islam. He changed his name and his habitual mode of dress and settled down in Qubā, a village near Medina. As he had been away for a long time and had altered his appearance and his dress, the people of Medina did not recognize him. Only those hypocrites recognized him with whom he had relations in secret. He took the hypocrites of Medina into his confidence and with their concurrence planned to go to Syria and excite and provoke the Christian rulers and Christian Arabs into attacking Medina. While he was engaged in his sinister mission in the north, he had planned for the spread of disaffection in Medina. His colleagues, the hypocrites, were to spread rumours that Medina was going to be attacked by Syrian forces. As a result of this dual plot 'Abū 'Āmir hoped that Muslims and Syrian Christians would go to war. If his plot did not succeed, he hoped that Muslims would themselves be provoked into attacking Syria. Even thus a war might start between Muslims and Syrians and Abū 'Āmir would have something to rejoice over. Completing his plans, he went to Syria. While he was away the hypocrites at Medina—according to plan—began to spread rumours that caravans had been sighted which were coming to attack Medina. When no caravan appeared, they issued some kind of explanation.

THE EXPEDITION OF TABŪK

These rumours became so persistent, that the Prophet[sa] thought it worth while to lead in person a Muslim army against Syria. These were difficult times.

Arabia was in the grip of a famine. The harvest in the previous year had been poor and both grain and fruit were in short supply. The time for the new harvest had not yet come. It was the end of September or the beginning of October when the Prophet[sa] set out on this mission. The hypocrites knew that the rumours were their own inventions. They knew also that their design was to provoke Muslims into an attack on the Syrians if the Syrians did not attack Muslims. In either case, a conflict with the great Roman Empire was to result in the destruction of Muslims. The lesson of Mauta was before them. At Mauta Muslims had to face such a huge army that it was with great difficulty that they were able to effect a retreat. The hypocrites were hoping to stage a second Mauta in which the Prophet[sa] himself might lose his life. While the hypocrites were busy spreading rumours about the Syrian attack on Muslims, they also made every effort to strike fear in the minds of Muslims. The Syrians could raise very large armies which Muslims could not hope to stand against. They urged Muslims not to take part in the conflict with Syria. Their plan was, on the one hand, to provoke Muslims into attacking Syria and, on the other, to discourage them from going in large numbers. They wanted Muslims to go to war against Syria and meet with certain defeat. But as soon as the Prophet[sa] announced his intention of leading this new expedition, enthusiasm ran high among Muslims. They went forward with offers of sacrifice for the sake of their faith. Muslims were ill-equipped for a war on such a scale. Their treasury was empty. Only the more prosperous Muslims had means to pay for the war. Individual Muslims vied with one another in the spirit of sacrifice for the sake of their faith. It is said that when the expedition was under way and the Prophet[sa] appealed for funds, 'Uthman[ra] gave away the greater part of his wealth. His contribution is said to have amounted to about one thousand gold dinars, equivalent to about twenty-five thousand rupees. Other Muslims also made contributions according to their capacity. The poor Muslims were also provided with riding animals, swords and lances. Enthusiasm prevailed. There was at Medina at the time a party of Muslims who had migrated from Yemen. They were very poor. Some of them went to the Prophet[sa] and offered their services for this expedition. They said, "O Prophet[sa] of God, take us with you. We want nothing beyond the means of going." The Qur'an makes a reference to these Muslims and their offers in the following words:

> **Nor against those to whom, when they came to thee that thou shouldst mount them, thou didst say, 'I cannot find whereon I can mount you'; they turned back, their eyes overflowing with tears, out of grief that they could not find what they might spend (9: 92).**

That is to say, they are not to blame who did not take part in the war because they were without means and who applied to the Prophet[sa] to provide them with the means of transport to the battlefield. The Prophet[sa] was unable to provide the transport, so they left disappointed feeling they were poor, and were unable to contribute to the war between Muslims and Syrians. Abū Mūsā[ra] was the leader of this group. When asked what they had asked for, he said, "We did not ask for camels or horses. We only said we did not have shoes and could not cover the long journey bare-footed. If we only had shoes, we would have gone on foot and taken part in the war alongside of our Muslim brethren." As this army was going to Syria and Muslims had not yet forgotten what they had suffered at Mauta, every Muslim was full of anxiety with regard to the personal safety of the Prophet[sa]. The women of Medina played their part. They were busy inducing their husbands and sons to join the war. One Companion who had gone out of Medina returned when the Prophet[sa] had already set out with the army. This Companion entered his house and was expecting his wife to greet him with the affection and emotion of a woman who meets her husband after a long time. He found his wife sitting in the courtyard and went forward to embrace and kiss her. But the wife raised her hands and pushed him back. The astonished husband looked at his wife and said, "Is this the treatment for one who comes home after a long time?"

"Are you not ashamed?" said the wife. "The Prophet[sa] of God should go on dangerous expeditions, and you should be making love to your wife? Your first duty is to go to the battle-field. We shall see about the rest." It is said the Companion went out of the house at once, tightened the girths of his mount and galloped after the Prophet[sa]. At a distance of about three days' journey he overtook the Muslim army. The disbelievers and the hypocrites had probably thought that the Prophet[sa] acting upon rumours, invented and spread by them, would spring upon the Syrian armies without a thought. They forgot that the Prophet[sa] was concerned to set an example to generations of followers for all time to come. When the Prophet[sa] neared Syria, he stopped and sent his men in different directions to report on the state of affairs. The men returned and reported there were no Syrian concentrations anywhere. The Prophet[sa] decided to return, but stayed for a few days during which he signed agreements with some of the tribes on the border. There was no war and no fighting. The journey took the Prophet[sa] about two months and a half. When the hypocrites at Medina found that their scheme for inciting war between Muslims and Syrians had failed and that the Prophet[sa] was returning safe and sound, they began to fear that their intrigue had been exposed. They were afraid of the punishment which was now their due. But they did not halt their sinister plans. They equipped a party and posted it on the two sides of a narrow pass some distance from Medina. The pass was so narrow that only a single file could go through it. When the Prophet[sa] and the Muslim army approached the spot, he had a warning by revelation that the enemy was in ambush on both sides of the narrow pass. The Prophet[sa] ordered his Companions to reconnoitre. When they reached the spot they saw men in hiding with the obvious intent to attack. These men, however, fled as soon as they saw this reconnoitring party. The Prophet[sa] decided not to pursue them.

When the Prophet[sa] reached Medina, the hypocrites who had kept out of this battle began to make lame excuses. But the Prophet[sa] accepted them. At the same time he felt that the time had come when their hypocrisy should be exposed. He had a command from God that the mosque at Qubā, which the hypocrites had built in order to be able to hold their meetings in secret, should be demolished. The hypocrites were compelled to say their prayers with other Muslims. No other penalty was proposed.

Returning from Tabūk, the Prophet[sa] found that the people of Ṭā'if also had submitted. After this the other tribes of Arabia applied for admission to Islam. In a short time the whole of Arabia was under the flag of Islam.

THE LAST PILGRIMAGE

In the ninth year of the Hijra the Prophet[sa] went on a pilgrimage to Mecca. On the day of the Pilgrimage, he received the revelation containing the famed verse of the Qur'an which says:

> **This day have I perfected your religion for you and completed My favour upon you and have chosen for you Islam as religion (5:4).**

This verse said in effect that the Message which the Holy Prophet[sa] had brought from God and which by word and deed he had been expounding all these years, had been completed. Every part of this Message was a blessing. The Message now completed embodied the highest blessings which man could receive from God. The Message is epitomized in the name 'al-Islam', which means submission. Submission was to be the religion of Muslims, the religion of mankind. The Holy Prophet[sa] recited this verse in the valley of Muzdalifa, where the pilgrims had assembled. Returning from Muzdalifa, the Prophet[sa] stopped at Minā. It was the eleventh day of the month of Dhu'l-Ḥijja. The Prophet[sa] stood before a large gathering of Muslims and delivered an address, famed in history as the fare-well address of the Prophet[sa]. In the course of this address he said:

> **O men, lend me an attentive ear. For I know not whether I will stand before you again in this valley and address you as I address you now. Your lives and your possessions have been made immune by God to attacks by one another until the Day of Judgement. God has appointed for every one a share in the inheritance. No 'will' shall now be admitted which is prejudicial to the interests of a rightful heir. A child born in any house will be regarded as the child of the father in that house. Whoever contests the parentage of this child will be liable to punishment under the Law of Islam. Anyone who attributes his birth to some one else's father, or falsely claims someone to be his master, God, His angels and the whole of mankind will curse him.**
>
> **O men, you have some rights against your wives, but your wives also have some rights against you. Your right against them is that they should live chaste lives, and not adopt ways which may bring disgrace to the husband in the sight of his people. If your wives do not live up to this, then you have the right to punish them. You can punish them after due inquiry has been made by a competent authority, and your right to punish has been established. Even so, punishment in such a case must not be very severe. But if your wives do no such thing, and their behaviour is not such as would bring disgrace to their husbands, then your duty is to provide for them food and garments and shelter, according to your own standard of living. Remember you must always treat your wives well. God has charged you with the duty of looking after them. Woman is weak and cannot protect her own rights. When you married, God appointed you the trustees of those rights. You brought your wives to your homes under the Law of God. You**

must not, therefore, insult the trust which God has placed in your hands.

O men, you still have in your possession some prisoners of war. I advise you, therefore, to feed them and to clothe them in the same way and style as you feed and clothe yourselves. If they do anything wrong which you are unable to forgive, then pass them on to someone else. They are part of God's creation. To give them pain or trouble can never be right.

O men, what I say to you, you must hear and remember. All Muslims are as brethren to one another. All of you are equal. All men, whatever nation or tribe they may belong to, and whatever station in life they may hold, are equal.

While he was saying this the Prophet[sa] raised his hands and joined the fingers of the one hand with the fingers of the other and then said:

Even as the fingers of the two hands are equal, so are human beings equal to one another. No one has any right, any superiority to claim over another. You are as brothers.

Proceeding the Prophet[sa] said:

Do you know what month this is? What territory we are in? What day of the year it is today?

The Muslims said in reply, they knew it was the sacred month, the sacred land and the day of the Hajj.

Then the Prophet[sa] said:

Even as this month is sacred, this land inviolate, and this day holy, so has God made the lives, property and honour of every man sacred. To take any man's life or his property, or attack his honour, is as unjust and wrong as to violate the sacredness of this day, this month, and this territory. What I command you today is not meant only for today. It is meant for all time. You are expected to remember it and to act upon it until you leave this world and go to the next to meet your Maker.

In conclusion, he said:

What I have said to you, you should communicate to the ends of the earth. Maybe those who have not heard me may benefit by it more than those who have heard (*Siḥāḥ Sitta, Ṭabarī, Hishām* and *Khamīs*).

The Prophet's[sa] address is an epitome of the entire teaching and spirit of Islam. It shows how deep was the Prophet's[sa] concern for the welfare of man and the peace of the world; also how deep was his regard for the rights of women and other weak creatures. The Prophet[sa] knew his end was near. He had had hints from God about his death. Among the cares and anxieties to which he gave expression were his care and anxiety about the treatment women received at the hands of men. He took care that he should not pass away from this world to the next without assuring to women the status which was theirs by right. Since the birth of man, woman had been regarded as the slave and handmaid of man. This was the Prophet's[sa] one care. His other care was for prisoners of war. They were wrongly looked on and treated as slaves and were subjected to cruelties and excesses of all kinds. The Prophet[sa] felt he should not leave this world without assuring to prisoners of war the rights which were theirs in the sight of God. Inequality between man and man also oppressed the Prophet[sa]. Occasionally differences were stressed to a degree which could not be endured. Some men were raised to the skies and others were degraded to the depths. The conditions which made for this inequality were conditions which made for antagonism and war between nation and nation and country and country. The Prophet[sa] thought of these difficulties, also. Unless the spirit of inequality was killed and conditions which induced one people to usurp the rights of another and to attack their lives and their possessions—unless these conditions which become rampant at times of moral decay were removed, the peace and progress of the world could not be assared. He taught that human life and human possessions had the same sacredness which belonged to sacred days, sacred months and sacred places. No man ever showed such concern and such care for the welfare of women, the rights of the weak, and for peace between nations as did the Prophet[sa] of Islam. No man ever did as much as the Prophet[sa] to promote equality among man-kind. No man pined as much as he for the good of man. No wonder, Islam has always upheld the right of women to hold and to inherit property. European nations did not conceive of this right until about one thousand three hundred years after the advent of Islam. Every person who enters Islam becomes the equal of everyone else, no matter how low the society from which he comes. Freedom and equality are characteristic contributions of Islam to the culture of the world. The conceptions which other religions hold of freedom and equality are far behind those which Islam has preached and practised. In a Muslim mosque, a king, a religious leader and a common man have the same status; there is no difference between them. In the places of worship of other religions and other nations these differences exist to this day, although those religions and nations claim to have done more than Islam for freedom and equality.

THE PROPHET[sa] GIVES HINTS OF HIS DEATH

On the way back, the Prophet[sa] again informed his Companions of his approaching death. He said, "O men I am but one like you. I may receive the Call any day and I may have to go. My Kind and Vigilant Master has informed me that a Prophet[sa] lives up to half the years of the Prophet[sa] before him.[1] I think I shall soon receive the Call and I shall depart. O my Companions, I shall have to answer God, and you will have to answer also. What will you then say? "

---

1 This was not meant as a general law. It referred only to the Holy Prophet[sa]. A tradition puts down the age of Jesus at one hundred and twenty or so. As he had already attained to sixty-two or sixty-three, he thought his death must be near.—Ed.

Upon this the Companions said, "We will say that you delivered well the Message of Islam and devoted all your life to the service of the Faith. You had the most perfect passion for the good of man: We will say: Allah, give him the best of rewards."

Then the Prophet[sa] asked, "Do you bear witness that God is One, that Muḥammad[sa] is His Servant and Prophet[sa], that Heaven and Hell are true, that death is certain, that there is life after death, that the Judgement Day must come, and that all the dead will one day be raised from their graves, restored to life and assembled?"

"Yes," said the Companions. "We bear witness to all these truths."

Turning to God, the Prophet[sa] said, "Be Thou also a witness to this—that I have explained Islam to them."

After this Pilgrimage, the Prophet[sa] was very busy teaching and training his followers, trying to raise their moral standard and to reform and refine their conduct. His own death became his frequent theme and he prepared the Muslims for it.

One day, rising for an address to the Faithful, he said, "Today I have had the revelation:

> **When the help of Allah comes, and victory, and thou seest men entering into the religion of Allah in troops, extol thou the glory of thy Lord, with His praise, and seek forgiveness of Him. Verily He is Oft-Returning with compassion " (110: 2-4).**

That is to say, the time was coming when, with the help of God, multitudes were to join the Faith of Islam. It was then to be the duty of the Prophet[sa]—and of his followers—to praise God and pray to Him to remove all obstacles in the way of the establishment of the Faith.

The Prophet[sa] made use of a parable on this occasion: God said to a man, 'If it please you, you may return to Me, or you may work a little longer at reforming the world.' The man said that he preferred to return to his Lord.

Abū Bakr[ra] was among the audience. He had been listening to this last address of the Prophet[sa], with fervour and anxiety the fervour of a great believer and the anxiety of a friend and follower who could see in this address the portents of the Prophet's[sa] death. On hearing the parable Abū Bakr[ra] could contain himself no longer. He broke down. The other Companions, who had taken a surface view of what they had been listening to, were amazed when Abū Bakr[ra] burst into tears. What could be the matter with Abū Bakr[ra]? they asked. The Prophet[sa] was relating the coming victories of Islam, yet he was weeping. 'Umar[ra], particularly, felt annoyed at Abū Bakr[ra]. The Prophet[sa] was giving glad news, yet this old man was crying. But only the Prophet[sa] understood what was happening. Only Abū Bakr[ra], he thought had understood him. Only he had perceived that the verses which promised victories also portended the Prophet's[sa] approaching death.

The Prophet[sa] went on to say, "Abū Bakr[ra] is very dear to me. If it were permissible to love anyone more than others, I would so have loved Abū Bakr[ra]. But that degree of love is only for God. O my people, all the doors which open to the mosque should be closed from today except the door of Abū Bakr[ra]."

There was no doubt that this last instruction implied a prophecy that after the Prophet[sa] Abū Bakr[ra] would be the First Khalifah. To lead the Faithful in prayers he would have to come to the mosque five times a day and, for this, he would have to keep open the door of his house into the mosque. Years afterwards, when 'Umar[ra] was Khalifah, he asked some of those present the meaning of the verse, "When the help of God and victory come." Evidently he remembered the circumstances in which the Prophet[sa] taught Muslims this and the verses which follow. He must have remembered also that then only Abū Bakr[ra] understood the meaning of these verses. 'Umar[ra] was trying to test Muslims for their knowledge of these verses. They had failed to understand them at the time of their revelation: did they know the meaning now? Ibni 'Abbāsra, who must have been ten or eleven years of age at the time of their revelation and who was now seventeen or eighteen, volunteered to answer. He said, "Leader of the Faithful, these verses contained a prophecy about the death of the Holy Prophetsa. When a Prophet'ssa work is done, he wishes no longer to live in the world. The verses spoke of the imminent victory of Islam. This victory had a sad side and that was the impending departure of the Prophetsa from this world." 'Umarra complimented Ibn 'Abbāsra and said that when the verses were revealed only Abū Bakrra understood their meaning.

LAST DAYS OF THE PROPHETsa

At last the day drew near which every human being must face. The Prophet'ssa work was done. All that God had to reveal to him for the benefit of man had been revealed. The spirit of Muḥammadsa had infused new life into his people. A new nation had arisen, a new outlook on life and new institutions; in short, a new heaven and a new earth. The foundations of a new order had been laid. The land had been ploughed and watered and the seed scattered for a new harvest. And now the harvest itself had begun to show. It was not, however, for him to reap it. It was for him only to plough, to sow and to water. He came as a labourer, remained a labourer and was now due to depart as a labourer. He found his reward not in the things of this world but in the pleasure and the approval of his God, his Maker and Master. When the time came for reaping the harvest, he preferred to go to Him, leaving others to reap.

The Holy Prophetsa fell ill. For some days he continued to visit the mosque and lead the prayers. Then he became too weak to do this. The Companionsra were so used to his daily company that they could hardly believe he would die. But he had been telling them of his death again and again. One day, touching upon this very theme, he said, "If a man make a mistake, it is better he should make amends for it in this very world so that he should have no regrets in the next. Therefore I say, if I have done any wrong to any of you, it may be only unwittingly, let him come forward and ask me to make amends. If even unknowingly I have injured any one of you, let him come forward and take his revenge. I do not wish to be put to shame when I face my God in the next world. The Companions[ra] were moved. Tears sprang to their eyes. What pains had he not taken and what sufferings had he not endured for their sake? He put up with hunger and thirst in order that others might have enough to eat and to drink. He mended his own clothes and cobbled his own shoes in order that others might dress well. And yet here he was, eager to right even fancied wrongs he might have done to others; so much did he respect the rights of others.

All the Companions received the Prophet's[sa] offer in solemn silence. But one came forward and said, "O Prophet[sa] of God, I once received an injury from you. We were lining up for battle when you passed by our line and while passing you dug your elbow in my side. It was all done unwittingly, but you said we could avenge even unintentional wrongs. I want to avenge this wrong." The Companions, who had received the Prophet's[sa] offer in solemn silence, were full of wrath. They became enraged at the insolence and stupidity of this man who had failed completely to understand the spirit of the Prophet's[sa] offer and the solemnity of the occasion. But the Companion seemed adamant—determined to take the Prophet[sa] at his word.

The Prophet[sa] said, "You are welcome to take your revenge."

He turned his back to him and said, "Come and hit me as I hit you."

"But," explained this Companion, "when you hit me my side was bare, because I was wearing no shirt at the time."

"Raise my shirt," said the Prophet[sa], "and let him hit my side with his elbow." They did so but, instead of hitting the bare side of the Prophet[sa], this Companion bent forward with bedewed eyes and kissed the Prophet's[sa] bare body.

"What is this?" asked the Prophet[sa].

"Didn't you say that your days with us were numbered? How many more occasions can we then have of touching you, in the flesh and expressing our love and affection for you? True, you did hit me with your elbow, but who could think of avenging it. I had this idea here and now. You offered to let us take revenge. I said to myself—let me kiss you under cover of revenge."

The Companions full of wrath until then began to wish the thought had occurred to them.

THE PROPHET[sa] PASSES AWAY

But the Prophet[sa] was ill and the ailment seemed to advance. Death seemed to draw nearer and nearer, and depression and gloom descended over the hearts of the Companions. The sun shone over Medina as brightly as ever, but to the Companions it seemed paler and paler. The day dawned as before but it seemed to bring darkness, not light. At last came the time when the soul of the Prophet[sa] was to depart from its physical frame and meet its Maker. His breathing became more and more difficult. The Prophet[sa], who was spending his last days in 'Ā'isha[ra]'s chamber, said to her, "Raise my head a little and bring it near to your side. I cannot breathe well." 'Ā'isha[ra] did so. She sat up and held his head. The death-pangs were visible. Greatly agitated, the Prophet[sa] looked now to this side and now to that. Again and again he said, "Woe to the Jews and the Christians. They encouraged the worship of the graves of their Prophets." This, we might say, was his dying message for his followers. While he lay on his death-bed, he seemed to say to his followers, "You will learn to hold me above all other Prophets[as], and more successful than any of them. But take care, do not turn my grave into an object of worship. Let my grave remain only a grave. Others may worship the graves of their Prophets[as] and turn them into centres of pilgrimage, places where they may repair and perform austerities, make their offerings, and do their thanksgiving. Others may do this, but not you. You must remember your one and only objective—that is, the worship of the One and Only God."

After he had thus warned Muslims about their duty to guard the hard-won idea of One God and the distinction between God and Man, his eyelids began to droop. His eyes began to close. All he then said was, "To my Friend the Highest of the High—to my Friend the Highest of the High," meaning evidently that he was heading towards God. As he said this he gave up the ghost.

The news reached the mosque. There many Companions[ra] had assembled, having given up their private tasks. They were expecting to hear better news but instead heard of the Prophet's[sa] death. It came like a bolt from the blue. Abū Bakr[ra] was out. 'Umar[ra] was in the mosque, but he was utterly stupefied with grief. It angered him if he heard anyone say the Prophet[sa] was dead. He even drew his sword and threatened to kill those who should say the Prophet[sa] had died. There was much the Prophet[sa] had yet to do, so the Prophet[sa] could not die. True, his soul had departed from his body, but it had gone only to meet its Maker. Just as Moses[as] had gone for a time to meet his Maker only to return, the Prophet[sa] must return to do what had been left undone. There were the hypocrites, for instance, with whom they had yet to deal. 'Umar[ra] walked about sword in hand almost as a mad man. As he walked he said: "Whosoever says the Prophet[sa] has died will himself die at 'Umar[ra]'s hands." The Companions felt braced and they half-believed what 'Umar[ra] said. The Prophet[sa] could not die. There must have been a mistake. In the meantime some Companions went in search of Abū Bakr[ra], found him and told him what had happened. Abū Bakr[ra] made straight for the mosque at Medina and speaking not a word to anyone, entered 'Ā'isha's[ra] room and asked her, "Has the Prophet[sa] died?"

"Yes," replied 'Ā'isha[ra]. Then he went straight to where the Prophet's[sa] body was lying, uncovered the face, bent down and kissed the forehead. Tears laden with love and grief fell from his eyes and he said, "God is our witness. Death will not come upon you twice over."

It was a sentence full of meaning. It was Abū Bakr[ra]'s reply to what 'Umar[ra] had been saying out of his mad grief. The Prophet[sa] had died once. That was his physical death—the death everyone must die. But he was not to have a second death. There was to be no spiritual death—no death to the beliefs which he had established in his followers and for the establishment of which he had taken such pains. One of those beliefs—one of the more important beliefs—he had taught was that even Prophets[as] were human and even they must die. Muslims were not going to forget this so soon after the Prophet[sa]'s own death. Having said this great sentence over the dead body of the Prophet[sa], Abū Bakr[ra] came out and, piercing through the lines of the Faithful, advanced silently to the pulpit. As he stood, 'Umar[ra] stood by him, his sword drawn as before, determined that if Abū Bakr[ra] said the Prophet[sa] had died Abū Bakr[ra] must lose his head. As Abū Bakr[ra] started to speak, 'Umar[ra] pulled at his shirt, wanting to stop him from speaking but Abū Bakr[ra] snatched back his shirt and refused to stop.

He then recited the verse of the Qur'an:

And Muḥammad[sa] is only a Messenger. Verily, all Messengers have passed away before him. If then he die or be slain, will you turn back on your heels? (3: 145).

That is to say, Muḥammad[sa] was a man with a Message from God. There had been other men with Messages from God, and all of them had died. If Muḥammad[sa] should die, would they turn back upon everything which they had been taught and which they had learnt? This verse was revealed at the time of Uḥud. Rumour had then gone round that the Prophet[sa] had been killed by the enemy. Many Muslims lost heart and withdrew from the battle. The verse came from heaven to brace them. It had the same effect on this occasion. Having recited the verse, Abū Bakr[ra] added to it a word of his own. He said, "Those amongst you who worship God, let them know that God is still alive, and will ever remain alive. But those amongst you who worshipped Muḥammad[sa], let them know it from me that Muḥammad[sa] is dead." The Companions recovered their balance on hearing this timely speech. 'Umar[ra] himself was changed when he heard Abū Bakr[ra] recite the verse quoted above. He began to return to his senses, and to recover his lost judgement. By the time Abū Bakr[ra] had finished the recitation of the verse 'Umar's[ra] spiritual eye was fully opened. He understood that the Prophet[sa] had really died. But no sooner had he realized it, than his legs began to tremble and give way. He fell down exhausted. The man who wanted to terrorize Abū Bakr[ra] with his bare sword had been converted by Abū Bakr's[ra] speech. The Companions felt the verse had been revealed for the first time on that day, so strong and so new was its appeal. In a paroxysm of grief, they forgot that the verse was in the Qur'an.

Many expressed the grief which overtook Muslims on the death of the Prophet[sa], but the pithy and profound expression which Ḥassān[ra], the poet of early Islam, gave to it in his couplet remains to this day the best and the most enduring. He said: 'Thou wast the pupil of my eye. Now that thou hast died my eye hath become blind. I care not who dies now. For I feared only thy death.'

This couplet voiced the feeling of every Muslim. For months in the streets of Medina men, women and children went about reciting this couplet of Ḥassān bin Thābit[ra].

THE PROPHET'S[sa] PERSONALITY AND CHARACTER

HAVING briefly described the outstanding events in the life of the Holy Prophet[sa] we would now attempt a short sketch of his character. In this connection we have available the collective testimony of his own people which they bore to his character before he claimed to be a Prophet[sa]. At that stage he was known among his people as "The Trusty" and "The True" (*Hishām*). There are living at all times large numbers of people against whom no charge of dishonesty is preferred. There are also large numbers who are never exposed to a severe trial or temptation and in the ordinary affairs and concerns of life they behave with honesty and integrity, yet they are not regarded as worthy of any special distinction on that account. Special distinctions are conferred only when the life of a person illustrates in a conspicuous degree some high moral quality. Every soldier that goes into battle puts his life in jeopardy but not every such British soldier has been regarded as worthy of the award of the Victoria Cross, nor every such German soldier of the Iron Cross. There are hundreds of thousands of people in France who occupy themselves with intellectual pursuits but not every one of them is decorated with the Legion of Honour. The mere fact, therefore, that a man is trustworthy and true does not indicate that he possesses eminence in these respects, but when a whole people combines to confer upon an individual the titles of "The Trusty" and "The True", that is evidence of the possession of exceptional qualities. Had it been the practice of the people of Mecca to confer such a distinction upon some individual in each generation, even then the recipient would have been looked upon as occupying a high position. But the history of Mecca and of Arabia furnishes no indication that it was customary for the Arabs to confer these or similar titles upon eminent individuals in each generation. On the contrary, through centuries of Arab history we find that it was only in the case of the Holy Prophet[sa] of Islam that his people conferred the titles of "The Trusty" and "The True". This is proof of the fact that the Holy Prophet[sa] possessed these qualities in so eminent a degree that within the knowledge and the memory of his people no other individual could be regarded as his equal in these respects. The Arabs were well known for their keenness of mind and what they chose to regard as rare must in truth have been rare and unique.

When the Holy Prophet[sa] was summoned by, God to assume the burden and responsibilities of prophethood, his wife, Khadīja[ra], testified to his high moral qualities—an incident which has been related in the biographical portion of this General Introduction. We shall now proceed to illustrate some of his high moral qualities so that the reader may be able to appreciate even those aspects of his character which are not generally well known.

THE PROPHET'S[sa] PURITY OF MIND AND CLEANLINESS OF BODY

It is related of the Holy Prophet[sa] that his speech was always pure and that he was (unlike most of his contemporaries) not given to the use of oaths (*Tirmidhī*). This was something exceptional for an Arab. We do not imply that the Arabs at the time of the Holy Prophet[sa] habitually indulged in foul language, but there is no doubt that they were in the habit of punctuating their speech with a generous measure of oaths, a habit that persists among them even to this day. The Holy Prophet[sa], however, held the name of God in such reverence that he never uttered it without full justification.

He was very particular, even punctilious, with regard to physical cleanliness. He used to brush his teeth several times a day and was so keen on the practice that he used to say that were he not afraid that the ordinance might prove onerous, he would make it obligatory upon every Muslim to brush his teeth before every one of the five daily prayers. He always washed his hands before and after each meal and, after eating anything that had been cooked, he always rinsed his mouth and considered it desirable that every person who had eaten anything cooked should rinse his mouth before joining in any of the prayers (*Bukhārī*).

In the polity of Islam a mosque is the only place of gathering prescribed for the Muslims. The Holy Prophet[sa], therefore, laid particular stress upon the cleanliness of mosques, especially on occasions when people were expected to collect in them. He had directed that on such occasions incense should be burnt in the mosques to purify the air (*Abū Dāwūd*). He also gave directions that nobody should go to a mosque on the occasion of a congregation or gathering after eating anything that was likely to exhale an offensive odour (*Bukhārī*).

He insisted upon streets being kept clean and clear of twigs, stones, and all articles or matter which was likely either to obstruct or to prove offensive. Whenever he himself found any such matter or article lying in a street he would remove it, and he used to say that a person who helps to keep streets and roads clean and clear, earns spiritual merit in the sight of God. He is also reported to have enjoined that public thoroughfares should not be so used as to cause obstruction nor should any unclean or undesirable matter or article be thrown on to a public street, nor should a street be defiled in any other way, as all such acts are displeasing to God. He was very keen that all supply of water conserved for human use should be kept clean and pure. For instance, he prohibited anything being thrown into standing water which might befoul it and any reservoir of water being used in a manner which would render it impure (*Bukhārī* and *Muslim, Kitāb al-Birr Waṣṣila*).

THE PROPHET'S[sa] SIMPLE LIFE

The Prophet[sa] was extremely simple in the matter of food and drink. He never expressed displeasure with ill-prepared or ill-cooked food. If he could eat such food he would do so to save the person who had prepared it from disappointment. If, however, a dish was uneatable, he merely refrained from partaking of it and never expressed his disapproval of it. When he sat down to a meal he paid attention to the food placed before him and used to say that he did not like an attitude of indifference towards food as if the person eating was above paying attention to mere matters of food and drink. When any eatable was presented to him he always shared it with those present. On one occasion somebody presented him with some dates. He looked round and after making an estimate of the number of people present divided the dates equally among them, each of them receiving seven. Abū Hurairā[ra] relates that the Holy Prophet[sa] never ate his fill even of barley bread (*Bukhārī*).

On one occasion while he was passing along a road he noticed some people gathered round a roast kid ready to enjoy the feast. When they saw the Holy Prophet[sa] they invited him to join them, but he declined. This was not due to his not having a liking for roast meat but to the fact that he did not approve of people indulging in a feast in the open where they could be observed by poor people who had themselves not enough to eat. It is related of him that on other occasions he did partake of roast meat. 'Ā'isha[ra] has related that the Holy Prophet[sa] did not, till the day of his death, on any occasion, eat his fill on three consecutive days. He was very particular that a person should not go to a meal in another person's house uninvited. On one occasion somebody invited him to a meal and requested that he might bring four other persons with him. When he arrived at the house of his host he found that a sixth person had also joined his party. The host came to the door to receive him and his party and the Holy Prophet[sa] drew his attention to the fact that there were now six of them and that it was for the host to decide whether he would permit the sixth person to join them in the meal or whether the latter should depart. The host, of course, readily invited the sixth person also (*Bukhārī, Kitāb al-Aṭ'ima*).

Whenever the Holy Prophet[sa] sat down to a meal he always began to eat by invoking the name and blessings of Allah, and as soon as he concluded he rendered thanks in these words: "All praise is due to Allah, Who has given us to eat: Praise, abundant and sincere and ever-increasing: Praise, which does not leave an impression upon one's mind that one has rendered enough praise but which creates in one's mind the feeling that enough has not been said and the praise which ought never to be terminated and which makes one think that every divine act is worthy of praise and should be praised. Oh Allah! do Thou fill our hearts with these sentiments." Sometimes he used these words: "All praise is due to God Who has satisfied our hunger and thirst. May our hearts ever yearn after His praise and never be ungrateful to Him." He always admonished his Companions to stop before they had eaten their fill and used to say that one man's food should always suffice for two. Whenever any special food was prepared in his house he used to suggest that a portion of it should be sent as a present to his neighbours; and presents of food and other articles used constantly to be sent from his house to his neighbours' houses (*Muslim* and *Bukhārī, Kitāb al-Adab*).

He always tried to ascertain from the faces of those who were in his company whether any of them was in need of sustenance. Abū Huraira[ra] relates the following incident: On one occasion he had been without food for over three days. He stood at the entrance to the mosque and observed Abū Bakr[ra] passing near. He asked Abū Bakr[ra] the meaning of a verse of the Qur'an which enjoins the feeding of the poor. Abū Bakr[ra] explained its meaning and passed on. Abū Huraira[ra] when relating this incident used to say with indignation that he too understood the Qur'an as well as Abū Bakr[ra] did. His object in asking the latter to explain the meaning of the verse had been that Abū Bakr[ra] might guess that he was hungry and might arrange to get food for him. Shortly after, 'Umar[ra] passed by and Abū Huraira[ra] asked him also to explain the meaning of the verse. 'Umar[ra] also explained its meaning and passed on. Abū Huraira[ra], like all Companions of the Holy Prophet[sa], was loath to make a direct request and when he perceived that his indirect attempts to draw attention to his condition had failed, he began to feel very faint. Thereupon he heard his name being called in a very soft and tender voice. Looking to the side from which the voice came he saw that the Holy Prophet[sa] was looking out from the window of his house and was smiling. He inquired of Abū Huraira[ra]: "Are you hungry?" to which Abū Huraira[ra] replied: "Verily, O Messenger of Allah[sa]! I am hungry."

The Holy Prophet[sa] said: "There is no food in our house either, but somebody has just sent us a cup of milk. Go to the mosque and see whether there are any other persons there who may be hungry like you." Abū Huraira[ra] goes on to relate: "I thought to myself, I am hungry enough to consume the whole of the milk in the cup, yet the Prophet[sa] has asked me to invite any other persons that may be in a similar situation, which means that I shall get very little of the milk. But I had to carry out the Prophet's[sa] orders, so I went into the mosque and found six persons sitting there whom I brought with me to the Prophet's[sa] door. He gave the cup of milk into the hands of one of them and asked him to drink. When he had finished and put away the cup from his mouth the Prophet[sa] insisted upon his drinking a second time and a third time till he had had his fill. In the same way he insisted upon every one of the six drinking his fill of the milk. Each time he asked anyone to drink I was afraid that little would be left for me. After all the six had drunk of the milk the Prophet[sa] gave the cup to me and I saw that there was still plenty of milk in it. In my case also he insisted that I should drink my fill and made me drink a second and a third time and at the end he drank what was left in the cup himself and rendered thanks to God and shut the door" (*Bukhārī, Kitābul Riqāq*). The Holy Prophet's[sa] object in offering the milk to Abū Huraira[ra] last of all may have been to indicate to him that he should have continued to endure the pangs of hunger, trusting in God, and should not have drawn attention to his condition even indirectly.

He always ate and drank with his right hand and always stopped three times to take breath in the middle of a drink. One reason for this may be that if a person who is thirsty drinks water at one stretch he is apt to drink too much and thus upset his digestion. In the matter of eating the rule that he followed was that he partook of all things that are pure and permissible but not in a manner which would savour of indulgence or would deprive other people of their due share. As has been stated, his normal food was always very simple but if anybody presented him with something specially prepared he did not decline it. He did not, however, hanker after good food, though he had a particular liking for honey and for dates. As regards dates, he used to say that there was a special relationship between a Muslim and the date tree whose leaves and bark and fruit, both ripe and unripe, and even the stones of whose fruit could all be put to some use or the other and no part of which was without its proper use. The same was the case with a true Muslim. No act of his was without its beneficence and all that he did promoted the welfare of mankind (*Bukhārī* and *Muslim*).

The Holy Prophet[sa] preferred simplicity in dress. His own dress normally consisted of a shirt and an *izār*[1] or a shirt and a pair of trousers. He always wore his *izār* or his trousers so that the garment covered his body up to

---

[1] A piece of cloth wrapped round the waist and hanging to the ankles—Ed.

a point above his ankles. He did not approve of the knee or any portion of the body above the knee being exposed without extreme necessity. He did not approve of the use, whether as part of dress or in the way of curtains, etc., of cloth which had figures embroidered or painted on it, especially if the figures were large and might be interpreted as representing gods or goddesses or other objects of worship. On one occasion he found a curtain hanging in his house bearing large figures and he directed it to be removed. He, however, saw no harm in the use of cloth bearing small figures which could not be so interpreted. He never wore silk himself and did not consider it permissible for Muslim men to wear it. For the purpose of authenticating the letters that he wrote to certain sovereigns inviting them to accept Islam he caused to be prepared a signet-ring, but directed that it should be made of silver and not of gold, for he said that the wearing of gold had been prohibited to Muslim men (*Bukhārī* and *Muslim*). Muslim women are permitted to wear silk and gold but in their case also the Holy Prophet's[sa] direction was that excess should be avoided. On one occasion he called for subscriptions for the relief of the poor and a lady took off one of her bracelets and placed it before him as her contribution. Addressing her, he said: "Does not your other hand deserve to be saved from the Fire?" The lady thereupon removed her bracelet from the other hand also and offered it for the purpose that he had in view. None of his wives possessed ornaments of any considerable value and other Muslim women also very seldom possessed any ornaments. In accordance with the teachings of the Qur'an he deprecated the hoarding of money or bullion, as he held that this was harmful to the interests of the poorer sections of the community and resulted in upsetting the economy of a community and was thus a sin.

'Umar[ra] suggested to the Holy Prophet[sa] on one occasion that as he had to receive Embassies from great monarchs, he should have a rich cloak prepared for himself which he could wear on such ceremonial occasions. The Prophetsa did not approve of the suggestion and said: "It would not be pleasing to God for me to adopt ways like this. I shall meet everybody in the clothes that I normally wear." On one occasion silk garments were presented to him and of these he sent one to 'Umarra. Upon this 'Umarra said, "How can I wear it when you have yourself disapproved of wearing silk garments." The Holy Prophetsa observed: "Every present is not meant for personal use." His meaning was that since the garment was of silk 'Umarra should have presented it to his wife or to his daughter or should have put it to some other use (*Bukhārī, Kitābul Libās*).

The Prophet'ssa bed was also very simple. He never used a bedstead or a couch but always slept on the ground, the bedding consisting of a piece of leather or of a piece of camelhair cloth. 'Ā'ishara relates: "Our bedding was so small that when the Holy Prophetsa used to get up at night for prayers I used to lie on one side of the bedding and stretched out my legs while he was in the standing posture and folded them back when he had to prostrate himself (*Muslim, Tirmidhī* and *Bukhārī*).

He adopted the same simplicity with regard to his residential arrangements. His house consisted normally of one room and a small courtyard. A rope used to be strung half way across the room so that when he had visitors a piece of cloth could be hung from the rope to convert a part of the room into an audience chamber separated from the portion occupied by his wife. His life was so simple that 'Ā'ishara related that during the lifetime of the Prophetsa they often had to sustain themselves on dates and water and that on the day of his death there was no food in the house except a few dates (*Bukhārī*).

RELATIONSHIP WITH GOD

Every aspect of the Holy Prophet's[sa] life appears to have been governed and coloured by his love for and devotion to God.

In spite of the very heavy responsibilities that had been laid upon his shoulders the greater portion of his time during the day as well as during the night was spent in the worship and praise of God. He would leave his bed at midnight and devote himself to the worship of God till it was time to go to the mosque for the morning prayers. He sometimes stood so long in prayer during the latter part of the night that his feet would get swollen, and those who saw him in that condition were always much affected. On one occasion 'Ā'isha[ra] said to him: "God has honoured you with His love and nearness. Why then do you subject yourself to so much discomfort and inconvenience?" He replied: "If God has by His Grace and Mercy conferred His love and nearness upon me, is it not my duty in return to be always rendering thanks to Him? Gratitude should increase in proportion to the favours received" (*Bukhārī, Kitābul Kusūf*).

He never entered upon any undertaking without divine command or permission. It has already been related in the biographical portion that, in spite of the very severe persecution to which he was subjected by the people of Mecca, he did not leave the town till he received the divine command to do so. When persecution became very severe and he gave permission to his Companions to migrate to Abyssinia, some of them expressed a desire that he should accompany them. He declined to do so on the ground that he had not received divine permission to that effect. Thus, during a period of hardships and persecution when people usually like to keep their friends and relations close to themselves, he directed his Companions to seek refuge in Abyssinia and himself stayed behind in Mecca, for God had not yet directed him to leave it.

Whenever he heard the word of God being recited, he was overcome by emotion and tears would start from his eyes, especially if he was listening to verses which emphasized his own responsibilities. 'Abdullāh bin Mas'ūd[ra] relates that he was on one occasion asked by the Holy Prophet[sa] to recite some verses of the Qur'an to him. He said: "O Messenger of Allah[sa]! The Qur'an has been revealed to you (i.e., you know it best of all). How then shall I recite it to you?" But the Holy Prophet[sa] said: "I love to hear it recited by other people also."

Thereupon 'Abdullāh bin Mas'ūd[ra] began to recite from Sūrah Al-Nisā'. When he recited the verse: "And how will it fare with them when We shall bring a witness from every people, and shall bring thee as a witness against them" (4: 42), the Holy Prophet[sa] exclaimed: 'Enough! Enough!" 'Abdullāh bin Mas'ūd[ra] looked up and saw that tears were streaming from the Holy Prophet's[sa] eyes (*Bukhārī, Kitāb Faḍā'ilul Qur'an*).

He was so particular about joining the congregational prayers that, even during severe illness when it is permissible not only to say one's prayers in one's room but even to say them lying in bed, he would go to the mosque to lead the prayers himself. On one occasion when he was unable to proceed to the mosque he directed that Abū Bakr[ra] should lead the prayers. Presently however, he felt some improvement in his condition and asked to be supported into the mosque. He rested his weight on the shoulders of two men but was in so feeble a condition that, according to 'Ā'isha[ra], his feet trailed along the ground (*Bukhārī*).

It is a common practice to give expression to one's pleasure or to draw attention to any particular matter by the clapping of hands and the Arabs used to follow the same practice. The Holy Prophet[sa], however, so loved the remembrance of God that for these purposes also he substituted the praise and remembrance of God in place of the clapping of hands. On one occasion while he was occupied with some important matter, the time of the next service drew near and he directed that Abū Bakr[ra] should lead the prayers. Shortly thereafter he was able to conclude the business upon which he was engaged and proceeded at once to the mosque. Abū Bakr[ra] was leading the prayers but when the congregation perceived that the Holy Prophet[sa] had arrived, they began to clap their hands for the purpose both of giving expression to their joy at his arrival and also to draw Abū Bakr[ra]'s attention to the fact that the Prophet[sa] himself had arrived. Thereupon Abū Bakr[ra] stepped back and made room for the Holy Prophet[sa] to lead the prayers. When the prayers were over, the Prophet[sa] addressed Abū Bakr[ra] and said: "Why did you step back after I had directed you to lead the prayers?" Abū Bakr[ra] replied: "O Messenger of Allah[sa]! How would it befit the son of Abū Quḥāfa[ra] to lead the prayers in the presence of the Messenger of Allah[sa]?" Then addressing the congregation the Prophet[sa] said: "Why did you clap your hands? It is not seemly that while you are engaged in the remembrance of God you should clap your hands. If it should so happen that during the course of prayers attention has to be drawn to some matter, instead of clapping your hands you should utter the name of God aloud. This would draw attention to whatever may have to be taken note of " (*Bukhārī*).

The Prophet[sa] did not approve of prayers or worship being carried on as a penance or imposition. On one occasion he came home and observed a rope dangling between two pillars. He inquired what its purpose was, and was informed that his wife Zainab[ra] was in the habit of supporting herself by means of the rope when she became tired in the course of her prayers. He directed the rope to be removed and said that prayers should be continued only so long as one felt easy and cheerful and that if a person became tired he should sit down. Prayers were not an imposition, and if carried on after the body became fatigued they failed of their purpose (*Bukhārī, Kitābul Kusūf*).

He abhorred every action and practice which savoured even remotely of idolatry. When his end was approaching and he was in the grip of the death agony he turned from side to side exclaiming: "May the curse of God descend upon those Jews and Christians who have converted the graves of their Prophets into places of worship" (*Bukhārī*). He had in mind those Jews and Christians who prostrated themselves at the graves of their Prophets and saints and addressed their prayers to them, and he meant that if Muslims fell into similar practices they would not be deserving of his prayers but would, on the contrary, cut themselves asunder from him.

His extreme sense of jealousy for the honour of God has already been referred to in the biographical portion. The people of Mecca sought to place all sorts of temptations in his way to persuade him to give up his opposition to idol-worship (*Ṭabarī*). His uncle Abū Ṭālib also tried to dissuade him and expressed his fear that if he persisted in his denunciation of idol-worship, Abū Ṭālib would have to choose between ceasing to give him his protection and the bitter opposition of his people. The only reply that the Prophet[sa] made to his uncle on that occasion was: "If these people were to place the sun on my right hand and the moon on my left, I would not desist from proclaiming and preaching the Unity of God" (*Zurqānī*). Again, during the Battle of Uḥud when a remnant of wounded Muslims were grouped round him at the foot of a hill and their enemies were giving vent to their feeling of jubilation at having broken the Muslim ranks in shouts of victory and their leader Abū Sufyān[ra] called out: "May Hubal (one of the idols worshipped by the Meccans) be exalted! May Hubal be exalted!" the Holy Prophet[sa], in spite of realizing that his own safety and that of the small band of Muslims who were gathered round him lay in keeping silent could restrain himself no longer and directed his Companions to shout in reply, "To Allah alone belongs victory and glory! To Allah alone belongs victory and glory!" (*Bukhārī*).

It was a common misconception among the followers of different religions before the advent of Islam that heavenly and terrestrial manifestations took place to mark occasions of joy and sorrow for Prophets, saints and other great men and that even the movements of the heavenly bodies could be controlled by them. For instance, it is related of some of them that they caused the sun to become stationary in its course or stopped the progress of the moon or caused running water to become still. Islam taught that such notions were baseless and that references to phenomena of this kind in religious Scriptures were only by way of metaphor which, instead of being interpreted in accordance with its correct significance, had given rise to superstitions. Nevertheless, some among Muslims were prone to attribute these phenomena to events in the lives of the great Prophets[as]. In the closing years of the Holy Prophet's[sa] life his son Ibrāhim died at the age of two and a half years. An eclipse of the sun occurred on the same day. Some Muslims in Medina gave currency to the idea that the sun had been darkened on the occasion of the death of the Prophet's[sa] son as a mark of divine condolence. When this was mentioned to the Holy Prophet[sa] he expressed great displeasure and severely condemned the notion. He explained that the sun and the moon and other heavenly bodies were all governed by divine laws and that their movements and the phenomena connected with them had no relation to the life or death of any person (*Bukhārī*).

Arabia is a very dry country and rain is always welcome and is eagerly waited for. The Arabs used to imagine that the coming of rain was controlled by the movements of stars. Whenever anybody gave expression to that idea, the Holy Prophet[sa] used to be very upset and admonished his people not to attribute favours bestowed upon them by Providence to other sources. He explained that rain and other natural phenomena were all governed by divine laws and that they were not controlled by the pleasure or displeasure of any god or goddess or of any other power (*Muslim, Kitābul Īmān*).

He had perfect trust in God which no combination of adverse circumstances could shake. On one occasion an enemy of his, finding him asleep and unguarded, stood over his head with drawn sword and threatened to despatch him at once. Before doing so he asked: "Who can rescue you from this predicament?" The Holy Prophet[sa] calmly replied: "Allah." He uttered this word with such perfect assurance that even the heart of his disbelieving enemy was forced to acknowledge the loftiness of his faith and trust in God. The sword fell from his hand, and he, who a moment before was bent upon his destruction, stood before him like a convicted criminal awaiting sentence (*Muslim, Kitābul Faḍā'il* and *Bukhārī, Kitābul Jihād*).

At the other end of the scale was his sense of perfect humility vis-a-vis the Divine. Abū Hurairā[ra] relates: "One day I heard the Holy Prophet[sa] say that no man would attain salvation through his own good deeds. Thereupon I said: 'O Messenger of Allah[sa]! 'Surely you will enter Paradise through your own good actions,' to which he replied: 'No, I too cannot enter Paradise through my own actions save only that God's Grace and Mercy should envelop me' " (*Bukhārī, Kitābur Riqāq*).

He always exhorted people to choose and follow the right path and to be diligent in their search for means whereby they could attain nearness to God. He taught that no man should desire death for himself, for if he is good he will, by living longer, be able to achieve greater good; and if he is evil, he may, if given time, be able to repent of his evil ways and start on a good way. His love for, and devotion to, God found expression in many ways. For instance, whenever after a dry season the first rain-drops began to descend, he would put out his tongue to catch a rain-drop and would exclaim: "Here is the latest favour from my Lord." He was constantly occupied in praying for God's forgiveness and beneficence, more particularly when he was sitting among people so that those who were in his company or were connected with him and Muslims generally should save themselves from divine wrath and should become deserving of divine forgiveness. The consciousness that he was always in the presence of God never deserted him. When he used to lie down to sleep, he would say: "O Allah! let me die (go to sleep) with Thy name on my lips and with Thy name on my lips let me rise." When he woke up, he would say: "All praise is due to God who has brought me to life after death (sleep) and one day we shall all be gathered unto Him" (*Bukhārī*).

He constantly yearned for nearness to God and one of his oft-repeated prayers was "O Allah! Do Thou fill my heart with Thy light and fill my eyes with Thy light and fill my ears with Thy light and put Thy light on my right and put Thy light on my left and put Thy light above me and put Thy light below me and put Thy light in front of me and put Thy light behind me and do Thou, O Allah, convert the whole of me into light" (*Bukhārī*).

Ibn 'Abbās[ra] relates: "Shortly before the Holy Prophet's[sa] death, Musailima (the false prophet) came to Medina and proclaimed that if Muḥammad[sa] would appoint him his successor he would be prepared to accept him. Musailima was accompanied by a very large retinue and the tribe with which he was connected was the largest among the tribes of Arabia. When the Holy Prophet[sa] was informed of his advent he went to meet him, accompanied by Thābit bin Qais bin Shams[ra]. He had in his hand a dried palm twig. When he arrived at Musailima's camp he went and stood in front of him. In the meantime some more of his Companions had come up and ranged themselves round him. Addressing Musailima he said, "It has been conveyed to me that you have said that if I were to appoint you my successor you would be ready to follow me, but I am not willing to bestow even this dried palm twig upon you contrary to God's commands. Your end will be as God has appointed. If you turn your back on me God will bring you to naught. I perceive very clearly that God will deal out to you what He has revealed to me." He then added: "I will now retire. If you have anything further to say, you may talk to Thābit bin Qais bin Shams[ra], who will act as my representative." He then returned. Abū Hurairā[ra] was also with him. Somebody inquired of the Prophet[sa] what he meant by saying that God would deal out to Musailima what had been revealed to him. The Holy Prophet[sa] replied: "I saw in a dream two bracelets round my wrists which I disliked. While still in my dream I was directed by God to blow upon the bracelets. When I blew upon them, both of them disappeared. I interpreted this to mean that two false claimants (to prophethood) would appear after me" (*Bukhārī, Kitābul Maghāzī*). This incident occurred towards the end of the Holy Prophet's[sa] life. The last and the largest of the Arab tribes who had not yet accepted him was prepared to make its submission and the only condition put forward by it was that the Holy Prophet[sa] should appoint its chief as his successor. Had the Prophet[sa] been actuated even remotely by any personal motives, nothing stood in the way of his securing the unity of the whole of Arabia by promising his succession to the chief of the largest tribe of Arabia. The Holy Prophet[sa] had no son of his own and no dynastic ambition could have stood in the way of such an arrangement, but he never regarded even the smallest thing as belonging to him and as being at his absolute disposal. He could, therefore, not deal with the leadership of Muslims as if it were in his gift. He regarded it as a sacred divine trust and believed that God would bestow it upon whomsoever He thought fit. He therefore rejected Musailima's offer with contempt, and told him that, let alone the leadership of Muslims, he was not prepared to bestow upon him even a dry palm twig.

Whenever he referred to or discoursed about God, it appeared to onlookers as if his whole being was in the grip of a passion of love for and devotion to God.

He always insisted upon simplicity in divine worship. The mosque, that he built in Medina and in which he always led prayers, had only a mud floor which was innocent of all covering or matting and the roof, which was made of dried palm branches and leaves, leaked whenever it rained. On such occasions the Holy Prophet[sa] and members of the congregation would be drenched with rain and mud but he would continue with the prayers till the end and on no occasion did he give any indication that he would postpone the service or remove to more weather-tight shelter (*Bukhārī, Kitābuṣ Ṣaum*).

He was also watchful regarding his Companions. 'Abdullāh bin 'Umar[ra] was a man of extreme piety and purity of life. Concerning him the Holy Prophet[sa] once said: " 'Abdullāh bin 'Umar[ra] would be an even better man if he were to be more regular with regard to his *Tahajjud* prayers."[1] When this was communicated to 'Abdullāh bin 'Umar[ra] he never thereafter missed these prayers. It is recorded that the Holy Prophet[sa], happening to be in the house of his daughter Fāṭima[ra], inquired of her and his son-in-law, 'Alī[ra], whether they were regular with regard to their *Tahajjud* prayers. 'Alī[ra] replied: "O Messenger of Allah[sa]! We try to get up for *Tahajjud* prayers but on occasion when God so wills that we are unable to wake up in time we miss them." He went back and, on the way, repeated several times a verse of the Qur'an which means that a man is often reluctant to admit his fault and tries to cover it up with excuses (*Bukhārī, Kitābul Kusūf*). The Prophet[sa] meant that 'Alī[ra] should not have attributed his default to God by saying that when God willed that they should not wake up they were unable to wake up in time, but should have admitted his own weakness in the matter.

DISAPPROVAL OF PENANCE

The Holy Prophet[sa], however, strongly disapproved of formality in the matter of worship and condemned the imposition of any penance upon oneself as a form of

---

[1] This is a voluntary prayer which is said in the latter part of the night and is not one of the daily prayers.—Ed.

worship. He taught that true worship consists in the beneficent use of the faculties with which God has endowed man. God having bestowed eyes upon man to see with, it would not be worship but impertinence to keep them shut or to have them removed. It is not the proper use of the faculty of sight which can be regarded as sinful, it is the improper use of the faculty that would be a sin. It would be ingratitude on the part of a man to have himself deprived of the faculty of hearing, though it would be sinful of him to use that faculty for the purpose of listening to slander and backbiting. Abstention from food (except on occasions when it is prescribed or is otherwise desirable) may amount to suicide and thus constitute an unforgivable sin, though it would also be sinful on the part of a man to devote himself entirely to food and drink or to indulge in the eating or drinking of prohibited or undesirable articles. This is a golden principle which was taught and emphasized by the Holy Prophet[sa] of Islam and which had not been inculcated by any previous Prophet.

The correct use of natural faculties constitutes high moral qualities; the frustration or stultification of those qualities is folly. It is their improper use that is evil or sinful. Their proper use is true virtue. This is the essence of the moral teachings inculcated by the Holy Prophet[sa] of Islam. And this, in brief, was also a picture of his own life and actions. 'Ā'isha[ra] relates: "Whenever the Holy Prophet[sa] had a choice of two courses of action he always chose the easier of the two, provided it was free from all suspicion of error or sin. Where a course of action was open to such suspicion, the Holy Prophet[sa] of all men gave it the widest berth" (*Muslim, Kitābul Faḍā'il*). This is indeed the highest and the most admirable course open to man. Many men voluntarily court pain and privations, not for the purpose of winning God's pleasure, for God's pleasure is not to be won by inflicting purposeless pain and privations upon oneself, but with the object of deceiving mankind. Such people possess little inherent virtue and wish to cover up their faults and to acquire merit in the eyes of others by assuming false virtues. The object of the Holy Prophet[sa] of Islam, however, was to attain to real virtue and to win the pleasure of God. He was, therefore, completely free from pretence and make-believe. That the world should regard him as bad or should appraise him as good was a matter of complete indifference to him. All that mattered to him was how he found himself and how God would judge him. If in addition to the testimony of his conscience and the approval of God he also won the true testimony of mankind he was grateful, but if men looked upon him with jaundiced eyes he was sorry for them and attached no value to their opinion.

ATTITUDE TOWARDS HIS WIVES

He was extremely kind and fair towards his wives. If on occasion any one of them failed to comport herself with due deference towards him he merely smiled and passed the matter over. He said to 'Ā'isha[ra] one day: " 'Ā'isha[ra], whenever you are upset with me I always get to know it." 'Ā'isha[ra] enquired: "How is that?" He said: "I have noticed that when you are pleased with me and in the course of conversation you have to refer to God, you refer to Him as the Lord of Muḥammad[sa]. But if you are not pleased with me, you refer to Him as the Lord of Ibrāhīm[as]." At this 'Ā'isha[ra] laughed and said he was right (*Bukhārī, Kitābun Nikdḥ*). Khadīja[ra] was his first wife and had made great sacrifices in his cause. She was much older than the Prophet[sa] After her death he married younger women but never permitted the memory of Khadīja[ra] to become dim. Whenever any of Khadīja[ra]'s friends visited him he would stand up to receive her (*Muslim*). If he chanced to see any article that had belonged to or had been connected with Khadīja[ra], he was always overcome by emotion. Among the prisoners taken by the Muslims in the Battle of Badr was a son-in-law of the Prophet[sa]. He possessed nothing which he could offer as ransom. His wife Zainab[ra] (the Prophet's[sa] daughter) sent to Medina a necklace which had belonged to her mother (Khadīja[ra]) and offered it as ransom for her husband. When the Prophet[sa] saw the necklace he recognized it and was much affected. He said to his Companions: "I have no authority to give any direction in this matter, but I know that this necklace is cherished by Zainab[ra] as a last memento of her deceased mother and, provided it commends itself to you, I would suggest that she should not be deprived of it and it may be returned to her." They intimated that nothing would give them greater pleasure and readily adopted his suggestion (*Ḥalbiyya, Vol. 2*). He often praised Khadīja[ra] to his other wives and stressed her virtues and the sacrifices that she had made in the cause of Islam. On one such occasion 'Ā'isha[ra] was piqued and said: "O Messenger of Allah, why go on talking of the old lady? God has bestowed better, younger and more attractive wives upon you." The Holy Prophet[sa] was overcome by emotion at hearing this and protested: "O no, 'Ā'isha[ra]! You have no idea how good Khadīja[ra] was to me" (*Bukhārī*).

HIGH MORAL QUALITIES

He was always very patient in adversity. He was never discouraged by adverse circumstances nor did he permit any personal desire to get a hold over him. It has been related already that his father had died before his birth and his mother died while he was still a little child. Up to the age of eight, he was in the guardianship of his grandfather and after the latter's death he was taken care of by his uncle, Abū Ṭālib. Both on account of natural affection and also because he had been specially admonished in that behalf by his father, Abū Ṭālib always watched over his nephew with care and indulgence but his wife was not affected by these considerations to the same degree. It often happened that she would distribute something among her own children, leaving out their little cousin. If Abū Ṭālib chanced to come into the house on such an occasion he would find his little nephew sitting apart, a perfect picture of dignity and without a trace of sulkiness or grievance on his face. The uncle, yielding to the claims of affection and recognizing his responsibility, would run to the nephew, clasp him to his bosom and cry out: "Do pay attention to this child of mine also! Do pay attention to this child of mine also!" Such incidents were not uncommon and those who were witnesses to them were unanimous in their testimony that the young Muḥammad[sa] never gave any indication that he was in any way affected by them or that he was in any sense jealous of his cousins. Later in life when he was in a position to do so, he took upon himself the care and upbringing of two of his uncle's sons, 'Alī[ra] and Ja'far[ra], and discharged this responsibility in the most excellent manner.

The Holy Prophet[sa], throughout his life, had to encounter a succession of bitter experiences. He was born an orphan, his mother died while he was still a small child and he lost his grandfather at the age of eight years. After marriage he had to bear the loss of several children, one after the other, and then his beloved and devoted wife Khadīja[ra] died. Some of the wives he married after Khadīja's[ra] death, died during his lifetime and towards the close of his life he had to bear the loss of his son Ibrahim. He bore all these losses and calamities cheerfully, and none of them affected in the least degree either his high resolve or the urbanity of his disposition. His private sorrows never found vent in public and he always met everybody with a benign countenance and treated all alike with uniform benevolence. On one occasion he observed a woman who had lost a child occupied in loud mourning over her child's grave. He admonished her to be patient and to accept God's will as supreme. The woman did not know that she was being addressed by the Holy Prophet[sa] and replied: "If you had ever suffered the loss of a child as I have, you would have realized how difficult it is to be patient under such an affliction." The Prophet[sa] observed: "I have suffered the loss not of one but of seven children," and passed on. Except when he referred to his own losses or misfortunes in this indirect manner, he never cared to dwell upon them nor did he permit them in any manner to interfere with his unceasing service to mankind and his cheerful sharing of their burdens.

HIS SELF-CONTROL

He always held himself under complete control. Even when he became a Sovereign he always listened to everybody with patience, and if a person treated him with impertinence he bore with him and never attempted any retaliation. In the East, one way of showing respect for a person whom one is addressing is not to address him by his personal name. The Muslims used to address the Holy Prophet[sa] as: "O Messenger of Allah[sa]", and non-Muslims used to address him as "Abū'l Qāsim[sa]" (i.e., Qāsim's father: Qāsim being the name of one of his sons). On one occasion a Jew came to him in Medina and started a discussion with him. In the course of the discussion he repeatedly addressed him as "O Muḥammad[sa], O Muḥammad[sa]". The Prophet[sa] paid no attention to his form of address and went on patiently expounding the matter under discussion to him. His Companions[ra], however, were getting irritated at the discourteous form of address adopted by his interlocutor till one of them, not being able to restrain himself any longer, admonished the Jew not to address the Prophet[sa] by his personal name but to address him as Abū'l Qāsim[sa]. The Jew said that he would address him only by the name which his parents had given him. The Prophet[sa] smiled and said to his Companions: "He is right. I was named Muḥammad[sa] at the time of my birth and there is no reason to be upset at his addressing me by that name."

Sometimes people stopped him in the way and engaged him in conversation, explaining their needs and preferring their requests to him. He always stood patiently and let them go on and proceeded only after they had done. On occasion people when shaking hands with him kept hold of his hand for some time and, though he found this inconvenient and it occasioned a loss of precious time also, he was never the first to withdraw his hand. People went freely to him and laid their troubles and difficulties before him and asked him for help. If he was able to help he never declined to do so. Sometimes he was pestered with requests and they were unreasonably pressed but he went on complying with them as far as he was able. On occasion, after complying with a request, he would admonish the person concerned to have greater trust in God and to avoid asking others for relief. On one occasion a devout Muslim asked him several times for money and each time he complied with his request but in the end said: "It is best for a man to put his trust in God and to avoid making requests." The person concerned was a sincere man. Out of regard for the feelings of the Prophet[sa], he did not offer to return what he had already received but he declared that in future he would never make a request to anybody under any circumstances. Years later, he was taking part in a battle, mounted on a charger, and in the thick of it when the din and confusion and the clash of arms were at their highest and he was surrounded by his enemies, his whip fell from his hand. A Muslim soldier who was on foot, perceiving his predicament, bent down to pick up the whip for him but the mounted man begged him to desist and jumped from his horse and picked up the whip himself, explaining to the soldier that he had long since promised the Holy Prophet[sa] that he would never make any request to anybody and that if he had permitted the soldier to pick up the whip for him it would have amounted to his having made an indirect request and would thus have rendered him guilty of breaking his promise to the Holy Prophet[sa].

JUSTICE AND FAIR DEALING

The Arabs were greatly given to favouritism and applied different standards to different persons. Even among the so-called civilized nations of today one observes a reluctance to bring prominent persons or persons occupying high positions or offices to account for their doings, though the law is enforced rigorously against the common citizen. The Holy Prophet[sa] was, however, unique in enforcing uniform standards of justice and fair dealing. On one occasion a case came before him in which a young woman belonging to a highly respectable family was found to have committed theft. This caused great consternation as, if the normal penalty were imposed upon the young woman, a leading family would be humiliated and disgraced. Many were anxious to intercede with the Prophet[sa] on behalf of the offender but were afraid to do so. Eventually Usāma[ra] was prevailed upon to undertake the mission. Usāma[ra] went to the Holy Prophet[sa] but the moment the latter perceived the trend of his submission he was much upset and said: "You had better desist. Nations have come to a bad end for showing favours to highly placed persons while pressing hard on the common people. Islam does not permit this and I will certainly not do it. Verily, if my own daughter, Fāṭima[ra], were to commit an offence I would not hesitate to impose the appropriate penalty" (*Bukhārī, Kitābul Ḥudūd*).

It has already been related that when the Prophet's uncle 'Abbās[ra] became a prisoner in the Battle of Badr, he was, like other prisoners, tied up with a rope to prevent his escape. The rope was so tightly secured that he groaned with pain during the night. The Prophet[sa] heard his groans and was unable to sleep. The

Companions of the Prophet[sa], perceiving this, loosened the rope that bound 'Abbās[ra]. When the Prophet[sa] got to learn of this, he directed that all prisoners should be treated alike, saying that there was no reason for showing favour to his own relative. He insisted that either they must loosen the bonds of all the prisoners or must tighten the bonds of 'Abbās[ra] like those of the others. As the Companions of the Prophet[sa] did not wish him to be subjected to uneasiness on account of his uncle they undertook to guard the prisoners carefully and loosened the bonds of all of them (*Zurqānī*, Vol. 3, p. 279).

Even during the exigencies of war he was most particular in observing all accepted rules and conventions. On one occasion he despatched a party of his Companions on a scouting expedition. They encountered some men of the enemy on the last day of the Sacred Month, Rajab. Thinking that it would be dangerous to let them escape and carry to Mecca the tidings of the scouting party being so near, they attacked them and in the course of the skirmish one of them was killed. After the scouting party had returned to Medina the Meccans began to protest that the Muslim scouts had killed one of their men in the Sacred Month. The Meccans had often been guilty of violating the sanctity of the Sacred Months vis-a-vis the Muslims whenever it suited them, and it would have been a suitable reply to their protest to say that as the Meccans had themselves set at naught the convention relating to the Sacred Months, so they were not entitled to insist upon their observance by Muslims. But the Prophet[sa] did not make this reply. He severely reprimanded the members of the party, refused to accept the booty and according to some reports even paid the blood-money for the person killed, till the revelation of 2: 218 cleared the whole position (*Ṭabarī* and *Ḥalbiyya*).

People are generally careful not to hurt the feelings of their friends and relations but the Holy Prophet[sa] was very particular in this respect even regarding people who were opposed to him. On one occasion a Jew came to him and complained that Abū Bakr[ra] had hurt his feelings by saying that God had exalted Muḥammad[sa] above Moses[as]. The Prophet[sa] summoned Abū Bakr[ra] and asked him what had transpired. Abū Bakr[ra] explained that the Jew had started by saying that he swore by Moses[as] whom God, he said, had exalted above the whole of mankind, and that he (Abū Bakr[ra]) had thereupon retorted by swearing by Muḥammad[sa], whom God had exalted above Moses[as]. The Prophet[sa] said: "You should not have said this as the feelings of other people should be respected. Nobody should exalt me above Moses[as]" (*Bukhārī, Kitābut Tauḥīd*). This did not mean that the Holy Prophet[sa] did not in fact occupy a higher position than Moses[as] but that an affirmation like this addressed to a Jew was likely to hurt his feelings and should have been avoided.

REGARD FOR THE POOR

The Holy Prophet[sa] was ever concerned to ameliorate the condition of the poorer sections of the community and to raise their status in society. On one occasion while he was sitting with his Companions[ra], a rich man happened to pass by.The Prophet[sa] inquired of one of his Companions[ra] what he thought of him. He replied "He is a well-to-do and well-connected man. If he were to ask for the hand of a girl in marriage the request would be favourably considered and if he were to intercede on behalf of anybody the intercession would be accepted." Shortly after, another man passed by who appeared to be poor and of no substance. The Prophet[sa] inquired of the same Companion[ra] what he thought of him. He replied: "O Messenger of Allah[sa]! He is a poor man. If he were to request the hand of a girl in marriage the request would not be favourably received and if he were to intercede on behalf of any person the intercession would be rejected and if he were to seek to engage anybody in conversation no attention would be paid to him." On hearing this the Prophet[sa] observed: "The worth of this poor man is much greater than the value of a quantity of gold sufficient to fill the whole universe" (*Bukhārī, Kitābur Riqāq*).

A poor Muslim woman used to clean out the Holy Prophet's[sa] mosque in Medina. The Prophet[sa] did not see her in the mosque for some days and made inquiries concerning her He was told that she had died. He said: "Why was I not informed when she died? I would have wished to join her funeral prayers," and added, "perchance you did not consider her worthy of consideration as she was poor. This was not right. Direct me to her grave." He then proceeded to her grave and prayed for her (*Bukhārī, Kitābuṣ Ṣalāt*). He used to say that there were people with tangled hair whose bodies were covered with dust and who were not welcomed by those who were well-to-do but who were so highly valued by God that if, trusting in God's beneficence, they swore in His name that a certain matter would take a certain turn He would support them." (*Muslim, Kitābul Birr Waṣ Ṣila*). On one occasion some Companions of the Holy Prophet[sa] who were freed slaves were sitting together when Abū Sufyān[ra] (who was a chieftain among the Quraish and had fought the Muslims up to the surrender of Mecca and had accepted Islam only on that occasion) happened to pass by. These Companions[ra], addressing him, recalled the victory that God had bestowed upon Islam. Abū Bakr[ra] also heard this and did not approve of a chieftain of the Quraish being reminded of their humiliation and he reprimanded the group of Companions[ra]. He then went to the Holy Prophet[sa] and related the incident to him. The Prophet[sa] said: "O Abū Bakr[ra]! I fear you may have hurt the feelings of these servants of God. If that should be so, God would be offended with you." Abū Bakr[ra] at once returned to those people and inquired: "Brothers of mine! Did you feel hurt over what I said?" To which they replied: "We felt no offence at what you said. May God forgive you!" (*Muslim, Kitābul Faḍā'l*).

While, however, the Prophet[sa] insisted that poor people should be respected and their feelings should not be injured and strove to fulfil their needs, he also sought to instil the sentiment of self-respect into them and taught them not to beg for favours. He used to say that it behoved a poor man not to seek to be content with a date or two or with a mouthful or two of food but to restrain himself from making a request, however severely he might be tried (*Bukhārī, Kitābul Kusūf*). On the other hand he used to say that no entertainment would be blessed unless some poor people were also invited to it. 'Ā'isha[ra] relates that a poor woman came to visit her on one occasion accompanied by her two little daughters. 'Ā'isha[ra] had nothing with her at the time except one date which she gave to the woman. The woman divided it between her little daughters and then they all departed. When the Prophet[sa] came home 'Ā'isha[ra] related this to him and he said: "If a poor man has daughters and he treats them with consideration, God will save him from the torments of Hell," and added: "God will bestow Paradise upon this woman on account of the consideration she showed towards her daughters" (*Muslim*). On one occasion he was told that one of his Companions, Sa'd[ra], who was a well-to-do person, was boasting of his enterprise to others. When the Prophet[sa] heard this, he said: "Let no man imagine that his wealth or standing or power is the result merely of his own efforts or enterprise. That is not so. Your power and your position and your wealth are all earned through the poor." One of his prayers was: "O God! Keep me humble while I am alive and keep me humble when I die and let my resurrection on the Day of Judgement be with the humble" (*Tirmidhī, Abwābul Zuhad*).

On one occasion during the hot weather when he was passing through a street, he observed a very poor Muslim carrying heavy loads from one place to another. He was very plain of features which were rendered still more unattractive by a heavy coating of perspiration and dust. He bore a melancholy look. The Holy Prophet[sa] approached him stealthily from the back and, as children sometimes do in fun, he put forward his hands and covered the labourer's eyes with them, expecting him to guess who he was. The man put back his own hands and feeling over the body of the Prophet[sa] realized that it was the Holy Prophet[sa] himself. He probably guessed also that nobody else would show such intimate affection for a man in his condition. Being pleased and encouraged, he pressed against the Holy Prophet's[sa] body and clasped him to himself from the back rubbing his dust and sweat-covered body against the clothes of the Prophet[sa], desiring perhaps to ascertain how far the Prophet[sa] would be willing to indulge him. The Prophet[sa] went on smiling and did not ask him to desist. When the man had been put in a thoroughly happy mood the Prophet[sa] said to him: "I possess a slave; do you think anybody will be willing to buy him?" The man realized that probably there was nobody in the whole world, save the Holy Prophet[sa] himself who would be ready to see any worth in him, and with a melancholy sigh he replied: "O Messenger of Allah[sa]! there is nobody in this world who would be prepared to purchase me." The Prophet[sa] said: "No! No! You must not say that. You are of great worth in the eyes of God" (*Sharḥussunna*).

Not only was he himself watchful of the welfare of the poor but he constantly exhorted others to be the same. Abū Mūsā Ash'arī[ra] relates that if a needy person approached the Holy Prophet[sa] and made a request, he would say to those around him, "You should also support his request so that you may acquire merit by becoming sharers in promoting a good deed" (*Bukhārī* and *Muslim*), his object being to create on the one side in the minds of his Companions a feeling of eagerness to help the poor and on the other in the minds of the needy a realization of the affection and sympathy felt for them by their better-off brethren.

SAFEGUARDING THE INTERESTS OF THE POOR

When Islam began to be generally accepted over the greater part of Arabia, the Holy Prophet[sa] often received large quantities of goods and money which he immediately distributed amongst those who were in need. On one occasion his daughter Fāṭima[ra] came to him and, showing him her hands which had become calloused by the labour involved in crushing grain with stones, requested that a slave might be allotted to her to lighten her labour. The Prophet[sa] replied: "I shall tell you something which will prove to be of far greater worth than a slave. When you go to bed at night you should utter the praise of God thirty-three times, and affirm His perfection an equal number of times and affirm His greatness thirty-four times. This will help you a great deal more than could the possession of a slave" (*Bukhārī*).

While distributing money on one occasion a coin fell from his hands and rolled out of sight. Having finished with the distribution he went to the mosque and led the prayers. It was his practice to remain sitting for a short while after the conclusion of the prayers, occupied in the remembrance of God and thereafter to let people approach him and put questions to him or proffer requests. On this occasion, as soon as the prayers were concluded, he got up and proceeded quickly to his house. He looked for the missing coin and, having recovered it, came back and bestowed it upon a needy person, explaining that the coin had fallen from his hands during the distribution of money and the matter had gone out of his mind but he suddenly recollected it while-leading the prayers and he was made uneasy by the thought that if he were to die before he could recover the coin and give it away to some person in need, he would be held responsible for it before God; that was the reason why he had left the mosque in such a hurry to recover the coin (*Bukhārī, Kitābul Kusūf*).

In his anxiety to fully safe-guard the interests of the poor and the needy he went so far as to lay down that no charity should ever be bestowed upon his descendants, fearing lest Muslims out of their love for and devotion towards himself should in course of time make his descendants the principal objects of their charity and thus deprive the poor and needy of their due share. On one occasion somebody brought to him a quantity of dates and offered them as charity. His grandson Imām Ḥasan[ra], who was then only two and a half years of age, happened to be sitting with the Prophet[sa]. He picked up one of the dates and put it into his mouth. The Prophet[sa] immediately put his finger into the child's mouth and forced the date out of it saying: "We have no right in this. This belongs to the poor among God's creatures" (*Bukhārī, Kitābul Kusūf*).

TREATMENT OF SLAVES

He constantly exhorted those who owned slaves to treat them kindly and well. He had laid down that if the owner of a slave beat his slave or abused him, the only reparation that he could make was to set the slave free (*Muslim, Kitābul Īmān*). He devised means for, and encouraged, the freeing of slaves on every pretext. He said: "If a person owning a slave sets him free, God will in recompense save every part of his body corresponding to every part of the slave's body from the torment of Hell." Again, he laid down that a slave should be asked to perform only such tasks as he could easily accomplish and that when he was set to do a task, his master should help him in performing it so that the slave should experience no feeling of humiliation or degradation (*Muslim*). If a master went on a journey accompanied by a slave, it was his duty to share his mount with the slave either by both riding together or each riding in turn. Abū Hurairā[ra], who used to spend the whole of his time after becoming a Muslim in the company of the Prophet[sa] and who had repeatedly heard the Prophet's[sa] injunctions regarding the treatment of slaves, has said: "I call God to witness in Whose hands is my life that were it not for the opportunities that I get of joining in holy war and of performing the Pilgrimage and were it not that I have opportunities of serving my old mother, I would have desired to die a slave, for the Holy Prophet[sa] constantly insisted upon slaves being well and kindly treated" (*Muslim*). Ma'rūr bin Suwaid[ra] relates: "I saw Abū Dharr Ghaffārī[ra] (a Companion[ra] of the Holy Prophet[sa]) wearing clothes exactly similar to those worn by his slave. I inquired of him the reason of this and he said: 'During the lifetime of the Holy Prophet[sa] I once taunted a man with his mother having been a slave. Upon this the Holy Prophet[sa] rebuked me and said: "You still seem to entertain pre-Islamic notions. What are slaves? They are your brethren and the source of your power. God in His wisdom confers temporary authority upon you over them. He who has such authority over his brother should feed him with the kind of food he himself eats; clothe him with the kind of clothes he himself wears and should not set him a task beyond his strength and should himself help him in whatever he is asked to do".' "On another occasion the Prophet[sa] said: "When your servant cooks food for you and sets it out before you, you should ask him to sit down with you to eat or at least to partake of a portion of it in your company, for he has established a right in it by working on it' (*Muslim*).

TREATMENT OF WOMEN

The Holy Prophet[sa] was very keen on improving the condition of women in society and on securing for them a position of dignity and fair and equitable treatment. Islam was the first religion which conferred upon women the right of inheritance. The Qur'an makes daughters along with sons heirs to the property left by their parents. In the same way a mother is made an heir to her son's or daughter's property and a wife is made an heir to her husband's property. When a brother becomes an heir of his deceased brother's property a sister is also an heir to that property. No religion before Islam had so clearly and firmly established a woman's right of inheritance and her right to possess property. In Islam a woman is the absolute owner of her own property and her husband cannot obtain any control over it by virtue merely of their relationship. A woman is at full liberty to deal with her property as she chooses.

The Holy Prophet[sa] was so careful with regard to the kind treatment of women that those around him who had not previously been accustomed to looking upon women in the light of helpmates and partners found it difficult to accommodate themselves to the standards that the Prophet[sa] was anxious to see set up and maintained. 'Umar[ra] relates: "My wife occasionally sought to intervene in my affairs with her counsel and I would rebuke her, saying that the Arabs had never permitted their women to intervene in their affairs. She would retort: 'That is all past. The Holy Prophet[sa] lets his wives counsel him in his affairs and he does not stop them. Why don't you follow his example?' My reply used to be: As for 'Ā'isha[ra] the Prophet[sa] is particularly fond of her but as regards your daughter (Ḥafṣa[ra]), if she does this she will one day have to suffer the consequences of her impertinence.' It so happened that thereafter on one occasion the Holy Prophet[sa], being upset over something, decided to spend a period of time apart from his wives. When I learnt of this I said to my wife, What I had feared had come to pass. Then I went to the house of my daughter Ḥafṣa[ra] and found her crying. I inquired of her what the matter was and whether the Prophet[sa] had divorced her. She said: 'I don't know about divorce, but the Prophet[sa] has decided to remain away from us for some time.' I said to her: 'Did I not often tell you not to take the same liberties with him as 'Ā'isha[ra] does, for the Holy Prophet[sa] is particularly fond of 'Ā'isha[ra], but you seem to have brought upon yourself what I had feared.' I then went to the Holy Prophet[sa] and found him lying down on a rough matting. He was at that time wearing no shirt and his body bore the marks of the pattern of the matting. I sat down near him and said: 'O Messenger of Allah! the Kaiser and the Chosroes do not deserve any of God's favours and yet they pass their lives in great comfort and you who are His Messenger pass your days in such discomfort.' The Prophet[sa] replied: 'That is not so. The Messengers of Allah are not expected to spend their time in comfort. That kind of life befits only secular monarchs.' I then related to the Prophet[sa] all that had passed between me and my wife and daughter. Hearing me, the Prophet[sa] laughed and said: 'It is not true that I have divorced my wives. I have merely thought it advisable to spend a little time away from them' " (*Bukhārī, Kitābun Nikāḥ*).

He was so careful concerning the sentiments of women that on one occasion when he was leading the prayers he heard the cry of a child and concluded the service quickly, explaining thereafter that as he had heard the cry of the child he imagined that the child's mother would be distressed at its cry and he had therefore concluded the service quickly so that the mother could go to the child and look after it.

When during any of his journeys women were also among the party he always gave directions that the caravan should move slowly and by easy stages. On one such occasion when the men were eager to push forward, he said: "Take care of glass! Take care of glass!" meaning thereby that women were of the party and that if camels and horses were put to the gallop they would suffer from the joltings of the animals (*Bukhārī, Kitābul Adab*). During a battle confusion arose among the ranks of the mounted soldiers and the animals became unmanageable. The Holy Prophet[sa] fell from his horse and some of the women also fell from their mounts. One of his Companions[ra], who was riding a camel immediately behind the Prophet[sa] jumped down and ran towards him crying: "May I be your sacrifice, O Messenger of Allah[sa]." The Prophet's[sa] foot was still in the stirrup. He released it hastily and said to his Companion: "Don't bother about me, go and help the women." Just before his death one of the injunctions he addressed to Muslims and laid stress upon was that they should always treat women with kindness and consideration. It was an oft-repeated saying of his that if a man had daughters and he arranged to have them educated and took pains with their upbringing, God would save him from the torment of Hell (*Tirmidhī*).

It was a common practice with the Arabs to inflict physical chastisement upon women for every little fault. The Holy Prophet[sa] taught that women were equally with men the creatures of God and were not the slaves of men and should not be beaten. When women got to know of this they went to the other extreme and began to oppose men in everything, with the result that in many homes domestic peace was continually disturbed. 'Umar[ra] complained of this to the Holy Prophet[sa] and said that unless women could on occasion be chastised they would become unruly and there would be no holding them in check. As detailed Islamic teachings with regard to the treatment of women had not yet been revealed, the Prophet[sa] said that if a woman was guilty of serious transgression she might be chastised. This in its turn led the men in many cases to revert to the old Arab practice. It was now the turn of the women to complain and they laid their grievances before the Prophet's[sa] wives. Thereupon, the Prophet[sa] admonished men and told them that those who treated women with unkindness could never win the favour of God. Thereafter the rights of women were established, and for the first time women began to be treated as free individuals in their own right (*Abū Dāwūd, Kitābun Nikāḥ*).

Mu'āwiya al-Qushairī[ra] relates: "I inquired of the Holy Prophet[sa] what claim my wife had upon me," and he replied: "Feed her with that which God bestows upon you in the way of food, and clothe her with that which God bestows upon you in the way of clothes and do not chastise her nor abuse her nor put her out of your house." He was so careful of the feelings and sentiments of women that he always exhorted those who had to go upon a journey to finish their errands quickly and return home as soon as possible so that their wives and children should not suffer separation longer than was necessary. Whenever he returned from a journey he always came home during the day-time. If he found night approaching towards the end of his journey, he would camp outside Medina for the night and enter it next morning. He also told his Companions that when they returned from a journey they should not come home suddenly without notice of their return (*Bukhārī* and *Muslim*). In giving this direction he had in mind the fact that the relations between the sexes are largely governed by sentiment. In the absence of the husband a wife may often neglect the care of her body and of her dress and if the husband were to return home unexpectedly the finer sentiments of the wife or the husband might be upset. By giving the direction that when a man returns from a journey he should contrive to arrive home during the day-time and after intimation to the members of his family of his return, he ensured that the members of his family would be ready to receive the returning member in a befitting manner.

ATTITUDE TOWARDS THE DEAD

He enjoined that every person should make a will concerning the regulation of his affairs after his death so that those connected with him should suffer the minimum of inconvenience after his demise.

He laid down that no man should speak ill of a person who was dead but that whatever of good he had possessed should be emphasized, for no benefit could result to anybody from mentioning the weaknesses or vices of the deceased but by emphasizing his virtues people would be inclined to pray for him (*Bukhārī*). He insisted upon a deceased person's debts being paid before he was buried. He very often satisfied the liabilities of a deceased person himself, but if he was not able to do this, he exhorted the heirs and relatives of the deceased or other persons to discharge his liabilities and would not say the funeral prayers over a deceased person till his liabilities had been discharged.

TREATMENT OF NEIGHBOURS

He always treated his neighbours with extreme kindness and consideration. He used to say that the angel Gabriel had emphasized consideration towards one's neighbours so often that he sometimes began to think that a neighbour would perhaps be included among the prescribed heirs. Abū Dharr[ra] relates that the Holy Prophet[sa] said to him: "Abū Dharr[ra], while broth is being cooked for your family, add a little more water to it so that your neighbour might also share in it." This does not mean that the neighbour should not be invited to share in other things but, as the Arabs were mostly a migratory people and their favourite dish was broth, the Holy Prophet[sa] referred to this dish as a typical one and taught that one should not think so much of the taste of the food as of the obligation to share it with one's neighbour.

Abū Hurairā[ra] relates: "On one occasion the Holy Prophet[sa] exclaimed: 'I call God to witness that he is not a believer! I call God to witness that he is not a believer! I call God to witness that he is not a believer!' The Companions inquired: 'Who is not a believer, O Messenger of Allah[sa]?' and he replied: 'He whose neighbour is not secure against injury and ill-treatment at his hands.' On one occasion when he was addressing women, he said: 'If anybody finds only the foot of a goat to cook, that person should share it with his or her neighbour.' He asked people not to object to their neighbours driving pegs into their walls or putting them to any other use which occasioned no injury." Abū Huraira[ra] relates: "The Prophet[sa] said: 'He who believes in God and in the Day of Judgement should occasion no inconvenience to his neighbour: he who believes in God and in the Day of Judgement should occasion no inconvenience to his guest, and he who believes in God and in the Day of Judgement should utter only words of virtue or should keep quiet' " (*Muslim*).

TREATMENT OF RELATIVES

Most people suffer from the failing that when they marry and set up house for themselves, they begin to neglect their parents. The Holy Prophet[sa], therefore, laid great stress upon the meritoriousness of serving one's parents and treating them with kindness and consideration. Abū Hurairā[ra] relates: "A man came to the Holy Prophet[sa] and asked to be told who was most deserving of kind treatment at his hands. The Prophet[sa] replied: 'Your mother'. The man asked 'And next to her?' The Prophet[sa] repeated, 'Again thy mother'. The man asked a third time, 'And after my mother?' and the Prophet[sa] again replied, Still thy mother', and when the man asked him a fourth time, he said: 'After her thy father and after him thy nearest relatives and after them thy more remote relatives.' "The Prophet's[sa] own parents and grand parents had died while he was still a child. The parents of some of his wives were, however, alive and he always treated them with great consideration and deference. On the occasion of the surrender of Mecca when the Holy Prophet[sa] entered the town as a victorious general, Abū Bakr[ra] brought his father to meet him. He said to Abū Bakr[ra]: "Why did you trouble your father to come to me? I would gladly have gone to him myself" (*Ḥalbiyya*, Vol. 3, p. 99). One of his sayings was: "Unlucky is the man whose parents live to old age and he fails to earn Paradise even then", meaning that the service of one's parents particularly when they reach old age attracts the grace and favour of God and, therefore, a person to whom is afforded the opportunity of serving his aged parents and who avails himself of the opportunity to the full is bound to become confirmed in righteous ways and a recipient of the grace of God.

A man once complained to the Holy Prophet[sa] that the more benevolence he exercised towards his relations the more hostile they became towards him; and that the more he treated them with kindness the more they persecuted him; and the more he demonstrated affection towards them the more they frowned upon him. The Prophet[sa] said: "If what you say is true you are very fortunate, for you will ever be the recipient of God's succour" (*Muslim, Kitābul Birr Waṣ Ṣila*). On one occasion when the Holy Prophet[sa] was exhorting people to give alms and charity one of his Companions, Abū Ṭalḥa Anṣāri[ra], came to him and offered to dedicate an orchard for charitable purposes. The Prophet[sa] was very pleased and exclaimed, "What an excellent charity! What an excellent charity! What an excellent charity!" and added: "Having dedicated this orchard to the service of the poor, I want you now to divide it among your poor relatives" (*Bukhārī, Kitābut Tafsīr*). A man came to him on one occasion and said: "O Messenger of Allah[sa]! I am prepared to make a covenant of Hijrat and I am prepared to make a covenant to take part in the holy war, for I am anxious to win the pleasure of God." The Holy Prophet[sa] inquired whether either of his parents was alive and the man told him that both were alive. He then asked: "Are you indeed anxious to win the pleasure of God?" and on the man replying in the affirmative the Prophet[sa] said: "Then go back to your parents and serve them and serve them well." He pointed out that one's non-Muslim relations were equally entitled to be treated kindly and with consideration along with one's Muslim relations. One of Abū Bakr's[ra] wives, who was a non-Muslim, visited her daughter Asmā'[ra] and the latter inquired of the Holy Prophet[sa] whether she might serve her and make presents to her, to which the Holy Prophet[sa] replied: "Certainly, for she is thy mother" (*Bukhārī, Kitābul Adab*).

He treated not only his near relatives but even remote ones and anybody connected with them with great consideration. Whenever he sacrificed an animal he would send a portion of the meat to the friends of Khadīja[ra] (his deceased wife) and told his wives never to overlook them on such occasions. Many years after Khadīja's[ra] death when he was sitting with some of his Companions, Khadīja's[ra] sister, Ḥālah[ra], came to see him and asked permission to enter. Her voice sounded in the Prophet's[sa] ears very much like that of Khadīja[ra] and when he heard it he said: "Oh Lord! This is Hālah[ra], Khadija's[ra] sister." Indeed, true affection always manifests itself thus that one becomes fond of and considerate towards all those who may be connected with a person whom one loves or holds in high esteem.

Anas bin Mālik[ra] relates that during the course of a journey he found himself in the company of Jarīr bin 'Abdullāh[ra] and observed that the latter busied himself in looking after him as a servant looks after his master. As Jarīr bin 'Abdullāh[ra] was older than Anas[ra], the latter was embarrassed and protested that Jarir[ra] should not put himself out on his account. Jarīr[ra] replied: "I used to observe how devotedly the Anṣār served the Holy Prophet[sa] and, being impressed with their devotion to and love for the Holy Prophet[sa], I had resolved in my mind that if I ever happened to be in the company of an Anṣārī, I would serve him like a servant. I am, therefore, only carrying out my resolve and you should not seek to dissuade me" (*Muslim*). This incident affirms that where one person truly loves another, his affection extends also to those who sincerely serve the object of his attachment. In the same way those who truly honour their parents are always deferential and considerate towards those who may be connected with their parents through bonds of affection or relationship. On one occasion the Holy Prophet[sa] stressed it as the highest virtue for a man to honour the friends of his father. Among the persons addressed was 'Abdullāh bin 'Umar[ra]. Many years after, while proceeding on Pilgrimage, he met a Bedouin and he made over to him his own mount and also presented him with his turban. One of his companions observed that he had been over-generous as a Bedouin would be pleased with very little. 'Abdullāh bin 'Umar[ra] said: "This man's father was a friend of my father's and I have heard the Holy Prophet[sa] say that it is one of the highest virtues for a man to honour his father's friends."

KEEPING GOOD COMPANY

He always preferred to keep company with the virtuous and if he observed any weakness in any of his Companions[ra] he admonished him gently and in private. Abū Musā Ash'ari[ra] relates: "The Holy Prophet[sa] illustrated the benefit to be derived from good friends and virtuous companions and the injury to be apprehended from evil friends and vicious companions by saying: 'A man who keeps company with virtuous people is like a person who carries about musk with him. If he partakes of it he derives benefit from it, if he sells it he makes a profit out of it and if he merely keeps it he enjoys its perfume. A man who keeps company with evil persons is like one who blows into a charcoal furnace; all that he can expect is that a spark may alight upon his clothes and set them on fire or that the gas emitted by the charcoal may upset his brain'." He used to say that a man's character takes on the colour of the company he keeps and that therefore one should be careful to spend one's time in the company of the good (*Bukhārī* and *Muslim*).

SAFEGUARDING PEOPLE'S FAITH

The Holy Prophet[sa] was very careful to safe-guard against possible misunderstandings. On one occasion his wife Ṣafiyya[ra] came to see him in the mosque. When the time came for her to return home it had become dark and the Prophet[sa] decided to escort her to her house. On the way he passed by two men and, wishing to avoid any speculation on their part as to his companion, he stopped them and lifting the veil from the face of his wife said: "See, this is Ṣafiyya[ra] my wife." They protested saying: "O Messenger of Allah[sa]! why did you imagine that we should fall into any misconception regarding you?" The Prophet[sa] replied "Satan (i.e., evil thoughts) often courses through a man's blood. I was afraid lest your faith be affected" (*Bukhārī, Abwābul I'tikāf*).

OVERLOOKING FAULTS OF OTHERS

He never gave publicity to the faults and shortcomings of others and admonished people not to proclaim their own faults. He used to say: "If a person covers up the faults of another, God will cover up his faults on the Day of Judgement." And, "Every one of my followers can escape the consequences of his errors (i.e., by true repentance and reform) except those who go on proclaiming their wrongdoing" and illustrated this by saying: ,"A man commits a sin at night and God covers it up; in the morning he meets his friends and boasts before them:. 'I did this last night, I did that last night,' and thus he himself lays bare that which God had covered up" (*Bukhārī* and *Muslim*).

Some people foolishly imagine that a confession of sin helps towards repentance; the truth is that it only fosters immodesty. Sin is an evil and he who slips into it and becomes a prey to shame and remorse has a chance of climbing back into the path of purity and righteousness through repentance. His case is like that of a person who has been seduced by evil but is pursued by righteousness and as soon as a chance offers, the evil is vanquished and the sinner is claimed back by righteouness. Those, however, who proclaim their sins and take pride in them lose all sense of good and evil and become incapable of repentance.

On one occasion a man came to the Holy Prophet[sa] and said: "I have been guilty of adultery" (this when established by proper evidence being a punishable offence under Islamic Law). Hearing the man's confession, the Holy Prophet[sa] turned away from him and became occupied with something else. He meant to indicate that the proper remedy in such a case was repentance and not public confession. But the man did not realize this and imagining that the Prophet[sa] had not heard him, went and stood in front of him and, addressing him, repeated his confession. The Holy Prophet[sa] again turned away from him but the man again went and stood in front of him and repeated his confession. When he had done this four times the Prophet[sa] said "I had wished that this man should not have proclaimed his sin till God should have indicated His will with regard to him but, as he has repeated his confession four times, I am compelled to take action" (*Tirmidhī*). 'He then added: "This man has himself confessed and has not been charged by the woman concerning whom he makes the confession. The woman should be questioned and, if she denies her guilt, she should not be molested and only this man should be punished in accordance with his confession but, if she confesses she should also be punished." It was the practice of the Holy Prophet[sa] to follow the Law of the Torah in matters regarding which the Qur'an was silent, and as the Torah prescribes that an adulterer should be stoned to death he pronounced the sentence upon this man accordingly. When the sentence was being carried out the man tried to run away but the people pursued him and carried out the sentence. When the Prophet[sa] came to know of this he disapproved of it. He said that the man had been sentenced in accordance with his own confession. His attempt to run away was in effect a retraction of his confession and thereafter he should not have been subjected to a penalty which had been imposed upon him solely on account of his confession.

The Prophet[sa] laid down that the Law was concerned only with overt acts. During the course of a war, a party of Muslims came upon a non-Muslim who used to lie in wait in lonely places and whenever he found a solitary Muslim he would attack and kill him. On this occasion Usāma bin Zaid[ra] pursued him and, having overtaken and caught him, drew his sword to kill him. When the man found that no way of escape was left open to him he repeated the first portion of the Muslim confession of faith, viz., "There is no being worthy of worship save Allah," thereby indicating that he had accepted Islam. Usāma[ra] paid no heed to this and killed him. When this, among the other incidents of the campaign, was related to the Holy Prophet[sa] he sent for Usāma[ra] and questioned him. On his confirming the account of the incident the Prophet[sa] said: "How will it be with you on the Day of Judgement when his confession of faith will bear witness in his favour?" Usāma[ra] replied, "O Messenger of Allah[sa]! that man was a murderer of Muslims and his declaring himself to be a Muslim was merely a ruse to escape just retribution." But the Prophet[sa] went on repeating: "Usāma[ra], how will it be with you when the man's confession of faith will bear witness against you on the Day of Judgement?" meaning that God would hold Usāma[ra] to account for the man's death, for though he had been guilty of the murder of Muslims, his reciting the confession was an indication that he had repented of his misdeeds. Usāma[ra] protested that the man's reciting of confession of faith was due to his fear of death and was not an indication of repentance. Thereupon the Holy Prophet[sa] said:

> **"Did you peep into his heart to see whether he was telling the truth or not?" and went on repeating: "How will you answer on the Day of Judgement when his confession of faith will be cited in evidence against you?" Usāma[ra] says: "On hearing the Prophet[sa] repeat this so often I wished that I had become a convert to Islam only that moment**

and had not been guilty of what was charged against me" (*Muslim, Kitābul Īmān*).

The Holy Prophet[sa] was ever ready to forgive people their faults and trespasses. One of the persons concerned in the affair of the slander against his wife, 'Ā'isha[ra], was dependent for his living upon the charity of Abū Bakr[ra] ('Ā'isha[ra]'s father). When the falsehood of the allegation against 'Ā'isha[ra] was clearly established, Abū Bakr[ra] stopped his support of this man. Even this is evidence of Abū Bakr's[ra] commendable moderation and restraint. An average person would have proceeded to extreme lengths against a dependent who had been guilty of defaming his daughter. When the Prophet[sa] came to know of what Abū Bakr[ra] had done, he spoke to him and pointed out that though the man had been at fault, it did not behove a person like Abū Bakr[ra] to deprive him of his means of sustenance on account of his wrongdoing. Thereupon Abū Bakr[ra] resumed his patronage of the man (*Bukhārī, Kitābut Tafsīr*).

PATIENCE IN ADVERSITY

The Holy Prophet[sa] used to say: "For a Muslim, life is all full of good and nobody but a true believer finds himself in that position; for, if he meets with success he is grateful to God and becomes the recipient of greater favours from Him. On the other hand, if he suffers pain or tribulation he endures it with patience and thus again makes himself deserving of God's favours." When his end drew near and he gave vent to a groan in the extremity of his condition, his daughter Fāṭima[ra] exclaimed that she could not bear to see him in that state. Thereupon he said: "Have patience! Your father will suffer no pain after this day," meaning that all his troubles were confined to this world and from the moment that he was released from this life and entered the presence of his Maker he would be subject to no further pain. During the prevalence of an epidemic he would not approve of people moving out of an afflicted town into another, for this serves to enlarge the area of the pestilence. He used to say that in times of epidemic if a person stayed on in his own town and refrained from carrying infection into unaffected areas and died of the epidemic, he would be regarded as a martyr (*Bukhārī, Kitabuṭ Ṭibb*).

MUTUAL COOPERATION

He used to teach that one of the best Islamic characteristics was that a man should not interfere in matters with which he was not concerned and that people should not go about criticizing others and interfering in matters that were not their concern. This is a principle which if generally adopted and enforced would go a long way towards securing peace and orderliness in the world. A large part of our troubles is due to the tendency of the majority of people to indulge in undue interference and to hold back their co-operation when it may be needed in providing relief for those in distress.

The Holy Prophet[sa] laid great stress upon mutual cooperation. He had made it a rule that if any person was called upon to pay a sum of money by way of penalty and was unable to put up the whole amount, his neighbours or his fellow-citizens or his fellow-tribesmen should make up the amount by raising a subscription. People sometimes came and took up their residence near the Prophet[sa], devoting their time to the service of Islam in various ways. He always counselled their relatives to assume the responsibility of providing for their modest requirements. It is reported by Anas[ra] that during the time of the Holy Prophet[sa] two brothers accepted Islam and one of them stayed on with the Holy Prophet[sa] while the other continued with his normal occupation. The latter, later on, complained to the Holy Prophet[sa] that his brother was spending his time in idleness. The Holy Prophet[sa] said: "God provides for you also on account of your brother and it behoves you therefore to make provision for him and leave him free to serve the Faith" (*Tirmidhī*).

During the course of a journey, when the Prophet's[sa] party arrived at their camping place, his Companions immediately occupied themselves with their respective tasks in setting up camp for the night. The Holy Prophet[sa] said: "You have allotted no task to me. I shall go and collect fuel for cooking." His Companions protested and said: "O Messenger of Allah[sa]! why should you occupy yourself in that way when all of us are here to do whatever may be necessary?" He said: "No, No. It is my duty to do my share of whatever may have to be done," and he collected fire-wood from the jungle for cooking the food (*Zurqānī*, Vol. 4, p. 306).

TRUTHFULNESS

As has been related the Holy Prophet[sa] was himself so rigid in his standards of truthfulness that he was known among his people as "The Trusty" and "The True". He was equally anxious that Muslims should adopt the same standards of truth as were observed by himself. He regarded truth as the basis of all virtue, goodness and right conduct. He taught that a truthful person is one who is so confirmed in truth that he is counted truthful by God.

On one occasion a prisoner was brought to the Holy Prophet[sa] who had been guilty of the murder of many Muslims. 'Umar[ra], who was also present, believed that the man richly deserved the imposition of the death penalty and he looked repeatedly at the Prophet[sa] expecting that the Prophet[sa] would at any moment indicate that the man should be put to death. After the Holy Prophet[sa] had dismissed the man 'Umar[ra] submitted that he should have been put to death as that was the only appropriate penalty. The Prophet[sa] replied: "If that is so, why did you not kill him?" 'Umar[ra] replied:

"O Messenger of Allahsa! if you had but given me an indication even by a flicker of your eyelids, I would have done so." To this the Prophetsa rejoined: "A Prophetsa does not act equivocally. How could I have employed my eye to indicate the imposition of a death penalty upon the man while my tongue was employed in talking amicably to him?" (*Hishām,* Vol. 2, p. 217).

A man once came to the Holy Prophetsa and said: "O Messengersa of Allah! I suffer from three evils: falsehood, indulgence in strong drinks and fornication. I have tried my utmost to get rid of them but have not succeeded. Will you tell me what to do? " The Prophetsa replied: "If you make a firm promise to me to give up one of them I guarantee that you will be rid of the other two." The man promised and asked the Prophetsa to tell him which of the three he should give up. The Prophetsa said: "Give up falsehood." Some time later the man came back and told the Holy Prophetsa that, having followed his advice, he was now free from all three vices. The Prophetsa asked him for the details of his struggle and the man said: "One day I wanted to indulge in liquor and was about to do so when I bethought myself of my promise to you and realized that if any of my friends asked me whether I had taken liquor, I would have to admit it as I could no longer utter a falsehood. This would mean that I would acquire an evil reputation among my friends and they would in future avoid me. Thinking thus, I persuaded myself to postpone drinking to some later occasion and was able to withstand the temptation at the time. In the same way when I found myself inclined towards fornication I argued with myself that indulgence in the vice would expose me to the loss of the esteem of my friends as I would either have to tell a falsehood if questioned by them, thus breaking my promise to you, or I would have to admit my sin. In this way I continued to struggle between my resolve to fulfil my promise to you and my desire to indulge in liquor and in adultery. When some time had passed I began to lose the inclination to indulge in these vices and the resolve to keep away from falsehood has now saved me from the other two also."

INQUISITIVENESS

The Holy Prophetsa always exhorted people against inquisitiveness and to think well of each other. Abū Hurairara relates: "The Prophetsa said: 'Save yourselves from thinking ill of others for this is the greatest falsehood, and do not be inquisitive or apply epithets to each other out of contempt nor be envious of each other and do not entertain ill feelings towards each other; let each of you regard himself as the servant of God and treat others as his brothers as God has commanded,' and also 'Remember that every Muslim is a brother to every other Muslim. No Muslim should trespass against another or desert another in times of distress or look down upon another on account of his lack of substance or learning or any other thing. Purity springs from the heart and it is enough to defile a man's heart that he should look down upon his brother. Every Muslim must regard another Muslim's life, honour and property as sacred and inviolate. God does not regard your bodies nor your countenances nor your external actions but looks into your hearts" (*Muslim, Kitābul Birr Waṣ Ṣila*).

FRANK AND STRAIGHTFORWARD DEALING

He was anxious to safeguard Muslims against indulgence in any form of unfairness in their transactions. Passing through the market-place on one occasion, he observed a heap of corn which was being put to auction. He thrust his arm into the heap and found that though the outer layer of the corn was dry the corn inside was wet. He inquired from the owner the cause of this. The man explained that a sudden shower of rain had made part of the corn wet. The Prophetsa said that in that case he should have allowed the wet layer of corn to remain on the outside so that prospective purchasers could have appraised its real condition. He observed: "He who deals unfairly with others can never become a useful member of society" (*Muslim*). He insisted upon trade and commerce being entirely free from every suspicion of sharp practice. He exhorted purchasers always to inspect the goods and articles they proposed to purchase, and forbade any person to open negotiations for a transaction while negotiations about it were in progress with any other person. He also forbade the hoarding of commodities against a rise in the market and insisted that the market should be regularly supplied.

PESSIMISM

He was an enemy of pessimism. He used to say that whoever was guilty of spreading pessimism among the people was responsible for the downfall of the people, for pessimistic ideas have a tendency to discourage people and arrest progress (*Muslim*, Part II, Vol. 2). He warned his people against pride and boastfulness on the one hand and against pessimism on the other. He exhorted them to tread the middle path between these extremes. Muslims must work diligently in the trust that God would bless their efforts with the best results. Each should strive to go forward and should seek to promote the welfare and progress of the community, but everyone should be free from any feeling of pride or any tendency towards boastfulness.

CRUELTY TO ANIMALS

He warned people against cruelty to animals and enjoined kind treatment to them. He used to relate the instance of a Jewish woman who was punished by God for having starved her cat to death. He also used to relate the story of a woman who found a dog suffering from thirst near a deep well. She took off her shoe and lowered it into the well and thus drew up some water. She gave the water to the thirsty dog to drink. This good deed earned her God's forgiveness for all her previous sins.

'Abdullāh bin Mas'ūd[ra] relates: "While we were in the course of a journey along with the Holy Prophet[sa] we saw two young doves in a nest and we caught them. They were still very small. When their mother returned to the nest, not finding her little ones in it, she began to fly wildly round and round. When the Holy Prophet[sa] arrived at the spot he observed the dove and said, 'If any one of you has caught its young ones he must release them at once to comfort it' " (*Abū Dawūd*). 'Abdullāh bin Mas'ūd[ra] also relates that on one occasion they observed an ant-hill and, placing some straw on top of it, they set fire to it; whereupon they were rebuked by the Holy Prophet[sa]. On one occasion the Prophet[sa] observed a donkey being branded on the face. He inquired the reason for this and was told that the Romans had recourse to this practice for the purpose of identifying high-bred animals. The Prophet[sa] said that as the face was a very sensitive part of the body, an animal should not be branded on the face and that if it had to be done the branding should be done on its haunches (*Abū Dāwūd* and *Tirmidhī*). Since then Muslims always brand animals on their haunches and, following this Muslim practice, Europeans also do the same.

TOLERANCE IN RELIGIOUS MATTERS

The Holy Prophet[sa] not only emphasized the desirability of tolerance in religious matters but set a very high standard in this respect. A deputation from a Christian tribe of Najran visited him in Medina to exchange views on religious matters. It included several Church dignitaries. The conversation was held in the mosque and extended over several hours. At one stage the leader of the deputation asked permission to depart from the mosque and to hold their religious service at some convenient spot. The Holy Prophet[sa] said that there was no need for them to go out of the mosque, which was itself a place consecrated to the worship of God, and they could hold their service in it (*Zurqānī*).

BRAVERY

Several instances of his courage and bravery have been set out in the biographical portion. It suffices to relate one here. At one time Medina was full of rumours that the Romans were preparing a large army for its invasion. During that time Muslims were always on the *qui vive* at night. One night sounds of an uproar came from the desert. Muslims hurried out of their homes and some of them collected in the mosque and waited for the Holy Prophet[sa] to appear and to give them directions to meet the contingency. Presently they saw the Holy Prophet[sa] on a horse coming back from the direction of the sounds. They then discovered that at the very first sound of alarm the Prophet[sa] had mounted a horse and gone in the direction from which the sounds had come to find out whether there was any reason for alarm and had not waited for people to collect together so that he could proceed in company. When he came back he assured his Companions that there was no cause for alarm and that they could return to their homes and go to sleep (*Bukhārī, chap. on Shujā'at fil Ḥarb*).

CONSIDERATION TOWARDS THE UNCULTURED

He was particularly considerate towards those who from lack of cultural training did not know how to behave. On one occasion a dweller of the desert who had only recently accepted Islam and who was sitting in the company of the Holy Prophet[sa] in the mosque got up and walking away a few paces sat down in a corner of the mosque to pass water. Some of the Companions of the Prophet[sa] got up to stop him from doing so. The Prophet[sa] restrained them, pointing out that any interference with the man was bound to cause inconvenience to him and might possibly cause him injury. He told his Companions to let the man alone and to clean the spot later.

THE FULFILLING OF COVENANTS

The Holy Prophet[sa] was very particular with regard to the fulfilling of covenants. On one occasion an envoy came to him on a special mission and, after he had remained in his company for some days, he was convinced of the truth of Islam and suggested that he might declare his adherence to it. The Prophet[sa] told him that this would not be proper as he was there in a representative capacity and it was incumbent upon him to return to the headquarters of his Government without acquiring a fresh allegiance. If, after he had returned home, he still felt convinced of the truth of Islam he could return as a free individual and declare his acceptance of it (*Abū Dāwud, chap. on Wafā bil 'Ahd*).

DEFERENCE TOWARDS SERVANTS OF HUMANITY

He paid special deference to those who devoted their time and substance to the service of mankind. The Arab tribe, the Banū Ṭā'i started hostilities against the Prophet[sa] and in the ensuing battle their forces were defeated and some were taken prisoner. One of these was the daughter of Ḥātim Ṭā'i, whose generosity had become a proverb amongst the Arabs. When Ḥātim's daughter informed the Holy Prophet[sa] of her parentage he treated her with great consideration and as the result of her intercession he remitted all the penalties imposed upon her people on account of their aggression (*Ḥalbiyya,* Vol. 3, p. 227).

The character of the Holy Prophet[sa] is so many-sided that it is not possible to deal adequately with it within the space of a few pages.

LIFE OF THE PROPHET[sa] AN OPEN BOOK

The life of the Holy Founder of Islam[sa] is like an open book, to any part of which one may turn and meet with interesting details. The life of no other Teacher or Prophet is as well-recorded and as accessible to study as is the life of the Holy Prophet[sa]. True, this abundance of recorded fact has given malicious critics their opportunity. But it is also true that when the criticisms have been examined and disposed of, the faith and devotion which result cannot be inspired by any other life. Obscure lives escape criticism, but they fail to produce conviction and confidence in their devotees. Some disappointments and difficulties are bound to remain. But a life as rich in recorded detail as the Prophet's[sa] inspires reflection and, then, conviction. When criticism and false constructions have been liquidated, such a life is bound to endear itself to us completely and for ever.

It should be evident, however, that the story of a life so open and so rich cannot even briefly be told. Only a glimpse of it can be attempted. But even a glimpse is worth while. A religious book, as we say, can have little appeal unless a study of it can be supplemented by a knowledge of its Teacher. The point has been missed by many religions. The Hindu religion, for instance, upholds the Vedas, but of the Rishis who received the Vedas from God it is able to tell us nothing. The need to supplement a message by an account of the messenger does not seem to have impressed itself upon Hindu exponents. Jewish and Christian scholars, on the other hand, do not hesitate to denounce their own Prophets. They forget that revelation which has failed to reclaim its recipient cannot be of much use to others. If the recipient is intractable the question arises, why did God choose him? Must He have done so? Neither supposition seems reasonable. To think that revelation fails to reclaim some recipients is as unreasonable as to think that God has no alternative except to choose incompetent recipients for some of His revelations. Yet ideas of this kind have found their way into different religions, possibly because of the distance which now divides them from their Founders or because human intellect, until the advent of Islam, was incapable of perceiving the error of these ideas. How important and valuable it is to keep together a book and its Teacher was realized very early in Islam. One of the Prophet'ssa holy consorts was the young 'Ā'ishara. She was thirteen to fourteen years of age when she was married to the Prophetsa. For about eight years she lived in wedlock with him. When the Prophetsa died she was about twenty-two years of age. She was young and illiterate: Yet she knew that a teaching cannot be divorced from its teacher. Asked to describe the Prophet'ssa character, she answered at once that his character was the Qur'an (*Abū Dāwūd*). What he did was what the Qur'an taught; what the Qur'an taught was nothing else than what he did. It redounds to the glory of the Prophetsa that an illiterate young woman was able to grasp a truth which escaped Hindu, Jewish and Christian scholars.

'Ā'ishara expressed a great and an important truth in a crisp little sentence: it is impossible for a true and honest teacher to teach one thing but practise another, or to practise one thing but teach another. The Prophetsa was a true and honest Teacher. This is what 'Ā'ishara evidently wanted to say. He practised what he preached and preached what he practised. To know him is to know the Qur'an and to know the Qur'an is to know him.

Index of Subject Matter

(This index covers, under various heads, the account of the life of the Holy Prophet[sa] given in *Life of Muhammad[sa]*).

Jews
Banū Quraiẓa punished after the battle of Ditch 97
continously intrigued against the Holy Prophet[sa].................. 45
mischiefs of, of Medina after the battle of Uḥud 72
preferred Sa'd bin Mu'ādh[ra] as judge than the Holy Prophet[sa]................... 99
Sa'd's award for Banū Quraiẓa in harmony with the Bible 100
treachery of Banū Quraiẓa..................... 88
Ka'ba
360 idols in, ... 2
all the pictures on the walls of, wiped out ... 164
cleared of idols............ 163
the Holy Prophet[sa] left for Mecca for the circuit of, ... 144
Khadīja[ra]
death of, ... 26
first among women who became Muslim.......... 11
the Holy Prophet[sa] lead trading caravan of, to Syria.......................... 7
the Holy Prophet[sa] narrated his first revelation to, ... 11
took Muḥammad[sa] to Waraqa bin Naufal 11
Khaibar, fall of
at the hands of 'Alī[ra] 141
Ṣafiyya's dream came true 142
Khubaib[ra]
showed high standards of morality 76
Life of the Holy Prophet[sa]
a rock fragmented by the Holy Prophet[sa] on the occasion of the battle of Ditch 84
Abū Ṭālib became his guardian 5
address on the occasion of last pilgrimage...... 183
approved of the idea of digging a ditch for the battle of Ditch 83
became guest of Abū Ayyūb Anṣārī[ra] on arrival at Medina........ 43
birth of the Holy Prophet[sa]..................... 1
death of the Holy Prophet[sa]................ 191
declared that Zaid[ra] was his son........................ 9
did not seek to continue warfare after the battle of Ditch 104
distributed booty on the occasion of battle of Ḥunain among Meccans and who lived round about Mecca 175
entered Mecca on the occasion of fall of Mecca 158
first pledge of 'Aqaba 35
gave hints of his death . 186
got wounded in the Battle of Uḥud 67
grandfather died when he was eight................ 5

Index of Names

Index of Places